A COMMERCE OF TASTE

McGill-Queen's Studies in the History of Religion
Volumes in this series have been supported by the Jackman Foundation of Toronto.

SERIES ONE G.A. Rawlyk, Editor

1 Small Differences
Irish Catholics and Irish
Protestants, 1815–1922
An International Perspective
Donald Harman Akenson

2 Two Worlds
The Protestant Culture of
Nineteenth-Century Ontario
William Westfall

3 An Evangelical Mind
Nathanael Burwash and the
Methodist Tradition in Canada,
1839–1918
Marguerite Van Die

4 The Dévotes
Women and Church in Seventeenth-
Century France
Elizabeth Rapley

5 The Evangelical Century
College and Creed in English
Canada from the Great Revival
to the Great Depression
Michael Gauvreau

6 The German Peasants' War and
Anabaptist Community of Goods
James M. Stayer

7 A World Mission
Canadian Protestantism and the
Quest for a New International Order,
1918–1939
Robert Wright

8 Serving the Present Age
Revivalism, Progressivism, and the
Methodist Tradition in Canada
Phyllis D. Airhart

9 A Sensitive Independence
Canadian Methodist Women
Missionaries in Canada and
the Orient, 1881–1925
Rosemary R. Gagan

10 God's Peoples
Covenant and Land in South Africa,
Israel, and Ulster
Donald Harman Akenson

11 Creed and Culture
The Place of English-Speaking
Catholics in Canadian Society,
1750–1930
*Edited by Terrence Murphy and
Gerald Stortz*

12 Piety and Nationalism
Lay Voluntary Associations and the
Creation of an Irish-Catholic
Community in Toronto, 1850–1895
Brian P. Clarke

13 Amazing Grace
Studies in Evangelicalism in
Australia, Britain, Canada, and the
United States
*Edited by George Rawlyk and
Mark A. Noll*

14 Children of Peace
W. John McIntyre

15 A Solitary Pillar
Montreal's Anglican Church
and the Quiet Revolution
Joan Marshall

16 Padres in No Man's Land
Canadian Chaplains and the
Great War
Duff Crerar

17 Christian Ethics and Political
Economy in North America
A Critical Analysis
P. Travis Kroeker

18 Pilgrims in Lotus Land
Conservative Protestantism in
British Columbia, 1917–1981
Robert K. Burkinshaw

19 Through Sunshine and Shadow
The Woman's Christian Temperance
Union, Evangelicalism, and Reform
in Ontario, 1874–1930
Sharon Cook

20 Church, College, and Clergy
A History of Theological Education
at Knox College, Toronto, 1844–1994
Brian J. Fraser

21 The Lord's Dominion
   The History of Canadian Methodism
   Neil Semple

22 A Full-Orbed Christianity
   The Protestant Churches and Social Welfare in Canada, 1900–1940
   Nancy Christie and Michael Gauvreau

23 Evangelism and Apostasy
   The Evolution and Impact of Evangelicals in Modern Mexico
   Kurt Bowen

24 The Chignecto Covenanters
   A Regional History of Reformed Presbyterianism in New Brunswick and Nova Scotia, 1827–1905
   Eldon Hay

25 Methodists and Women's Education in Ontario, 1836–1925
   Johanne Selles

26 Puritanism and Historical Controversy
   William Lamont

SERIES TWO In memory of George Rawlyk
Donald Harman Akenson, Editor

1 Marguerite Bourgeoys and Montreal, 1640–1665
  Patricia Simpson

2 Aspects of the Canadian Evangelical Experience
  Edited by G.A. Rawlyk

3 Infinity, Faith, and Time
  Christian Humanism and Renaissance Literature
  John Spencer Hill

4 The Contribution of Presbyterianism to the Maritime Provinces of Canada
  Edited by Charles H.H. Scobie and G.A. Rawlyk

5 Labour, Love, and Prayer
  Female Piety in Ulster Religious Literature, 1850–1914
  Andrea Ebel Brozyna

6 The Waning of the Green
  Catholics, the Irish, and Identity in Toronto, 1887–1922
  Mark G. McGowan

7 Religion and Nationality in Western Ukraine
  The Greek Catholic Church and the Ruthenian National Movement in Galicia, 1867–1900
  John-Paul Himka

8 Good Citizens
  British Missionaries and Imperial States, 1870–1918
  James G. Greenlee and Charles M. Johnston

9 The Theology of the Oral Torah
  Revealing the Justice of God
  Jacob Neusner

10 Gentle Eminence
   A Life of Cardinal Flahiff
   P. Wallace Platt

11 Culture, Religion, and Demographic Behaviour
   Catholics and Lutherans in Alsace, 1750–1870
   Kevin McQuillan

12 Between Damnation and Starvation
   Priests and Merchants in Newfoundland Politics, 1745–1855
   John P. Greene

13 Martin Luther, German Saviour
   German Evangelical Theological Factions and the Interpretation of Luther, 1917–1933
   James M. Stayer

14 Modernity and the Dilemma of North American Anglican Identities, 1880–1950
   William H. Katerberg

15 The Methodist Church on the Prairies, 1896–1914
   George Emery

16 Christian Attitudes towards the State of Israel
   Paul Charles Merkley

17 A Social History of the Cloister
   Daily Life in the Teaching
   Monasteries of the Old Regime
   Elizabeth Rapley

18 Households of Faith
   Family, Gender, and Community
   in Canada, 1760–1969
   Edited by Nancy Christie

19 Blood Ground
   Colonialism, Missions, and the
   Contest for Christianity in the
   Cape Colony and Britain, 1799–1853
   Elizabeth Elbourne

20 A History of Canadian Catholics
   Gallicanism, Romanism, and
   Canadianism
   Terence J. Fay

21 The View from Rome
   Archbishop Stagni's 1915 Reports
   on the Ontario Bilingual Schools
   Question
   Edited and translated by John Zucchi

22 The Founding Moment
   Church, Society, and the
   Construction of Trinity College
   William Westfall

23 The Holocaust, Israel, and
   Canadian Protestant Churches
   Haim Genizi

24 Governing Charities
   Church and State in Toronto's
   Catholic Archdiocese, 1850–1950
   Paula Maurutto

25 Anglicans and the Atlantic World
   High Churchmen, Evangelicals,
   and the Quebec Connection
   Richard W. Vaudry

26 Evangelicals and the
   Continental Divide
   The Conservative Protestant
   Subculture in Canada and the
   United States
   Sam Reimer

27 Christians in a Secular World
   The Canadian Experience
   Kurt Bowen

28 Anatomy of a Seance
   A History of Spirit Communication
   in Central Canada
   Stan McMullin

29 With Skilful Hand
   The Story of King David
   David T. Barnard

30 Faithful Intellect
   Samuel S. Nelles and Victoria
   University
   Neil Semple

31 W. Stanford Reid
   An Evangelical Calvinist
   in the Academy
   Donald MacLeod

32 A Long Eclipse
   The Liberal Protestant Establishment
   and the Canadian University,
   1920–1970
   Catherine Gidney

33 Forkhill Protestants and Forkhill
   Catholics, 1787–1858
   Kyla Madden

34 For Canada's Sake
   Public Religion, Centennial
   Celebrations, and the Re-making
   of Canada in the 1960s
   Gary R. Miedema

35 Revival in the City
   The Impact of American Evangelists
   in Canada, 1884–1914
   Eric R. Crouse

36 The Lord for the Body
   Religion, Medicine, and Protestant
   Faith Healing in Canada, 1880–1930
   James Opp

37 Six Hundred Years of Reform
   Bishops and the French Church,
   1190–1789
   *J. Michael Hayden and
   Malcolm R. Greenshields*

38 The Missionary Oblate Sisters
   Vision and Mission
   Rosa Bruno-Jofré

39 Religion, Family, and Community in Victorian Canada
    The Colbys of Carrollcroft
    Marguerite Van Die

40 Michael Power
    The Struggle to Build the Catholic Church on the Canadian Frontier
    Mark G. McGowan

41 The Catholic Origins of Quebec's Quiet Revolution, 1931–1970
    Michael Gauvreau

42 Marguerite Bourgeoys and the Congregation of Notre Dame, 1665–1700
    Patricia Simpson

43 To Heal a Fractured World
    The Ethics of Responsibility
    Jonathan Sacks

44 Revivalists
    Marketing the Gospel in English Canada, 1884–1957
    Kevin Kee

45 The Churches and Social Order in Nineteenth- and Twentieth-Century Canada
    Edited by Michael Gauvreau and Ollivier Hubert

46 Political Ecumenism
    Catholics, Jews, and Protestants in De Gaulle's Free France, 1940–1945
    Geoffrey Adams

47 From Quaker to Upper Canadian
    Faith and Community among Yonge Street Friends, 1801–1850
    Robynne Rogers Healey

48 The Congrégation de Notre-Dame, Superiors, and the Paradox of Power, 1693–1796
    Colleen Gray

49 Canadian Pentecostalism
    Transition and Transformation
    Edited by Michael Wilkinson

50 A War with a Silver Lining
    Canadian Protestant Churches and the South African War, 1899–1902
    Gordon L. Heath

51 In the Aftermath of Catastrophe
    Founding Judaism, 70 to 640
    Jacob Neusner

52 Imagining Holiness
    Classic Hasidic Tales in Modern Times
    Justin Jaron Lewis

53 Shouting, Embracing, and Dancing with Ecstasy
    The Growth of Methodism in Newfoundland, 1774–1874
    Calvin Hollett

54 Into Deep Waters
    Evangelical Spirituality and Maritime Calvinist Baptist Ministers, 1790–1855
    Daniel C. Goodwin

55 Vanguard of the New Age
    The Toronto Theosophical Society, 1891–1945
    Gillian McCann

56 A Commerce of Taste
    Church Architecture in Canada, 1867–1914
    Barry Magrill

A COMMERCE OF TASTE

CHURCH ARCHITECTURE IN CANADA
1867–1914

BARRY MAGRILL

McGILL-QUEEN'S UNIVERSITY PRESS
Montreal & Kingston · London · Ithaca

© McGill-Queen's University Press 2012

ISBN 978-0-7735-3982-2 (cloth)
ISBN 978-0-7735-3983-9 (paper)

Legal deposit second quarter 2012
Bibliothèque nationale du Québec

Printed in Canada on acid-free paper that is 100% ancient forest free
(100% post-consumer recycled), processed chlorine free

This book has been published with the help of a grant from the Canadian
Federation for the Humanities and Social Sciences, through the Aid to
Scholarly Publications Program, using funds provided by the Social Sciences
and Humanities Research Council of Canada.

McGill-Queen's University Press acknowledges the support of the Canada
Council for the Arts for our publishing program. We also acknowledge the
financial support of the Government of Canada through the Canada Book
Fund for our publishing activities.

Library and Archives Canada Cataloguing in Publication

Magrill, Barry, 1964–
A commerce of taste : church architecture in Canada, 1867–1914 /
Barry Magrill.

(McGill-Queen's studies in the history of religion. Series two ; 56)
Includes bibliographical references and index.
ISBN 978-0-7735-3982-2 (bound).– ISBN 978-0-7735-3983-9 (pbk.)

1. Religious architecture–Canada. 2. Pattern books–Great Britain. 3. Gothic
revival (Architecture)–Canada. 4. Canada–Social conditions–19th century.
5. Canada–Economic conditions–19th century. I. Title. II. Series: McGill-
Queen's studies in the history of religion. Series two ; 56.

NA5244.M34 2012   726.5'0971   C2012-900172-4

Designed and typeset by studio oneonone in Minion 10/13.5

For
Judy, Jamie, Haley, and Geoffrey

CONTENTS

Acknowledgments · xiii
List of Illustrations · xv

Introduction · 3

1 The Rise of Commercial Society in Pre-Confederation Canada · 11

2 Economy and Religion from the Maritimes to Upper Canada · 48

3 Selling Ecclesiology as Identity in the Dominion of Canada · 67

4 Property Ownership and Church-Building: The Financial Structure of Churches in Ontario · 83

5 The Spread of Empire in Western Canada: Railway, Religion, and Church-Building · 107

6 An Unfinished Business of Western Expansion · 128

7 The Influence of US Artistic, Cultural, and Economic Capital · 166

Conclusion · 173
Appendix: Biographies of Pattern Book Authors · 177
Notes · 183
Bibliography · 195
Index · 213

ACKNOWLEDGMENTS

The research for this book was funded by a travel grant from the Art History, Visual Arts, and Theory Department at the University of British Columbia. The Université du Québec à Montréal together with the Society for the Study of Architecture in Canada provided funding through the Phyllis Lambert Prize that supported the manuscript's finalization.

Many individuals were helpful in the preparation of this book, sharing knowledge and expertise. I gratefully acknowledge the excellent advice of Rhodri Windsor-Liscombe at UBC. Without his insight into the broader web of social connections in the Canadian context my grappling with diverse data sets would have been in vain. I have benefited from the expertise of Malcolm Thurlby at York University, who became both guide and champion of this book even to the point of lending several key images from a personal collection of architectural pattern books. We also travelled together over many miles of roadway in search of the next church steeple, sharing ideas and case studies. Peter Coffman's work on churches in the Maritimes provided an invaluable resource.

In addition to being a study of the business of building churches, the book you are holding is also about the marketability of architecture books printed in the nineteenth and early twentieth centuries. In this regard, my research would not have been possible without the help of many fine librarians and archivists in Britain as well as Canada. It was my pleasure to have worked with the staff at the National Arts Library at the Victoria and Alberta Museum in London, Melanie Wallace at the Anglican Archives of New Westminster in Vancouver, British Columbia, and Nancy Mallet at the archives of the Cathedral of St James in Toronto. My research benefited from the assistance of several archives and libraries, including the Vaughan Memorial Library at Acadia University in Wolfville, Nova Scotia, the archives of Manitoba, the archives of

Edmonton, Alberta, The Royal BC Museum, the archives of St James Anglo-Catholic Church in Vancouver, and the archives of the Canadian Pacific Railway, as well as The Kelvin Smith Library at Case Western Reserve University, the Margaret M. Bridwell Art Library, University of Louisville Kentucky, and the National Arts Library in London, England. In that respect I would be remiss if I did not personally thank the following archivists and librarians: Twila Buttimer, William Claspy, Sharon Foley, Gail Gilbert, Ann Marie Holland, Bob Kennell, Jamie Miller, Wendy Robicheau, Kelly-Ann Turlington, Jane Turner, Diane Wardle, as well as James Wright and Anna Sheppard at the National Arts Library in London. Generous and welcoming support came from clergy and volunteers who opened the doors of their churches to me. As well, I sincerely acknowledge a debt of gratitude to my editors at McGill-Queen's University Press, Kyla Madden, Ryan Van Huijstee, and Claude Lalumière, whose help in putting this volume together was invaluable.

Finally, but in no way least, I wish to thank my family, who provided encouragement, support, love, and humour while this project progressed. Serendipitously, my parents provided an interest in history and business. My children Jamie, Haley, and Geoffrey learned great patience as they grew up wary of getting into our van for long car drives fearing unplanned stops at churches along any proposed route. The time needed to produce this work would not have been possible without the support of my spouse, Judy; I imagine the strength of our bond to be like the connective tissue holding together the complex data sets you are about to read.

LIST OF ILLUSTRATIONS

1.1 Specimen page of a watercolour of St Mary, Brook, Isle of Wight, from *Rural Churches, Their Histories, Architecture and Antiquities*. Sidney Corner, 1869. Photo courtesy of Rare Books and Special Collections, University of British Columbia. 12

1.2 The English Church (St George's Anglican Church). Fort George, British Columbia, c. 1911. Photo courtesy of Royal BC Museum and Archives D-08466. 12

1.3 Specimen page of an elevation of Netley Abbey from *Architectural Parallels; or the Progress in Ecclesiastical Architecture in England through the Twelfth and the Thirteenth Centuries Examined in a Series of Parallel Examples*, Edmund Sharpe. 1848. Photo courtesy of Rare Books and Special Collections, University of British Columbia. 14

1.4 Specimen page of Shiere Church from *Parish Churches*. Raphael and J. Arthur Brandon, 1847. Photo courtesy of Malcolm Thurlby. 17

1.5 Christ Church (Anglican). Maugerville, New Brunswick. Attributed to Frank Wills, 1856. Photo by the author. 18

1.6 Christ Church Anglican Cathedral, Montreal, Quebec. Published in the *Illustrated London News*. Frank Wills, 1856. 23

1.7 St Mary's, Snettisham, Norfolk, England, thirteenth century. Photo courtesy of Malcolm Thurlby. 24

1.8 Specimen page of St Peter's Church, Philadelphia, from *Ancient English Ecclesiastical Architecture and Its Principles Applied to the Wants of the Church at the Present Day*. Frank Wills, 1850. Photo courtesy of Malcolm Thurlby. 26

1.9 Specimen pages of Sens Cathedral (left), view of towers at Senlis and Covantres (right) from *Specimens of Medieval Architecture Chiefly Selected from Examples of the 12th and 13th Centuries in France and Italy*. William Eden Nesfield, 1862. Photo courtesy of Rare Books and Special Collections, University of British Columbia. 29

1.10 Specimen page of design no. 8, plate 15, from *Church Architecture: Plans, Elevations, and Views of Twenty-One Churches and Two School Houses*. Frederick Withers, 1873. Photo courtesy of the National Arts Library, London. 30

1.11 Specimen page of a photogravure illustration of Church of the Ascension, Washington, DC, from *King's Handbook of Notable Episcopal Churches in the United States*. Rev. George Wolfe Shinn, 1889. 33

1.12 Specimen page of Stone Capital, Arum and Hart's Tongue Fern from *Art Foliage*. James Kellaway Colling, 1874. 35

1.13 Specimen page showing a scissor truss from *Open Timber Roofs*. Raphael and J. Arthur Brandon, 1849. 44

2.1 West entrance of Christ Church (Anglican), the cathedral of Fredericton. Fredericton, New Brunswick. Frank Wills, 1845. Photo by the author. 52

2.2 West entrance of St Mary's Snettisham, Norfolk, England. Photo courtesy of Malcolm Thurlby. 53

2.3 East end of Christ Church (Anglican), the cathedral of Fredericton. Fredericton, New Brunswick. Frank Wills, 1845. Photo by the author. 53

2.4 St Mary's, Shottesbrooke (thirteenth century), Berkshire, England published in *Elevations, Sections Etc., of St John the Baptist at Shottesbrooke*. William Butterfield, 1844. Photo courtesy of Malcolm Thurlby. 54

2.5 St Anne's Chapel. Fredericton, New Brunswick. Architect: Frank Wills, 1847. Photo by the author. 60

2.6 Specimen page of St Michael's, Long Stanton, Cambridgeshire (thirteenth century) from *Parish Churches*. Raphael and J. Arthur Brandon, 1849. Photo courtesy of Malcolm Thurlby. 60

2.7 St Michael's Anglican Church. Sillery, Quebec. Frank Wills, 1852. Photo by the author. 61

2.8 Roman Catholic Church of Saint Michel. Sillery, Quebec. Goodlatte Richardson Browne, 1854. Photo by the author. 61

2.9 St Simon and St Jude. Tignish, Prince Edward Island. Patrick Keely, c.1860s. Photo courtesy of Malcolm Thurlby. 62

2.10 Specimen page of design no.5, plate 12, from *Rural Church Architecture*. George Woodward, 1868. Photo courtesy of the Margaret M. Bridwell Art Library, University of Louisville Kentucky. 64

3.1 St John the Baptist (Anglican Cathedral). St John's, Newfoundland. Sir George Gilbert Scott (begun 1846, damaged by fire 1892, rebuilt 1893). Photo by the author. 69

3.2 Specimen page from *Designs for Country Churches*. George Truefitt, 1850. Photo courtesy of The Thomas Fisher Rare Book Library, University of Toronto. 73

3.3 Specimen page of St Anne's Chapel, Fredericton, New Brunswick. From *Ancient Ecclesiastical Architecture*. Frank Wills, 1850. Photo courtesy of Malcolm Thurlby. 76

3.4 St John the Evangelist (Anglican). Oxford Mills, Ontario, 1869. Photo courtesy of Malcolm Thurlby. 77

3.5 Specimen page of a timber church from *Instrumenta Ecclesiastica*. William Butterfield, 1856. Photo courtesy of Malcolm Thurlby. 78

3.6 Specimen page from *Church Architecture: Plans Elevations and Views of Twenty-One Churches*. Frederick Withers, 1873. Photo courtesy of the National Arts Library, London. 79

3.7 St James-the-Less (Anglican), Toronto. Fred Cumberland and William Storm, 1857–61. Photo by the author. 80

3.8 Specimen page from *Designs for Country Churches*. George Truefitt, 1850. Photo courtesy of The Thomas Fisher Rare Books Library, University of Toronto. 81

4.1 St James' Anglican Cathedral, Toronto photographed in 1852 before the completion of the tower in 1874. Photo courtesy of Archives of St James Cathedral. 87

4.2 St James' Anglican Cathedral, Toronto. Architect: Fred Cumberland, 1852. Tower completed 1874; architect: Henry Langley. Photo by the author. 93

4.3 St Michael's Roman Catholic Church, Toronto. Architect: William Thomas, 1848. Tower architect: Henry Langley, c. 1867. Photo by the author. 95

4.4 St James Cathedral and environs, Toronto published in *The New Highway to the Orient*, 1890. Photo courtesy of Rare Books and Special Collections, University of British Columbia. 97

4.5 Specimen page of advertisement for "Dixon's Low Down Philadelphia Grate," for which the architect served as commercial agent. From *Woodward's National Architect*. George Woodward, 1869. 100

4.6 Specimen page of W.A. Langton submission from *Designs for Country, Town, and City Churches*, 1893. Photo courtesy of Vaughn Memorial Library, Acadia University. 102

4.7 Specimen page of Arthur E. Wells's winning entry for design of Presbyterian Church from *Designs for Village, Town and City Churches*, 1893. Photo courtesy of Vaughn Memorial Library, Acadia University. 102

4.8 Specimen page of "Design for a Large Town Church in the Scottish Baronial Style," by D.J. Creighton from *Designs for Country, Town and City Churches*, 1893. Photo courtesy of Vaughn Memorial Library, Acadia University. 104

4.9 St David's Presbyterian Church. Architect: David Stirling, 1866 (now Grafton Street Methodist). Photo the author. 105

4.10 Specimen page of a plan showing a precursor to the amphitheatrical layout from *Sketches of Churches: Designed for the Use of Nonconformists*. George Bidlake, 1865. Photo courtesy of the National Arts Library, London. 106

5.1 Holy Trinity Church, Stanley Mission. 1853–56. Showing similarities of nave and clerestory walls in High Victorian fashion omitting external buttresses. Photo by the author. 112

5.2 All Saint's Margaret Street (Anglican), London. William Butterfield, 1849–59. Photo by the author. 113

5.3 Specimen page of J. Roger Smith's design for the New Independent Chapel, Abergele, North Wales from *Examples of Modern Architecture Ecclesiastical and Domestic*. Davey James Brooks, 1873. Photo courtesy of Kelvin Smith Library, Case Western Reserve University. 114

5.4 Interior of T.N. Hibben and Company Bookseller, Victoria. Photo courtesy of the Archives of British Columbia G-02974. 117

5.5 Specimen page of design 13, plate 28, from *Church Architecture*. Henry Hudson Holly, 1871. Photo courtesy of the National Arts Library, London. 118

5.6 Holy Trinity, Winnipeg. Presentation drawing of design by Charles H. Wheeler, 1883. Photo courtesy of the Archives of Manitoba (N5063). 120

5.7 Specimen page of design of a church with corner tower and roof dormers detailing a hammerbeam roof in cross section from *Church Architecture: Plans Views and Perspectives of Twenty-One Churches* Frederick Withers, 1873. Photo courtesy of the National Arts Library, London. 121

5.8 St George's-in-the-Pines (Anglican). Banff, Alberta. F.P. Oakley, 1889. Photo by the author. 125

6.1 St Paul's Anglican Church. Metlakatla, British Columbia, c. 1874. Photo courtesy of the Archives of British Columbia AA-00043. 132

6.2 Specimen page from *Woodward's Rural Church Architecture*. George Woodward, 1876. Photo courtesy of the Margaret M. Bridwell Art Library, University of Louisville Kentucky. 133

6.3   Holy Cross Roman Catholic Church (Skatin First Nation), Skookumchuck, British Columbia, 1895–1905. Photo by the author. 136
6.4   Specimen page from *Rural Church Architecture*. George Woodward, 1868. Photo courtesy of the Margaret M. Bridwell Art Library, University of Louisville Kentucky. 138
6.5   Detail of tower from the Roman Catholic Church of St Louis. Bonaparte, British Columbia, c.1890. Photo by the author. 139
6.6   St Saviour's Anglican Church. Barkerville, British Columbia, 1869. Photo by the author. 141
6.7   St Anne's Anglican Church. Steveston, British Columbia, c. 1905. Photo courtesy of the City of Richmond, BC, Archives 1978 8-6. 144
6.8   Specimen page from *Chapel and Church Architecture with Designs for Parsonages*. Rev. George Bowler, 1856. Photo courtesy of the Victoria and Albert Museum, London. 145
6.9   St James' Anglo-Catholic Church. Vancouver, BC. Adrian Gilbert Scott, 1928–35. Photo by the author. 150
6.10 Postcard of Golder's Green Church, England. Designed by Giles Gilbert Scott, 1918. Photo courtesy of the Archives of St. James Anglo-Catholic Cathedral, Vancouver, BC. 151
6.11 St John the Divine Anglican Church, Victoria, BC. Col. William Ridway Wilson, 1912. Photo by the author. 153
6.12 Design of a Presbyterian Church by Arnold Woodroofe and C.O. Wickenden. Published in *Canadian Architect and Builder*, 1903. 155
6.13 Homer Street Methodist Church. Victoria, BC. Thomas Hooper, 1888. Photo by the author. 158
6.14 Prospective design for Palmerston Baptist Church by Henry Langley and Edmund Burke. Published in the *Canadian Architect and Builder*, 1888. Photo courtesy of the Archives of Ontario, Horwood Collection 546-0-2 (580). 159
6.15 The Reformed Episcopal Church of Our Lord, Victoria, BC. John Teague Victoria, 1876. Photo by the author. 162

7.1   St Mary's Roman Catholic Church, Indian River, Prince Edward Island. William Critchlow Harris, 1899–1092. Photo by the author. 167
7.2   Specimen page of "The Deformation and the Reformation" in the House of God from *Church Architecture*. Henry Hudson Holly, 1871. Photo courtesy of the National Arts Library, London. 172

A COMMERCE OF TASTE

INTRODUCTION

While writing this book about nineteenth-century religious architecture, economy, and taste during the global economic meltdown of 2008, I could not help but make connections to the troubled world during the lesser-known and little studied Depression of 1873–96. Some important connections in the social structure between religion and an emerging commercialism have been obscured to our generation by the devastation of the 1929 stockmarket crash and the subsequent Depression. But, like for the unfortunates caught in the 1873 Depression, unable to see ahead to changing fortunes, persistence in routine and faith provide rewards. Church-building characterized each of these traits, and it is the business of this book to illustrate how the post-Confederation social structure in Canada was formed alongside religious expansion. Yet, this does not mean that the role of economy was minimized in the material development of religious institution. Rather, the construction of churches in Canada represented the mobilization of significant amounts of community capital (financial, symbolic, and cultural) in an unselfconscious quest for identity, belonging, and spiritual reflection. Public finance in the form of tax-exemptions and private donations provided vital momentum for a range of projects from large-scale urban cathedrals to modest rural church buildings. At the core of these initiatives was volunteerism and community organization.

This is a book about the social and economic structures that constituted the Dominion of Canada. It introduces a new perspective into the way that money and print media intervened in the development of church architecture in Canada. For the reader interested in the early establishment of commercialism in the nineteenth century this manuscript and the specific case studies therein take into account the facts of economic life in a society clinging to a structure dependent upon religion's value system. As a function of the spread of Empire, the construction of Anglican churches was tied into Imperial and colonial politics. Newspaper announcements about church consecrations in the Canadian press, not unlike the popular British press, listed the architects, contractors, prominent patrons, and the cost of construction demonstrating the interrelatedness of economic and political power. What is more, these printed announcements were set pieces in a game of taste whose object was social dominance in an emerging nation. This book demonstrates how money and power were reflected in the way churches looked in the Canadas, but it is also about the social and economic formations around the instrumentalization of history and religion. Church pattern books of churches represented a build-up of cultural capital, and they were the shifting ground upon which taste, money, and architecture made exchanges.

ABOUT SOCIAL FORMATION AND IMPORTED CHURCH PATTERN BOOKS

Transatlantic shipments of books about England's medieval church architecture facilitated an unprecedented spread of the Gothic Revival in the Canadas. The dissemination of text and image was propelled by the advance of printing technology and rapid transoceanic and railway service, constituting a locus of identification in colonial – later, Canadian – architectural practice. Wooden crates packed with builder's newspapers, manufacturer's catalogues, picture postcards of England's cathedrals, and architectural pattern books were frequently unloaded at the Dominion's ports from massive cargo liners, such as the Cunard's Great Britain. The variety of plans, elevations, sections, and perspective drawings contained in pattern books of church architecture clearly marketed the Gothic Revival as a national style for the Canadas and claimed associative social enhancements. Church architecture's close connection with the structure of economic and political formations contextualizes the expansion of Christianity and settler society in the nineteenth century. More specifically, the church pattern books augmented religion's potency by marketing religion in association with taste and visual imagery. The production and consumption of the church pattern books in the Canadian context, in particular, demonstrated the close connection between the trans-Atlantic spread of cultural and religious identity and the marketability of taste in the politics of church-building committees.

The main objective of this text is a study of the business of building churches as it intersected with the church pattern book to provide a new ground for social change. It is not a study of pure economics, nor is it an analysis of architectural styles; instead, this book uses the interconnection between commerce and architectural taste in order to examine the spread of church-building in the colonies. As a new commercial practice no different than the railway and postal service, the church pattern books were responsible for spreading new design ideas in the Dominion, a system that employed a matrix of economy, religion, and, above all, the marketing of taste in the everyday world. Looking at the construction of churches in Canada as assertively affiliated with the spread of the pattern books, the industry of church-building as a form of business becomes apparent. The pattern book promoted neo-Gothic architecture, in a commercial manner, as the most suitable style for churches. The commercial nature of the pattern book relied heavily on variety, resulting in an associated amount of variance in the actual church buildings constructed in Canada between 1867 and 1914. The rise of consumer society during this period – between the negotiation of official Confederation and the outbreak of the First World War – opens up a critical terrain to question how history was instrumentalized to market new building techniques, how church-building was embedded in the expansion of social and economic infrastructures, and how architectural style played a significant role in the visible expression of social status and wealth. At the same time, the church pattern book was a point of convergence of lithographic art and architecture, religion and culture, as well as new commercial practices and commercially driven fashion. As a visual marker of wealth and social prestige the pattern book initially marketed, and eventually lost control of, the exclusivity associated with taste. As more church pattern books entered the marketplace and readerships expanded beyond the professional classes, taste became diluted and the architect lost his heroic status. The claims associated with taste developed into a series of banal and meandering arguments about the way churches should look.

The approach taken in this study uses Canada's social and economic history as a backdrop for a series of case studies of church-building projects. These case studies are linked to one another through their broad application of the styles advertised in church pattern books. The case studies illustrate in detail how the construction of a church in the Canadas expressed international affiliations through an attentive and logical adaptation to local economies. The spread of new church building projects, and of the pattern books themselves, is related to the expansion of new commercial practices in North America, which occurred alongside the growth of religion in a technocratic age and, most importantly, during a period when patterns of public taste became linked to identity.

To better understand how taste was used as a tool to legitimize social and economic dominance, a series of case studies examining Anglican churches in Canada shall be presented alongside comparative cases of churches built by Roman Catholic, Evangelical Christian, and even Jewish groups. The architectural activity of the Church of England in Canada represents the hub of this study because that denomination believed itself in control of the settlement process, even in places where their numbers were not superior. Politicizing taste, Anglicans exerted themselves to ensure the continuation of their social and economic status. The narrative sections of the church pattern book illustrate quite clearly how taste was used to maintain socioeconomic hierarchies, with religion playing a significant role.

Three key issues are focused on in examining the erection of religious monuments: the role of the church pattern books in circulating particular designs, the growing influence of economy in the development of print culture, and the development of national ideologies alongside religion. These concerns illustrate that the mechanical reproduction of the imagery contained in the church pattern books intensively amplified religion in society's consolidation. Meanwhile taste, and not religion, was diluted in the public sphere. The church pattern books operated as a locus of identification, across all denominations, through the publication of church plans and drawings. Meanwhile, new lithographic printing presses and the increased speed of delivery of goods via ship and rail contributed to a greater variety of church designs.

The case studies of church construction projects discussed in this book seek to recover the formation of the imagined "nationhood" that embraced political and commercial culture no less than religious practice. An integral part of Canada's imagined nationhood was the installation of real lines of communication, of which the pattern books may be included as a niche, claiming to offer the population access to new knowledge. Several of the churches examined in this book will be familiar ones to students of nineteenth-century architectural history, but here they receive a novel evaluation focused on cultural economics. In this way, the data – being the visual and textual material in the church pattern books and the actual churches constructed in the Canadas – meets a critical and qualitative analysis of settlement and social formation.

Of the hundreds of church pattern books published in the second half of the nineteenth century, only those known to have been used in Canada and those containing comparisons with Canadian churches have been included. Books key to the case studies include volumes produced in Britain by the architects George Truefitt (*Architectural Sketches on the Continent*, London: 1848, and *Designs for Country Churches*, London: 1850) and Raphael and J. Arthur Brandon (*Parish Churches*, 1st edition, London: 1849). In addition, volumes produced in the US by the architects Frederick Withers (*Church Architecture*, New York: 1873) and Davey James Brooks (*Examples of Modern Architecture*, Boston: 1873) are instrumental. A significant church pattern book compiled by the British-trained architect Frank Wills, *Ancient English Ecclesiastical Architecture and Its Principles Applied to the Wants of the Church at the Present Day* (New York: 1850), illustrates medieval European churches and contemporary designs by the author. Wills is a significant figure in Canadian architectural history, having immigrated to Canada, where he worked briefly in Montreal before leaving for New York.

Looking at the transmission of ideas in architecture via the pattern books imported from Britain and the US also enables a discussion of the different social economies of production as well as the interface between the pattern books and readers in the Dominion. The books also asserted a strong colonial mentality in the sense that the dominant economy superseded the local one. The full-page illustrations of churches in pattern books reflected the sociocultural geography of the authors living in Britain and the US. An architectural history of the books' places of publication in London, New York, and Boston was broadcast. Thus, authors illustrated churches known to them; British books contained British and European medieval churches while American books generally illustrated nineteenth-century North American neo-Gothic designs. The histories contained in the visual and textual material of the church pattern books were legitimized and marketed for adoption in the Canadas by church-building committees, contractors, and builders, as well as architects covertly seeking sources of fashion in Britain and the US.

A remarkably important pattern book for the study of church-building in Canada, as a form of commerce that marketed taste, was produced in 1893 by the General Assembly of Presbyterian Church. *Designs for Village, Town, and City Churches* collectively represented the modest output of several architects and builders working in Canada. This slim pattern book demonstrates the fashionable mode of marketing church designs as though they were not so different from other commercial goods advertised in the book's forward and rear sections. Like the US examples, the one produced in Canada resembled architectural magazines that sold advertising space, setting up a complex relationship between commerciality and authenticity.

ADVANTAGE FOR ANGLICAN CHURCH-BUILDERS

Builders of Anglican churches in the Canadas believed that the Church of England's social prestige and economic privilege ought to translate across the Atlantic Ocean. Since the established Church was a significant agent of the British imperial regime (its Monarch was styled supreme "Defender of the Faith" as constituted in the Church of England), they expected that the most advantageous real estate available for churches must accrue to the Church of England. In crowded towns and cities, corner lots became ideal real estate offering improved visibility. The Anglican Church prized these spaces, though other denominations seeking greater legitimacy in a public sphere quickly followed suit. In rural settings they benefited from large plots of land donated by congregants or purchased at discount from large commercial entities, most notably the Canadian Pacific Railway and the Hudson's Bay Company. Some of these sites included growing towns in the northwest benefiting from discounted prices on CPR land: Calgary in Alberta, as well as Moosejaw and Regina in Saskatchewan. Similar discounts on land were provided to a host of church-builders in small villages that included Rat Portage and Dominion City in Manitoba, as well as Turtle Mountain and Greenwood in British Columbia.[1]

As an expression of reality in this situation the Church of England became a competitor vying against other religious institutions for land, souls to convert, visibility in the community, and money to pay for architectural projects. The established Church of England failed, or refused, to recognize that they were outnumbered in some regions of the Canadas. The case study of St Saviour's Anglican Church in Barkerville, BC (1869) illustrates this concept quite well, since the prominent timber-frame church was located at the head of the only road in town. The building appeared to command the entire gold-rush town except that its Sunday services were markedly underattended as compared to those of the town's simple sawn-log Methodist church.

British immigrants affiliated with the Church of England initially benefited from a demographic head start in the Canadas, one that they often parlayed into a privileged role in the governance of the Dominion. Denying the same advantages to people of Roman Catholic, Methodist, and Baptist faiths, as well as to a large contingent of Eastern European immigrants, was their preferred method of assuring the status quo. This hierarchy in the Canadas was in actuality a complex and shifting terrain rather than the monolith early British settlers would have preferred. The situation was reflected in the way that Anglican church-builders received considerable financial backing from the Church of England, later replaced by local funding as the nineteenth-century wore on. Unable to finance a vast network of church-building campaigns across the immense Canadian landscape the Church of England empowered local church-building committees to erect modest structures. Indeed, the ebb and flow of commercial society across Canada can be traced according to the wealth displayed in the architecture of churches, especially since these projects were funded by community capital and private donation.

As the history of Confederation shows, and as accounted for in this text, the process of forming society in British North America was complex, conflicted, and even counter to the stabilizing logic of a dominant colonial narrative. Disagreement in the religious and political spheres appeared to underlie the daily routine. There was no uniform imperial policy and related colonial process. Confederation was a "deal-making" process reflecting diverse social and cultural interests within a loose association of regions, rather than a monolithic version of the superficially unifying "manifest destiny" of the United States. As with most negotiations, the parties accepted that Confederation meant different things to each participating region. In this sense, provincial politicians likely talked the Confederation into political reality.

Anglican church-building in the Canadas introduced imperial power relations that, positively and negatively, constituted the colonial situation. The imported church pattern books promoted Britain's architectural fashion and contributed to the reinforcement of British mores, cultural values, and economic structures in the Dominion of Canada. As a tool of Britain's power relations with its colonies, taste legitimized British and, to a considerable extent, Anglican cultural privilege. These patterns were eventually overwritten by US hegemony. The Dominion of Canada's population centres were located within relatively easy reach of US publishers' printing presses and their distribution networks. The outpouring of printed material and its accumulating variety of imagery read into, and out of, the pattern books' contributions to some intense architectural debates about the way churches should look. Those aesthetic debates reflected the interdenominational rivalries, as well as the internal tension within the Anglican Communion about the level of ritual observance in worship. For this reason, the iconography of neo-Gothic churches that reflected and reinforced British, and particularly Anglican, socioeconomic and cultural advantage, in essence became unanticipated points of contention.

It is also worth bearing in mind that the notion of a "modern colonial society" grew from the term *Empire*, coming into popular use to describe British expansion in all of its political, economic, and cultural – even religious

– associations. In that regard, the use of the term *Dominion* to describe British North America – months in advance of official Confederation 1 July 1867 – had biblical origins. This term suggested by the New Brunswick politician Samuel Leonard Tilley was found in Psalm 72:8, "His dominion shall be also from sea to sea." Church pattern books similarly wrapped themselves in the mantle of religion and thereby promoted religious institution as the essential practice devoted to community-building. The church pattern books were promoted as agents of social improvement, especially to emerging communities across the Dominion, where assumptions about new construction techniques were joined with the conviction in history's civilizing effect.

I

THE RISE OF COMMERCIAL SOCIETY IN PRE-CONFEDERATION CANADA

A "COMMERCE OF TASTE" IN CHURCH PATTERN BOOKS

Lithographs of churches displayed in pattern books, with spires reaching skyward against an idyllic forested scene, expressed a locus of religious values that became associated with the development of commercial society. Church-building projects in emerging towns and cities scattered across the Canadas that took English country churches as their models represented an imagined return to a romantic pastoral life rendered obsolete by modern economy (fig. 1.1). The strength of such imaginings brought similarly attired churches into existence in emerging Canadian railway towns like Fort George, British Columbia (fig. 1.2). Below the surface of the way things looked, the organization of building committees composed of businessmen, lawyers, architects, and builders demonstrated that erecting a church was dependent on the utilization of modern economic systems.

It is more than a little ironic that modern economy was exploited to produce an architectural fashion that embraced historical precedent. The illustrations of churches nestled in serene landscapes and unencumbered by signs of cluttered urban life reflect upon the perceived compassion and empathy of religious society. Beneath this superficial analysis is a much more complex series of commercial, political, social, and cultural affiliations. They can be described as the cultivated values associated with taste marking the stakes of social advantage, belonging, and group respectability as well as exclusion.[2]

These value systems were powerful, and often unconscious, expressions of individual and group positions and dispositions that defined power relationships. The cultural sociologist Pierre Bourdieu described such relationships in the literary field, intuitively understood on the basis of collective life experience in socioeconomic situations. Similar situations appeared as "rules of the game" for the architect turned pattern-book author and his reading

Fig. 1.1 Watercolour of St Mary, Brook, Isle of Wight.

Fig. 1.2 The English Church (St George's Anglican Church), Fort George, British Columbia, c. 1911.

public. This means, for instance, that an architect's rank in the profession, his social status, and even religious affiliation were deeply connected to his disposition toward his preferences for a particular architectural style. The space between an architect's position and his disposition in the game of outclassing competitors can be described, as Bourdieu explained, as the "habitus."[3] The habitus was akin to a trump card; that is, it was not only an architect's pedigree, but it was also the clubs he joined, the magazines he read, the class of designs he included in a pattern book he authored, and whether he was able to amass designs for a book in the first instance. It was all of the underlying connections that an architect's practice needed to thrive. As we will see, the habitus also marked out the space of architectural rivalries among religious denominations and it delineated the antagonisms between advocates of the revived Classical and Gothic architectural idioms, the aptly named "Battle of the Styles."

Architecture defined and distilled social and economic relationships in the public eye, especially when the issue of taste arose. People who stood to benefit from "enforcing" a connection between taste and the enduring, apparently permanent, aspects of antiquity intended to make this relationship proprietary to themselves alone. Church architecture became a field on which these struggles were played out, and books depicting illustrations of churches further extended that field into a commercial realm. Yet, this struggle was far from the only thing going on inside and outside of the church pattern books.

Inside the pattern books a collection of plans, elevations, sections, and perspective drawings of churches – mainly depicting medieval styles of the twelfth to the sixteenth centuries revived in the Victorian era – combined appropriate historical vocabulary and descriptive text (fig. 1.3). A pattern book generally offered practical building solutions while plainly characterizing a system dedicated to the proliferation of superficial variety, which was a chief characteristic of commercial society. The continued renewal of the images of churches promoted in a progression of pattern books brought the commercial aspects of marketing architecture into an uncomfortable association with religious identity.

The church pattern books boldly marketed a multitude of architectural plans by promising to enhance education and taste. Marketing the pattern books also promoted the imagery of churches, decisively locating fashion within the business of building churches. The competition between different pattern books for a share of the church-building consumer caused readerships to think of the lithographs of churches as both advertisement and educational material. Most pattern book authors were careful to promote taste-cum-fashion as a quality of education if not personal distinction. Readers who were

Fig. 1.3 Specimen page of an elevation of Netley Abbey.

accustomed to paying large sums for fashionable items also believed that the increased cost of erecting a complex church plan – as listed in the pattern books – was a sign of taste and consequently social status. Such readers thought that their appreciation for this system of economic and cultural exchange was the very sign of status they wished to project. For the wealthy and status-conscious church-builder, the look of a church in this printed format seemed to bestow social rank.

The relationship between taste – more properly defined as commercially driven fashion – education, and religion was unsustainable; the pattern book author George Truefitt, like many other architects authoring similar texts, was in the uncomfortable position of disavowing his intention to market taste while clearly defining the superiority of his designs on the basis of taste. As in the literary field, artists attempted to marshal their symbolic power by disavowing any interest in economy; however, artistry and economy were closely linked in the practice of architecture. Truefitt tried to navigate this difficulty with the following statement in the preface of his pattern book: "As the present work appeals principally to the eye, being composed of sketches, it may at first sight hardly seem to require a preface; but being intended to illustrate attempts at design, some explanation may be permitted with reference to its pretensions and the motives for submitting it to the Public; and for this purpose, a cursory retro-spective glance at the rise and progress of the revival of the *taste* for Pointed Architecture in this country appears necessary."[4] Truefitt assured his readership of the legitimacy of his artistic status, backfilling his position with claims to superior taste.

A "commerce of taste" could not truly be disavowed since it paralleled the production and consumption cycle evident in the construction of new churches in the Dominion and in the distribution of imported church pattern books. The rich quality of engraved images in the books helped to convey the sort of affluence to which wealthy church-builders in the Dominion aspired and to which ordinary folk could only imagine. The logic of the pattern book's organization, with more expensive-to-construct churches catalogued in the rear section of the book, fitted with a contemporary idea of upselling; that is, the cheap designs were placed up front in the books in order to entice patrons to self-identify with elaborate, exclusive, and more costly designs on subsequent pages. Architects were the direct beneficiaries of costlier projects, since their fee was based on a percentage of the construction expense. Poorer congregations able to build only modestly were encouraged to think that their first building was a temporary church intended for replacement on a grander architectonic scale. It appeared as if congregational growth and money was all that stood in their way.

The social and commercial realm around the pattern books was characterized by mobility and the constitution of historical references in architecture. Illustrated print-based books of church architecture signalled history's deployment as a stabilizing force on modernity. History was treated, like taste, as a commodity. The pattern books both purveyed an enduring sense of taste as well as acted as ciphers of the new transience of the economy linking architecture with the latest building fashions.

A "commerce of taste" enabled the exploitation of medieval aesthetics conceptualized in the pattern books as enduring and permanent.[5] The exchanges of social, cultural, and economic capital democratized the art of architecture and consequently destabilized the nascent stage of architectural professionalization in Canada. A remarkable aspect of the pattern book, and especially its representation in church-building enterprise, was the balance of commerciality and the sense of decorum that appealed to church-builders. The pattern books introduced in the Canadas new commercial and consumption practices that constituted new social identities. This new social order was particularly apparent in the development of a "modern" Dominion, despite its deep roots in British tradition, history, and values. Britain had already experienced a so-called transformation into "modern" society brought to the fore as much by economy as by technology. Goods, social veneers, and lifestyles that characterized modernity remade the substance of everyday life in Canada's expanding settlements.[6]

Taste was a marketable commodity in the church pattern books that manifested publicly in the fabric of a church. In the field of architectural practice, which was itself a commercial endeavour, the circulation of print constituted a parallel commercial culture. Architects, amateurs, and enthusiasts upheld the system that distributed church pattern books, which had economic, social, and cultural ramifications. Different groups of readers responded to the church pattern books according to their social positions. Advisory boards composed of merchant and professional classes, which formed church-building committees to choose an architect, approve a design, and fundraise for construction, used pattern books to familiarize themselves with the wide assortment of available church designs. They manifested in real space congregational and diocesan worldviews by identifying with particular architectural classifications. These categories were representations of style as well as money, each displayed in the pattern books. At the same time, pattern books were used extensively in the training process of new students in an architectural practice. Students learned the art of drawing through copying existing designs before the advent of schools dedicated to architectural and structural principles. At the heart of this educational and classifying structure was the power of marketing a broad historical canon. That canon most certainly included books illustrating a Classical grammar of architecture that reached all the way back to Ancient Greece. The canon of classical motifs and proportions represented in the architect Vitruvius's text *De Architectura*, written in the first century BCE, was rediscovered by Classical enthusiasts such as Sebastiano Serlio in *The General Rules of Architecture* (1537) and Andrea Palladio in *The Four Books of Architecture* (1570). There can be no doubt that these volumes canonized Classical architecture for generations of architects and designers that followed, influencing Colen Campbell's production of *Vitruvius Britannicus* in three volumes (1715, 1717, and 1725) and James Gibb's *A Book of Architecture* (1728). By the nineteenth century a "battle of the Styles" developed, in which medievalists exerted the influence of an alternate canon of architecture based not on the module and geometry but on a Romantic and flexible language of beauty. The battle fought on the field of illustrated print publications had each side claiming victory, the Classicists, whose book publication had evolved into the production of encyclopedias, and the Medievalists, whose books commercialized the Gothic idiom.

Like other new commercial practices, church pattern books were analogous to mail-order catalogues in which consumers shopped for "ancient-inspired" church designs. Though the church pattern books contained replicable plans of medieval and neo-Gothic churches, audiences opportunistically selected from the parts of the specimen designs that best suited them. Examples of Early English churches illustrated in Raphael and J. Arthur Brandon's pattern book, *Parish Churches* (1849), included Shiere Church, Surrey, England (fig. 1.4). The simplicity of the Early English architectural

Fig. 1.4 Specimen page of Shiere Church from *Parish Churches*.

Fig. 1.5 Christ Church (Anglican), Maugerville, New Brunswick.

vocabulary, with its thin lancet windows, simple corner buttresses, and meaty tower easily recreated in wood, appears at Christ Church in the village of Upper Maugerville, New Brunswick (1856) (fig. 1.5).

The circulation of print media gave taste-cum-fashion a complex spatial dimension. The spatial property of the "commerce of taste" was a major component channelling two-dimensional visual imagery into the built form, in a close and conflicted relationship. Transposing designs on paper into the built form was previously the privileged domain of the architect and builder. The advent of the pattern books extended this privilege to the reader, causing the professional architect to use claims of taste to control the whims of his client.[7] It was a dangerous game. The architect had to be careful to avoid offending his clientele, who ranged from church-building committees to bishops representing divinity on Earth. On the other hand, the pattern books, as commercial items, had no such social restrictions.

Without realizing the impact of the spatial dimension of taste coupled with modern science and technology, readers of the church pattern books disrupted religious institution's mystical authority. The mechanical spread of print-based visual and verbal imagery, thus, brought about a varied and opportunistic use of church illustrations. Public debates coalesced around the way churches should look, fuelled by the variety of church engravings in illustrated pattern books. The advantage in these debates was taste. Its power appeared to be derived from an extra-generational and perennial spring of social and economic status, when, in actuality, taste was never a fixed commodity but one always associated with changeable power structures. Public taste was a system of classificatory rules, habits, and customs that disposed people to certain preferences but also reflected the social norms and was embodied in the consumption that reproduced the social order.[8]

The commodification of taste in the church pattern books contributed to the dispersal of the aura associated with the "real" Gothic church. But, of course, Victorian church buildings were a substitution, and repetition, of a false image for a previous "real" one: the medieval church. Despite architects' efforts to create authenticity around the Gothic Revival, the pattern books actually reinforced the shadowy semblance of the simulacra. It was a temporal impossibility to build medieval churches in the nineteenth century, and so the pattern books represented an authoritative link to the past. The books constituted an aura of authenticity around the author's intent on gaining control over his clientele. An author also claimed to be able to elevate a reader's taste without also realizing that he was negating the exclusivity of taste through its broad public appeal. More widely available and cheaply produced pattern books meant greater public access to the visual language of church architecture and associated "commerce of taste." However, the increased public access to visual material associated with commercially based taste did not deliver on the books' promises to elevate the status of the masses. Instead, broad public participation in a "commerce of taste" eroded the "traditional" sacrosanct social distinctions. Consequently, the Dominion's church-builders used pattern books in ways unanticipated by the books' authors, picking from the parts of individual designs that appealed the most and recombining the vocabulary in eclectic ways. Public access to visual material in the pattern books tended to produce copies of British churches rather than flexible turns of an architectural Gothic phrase.

Commercialized taste became a component in the identity-making process associated with church-building in the decades after official Confederation. The result of marketing taste in the public domain, especially in print media, conflated the transience of fashion with the enduring and permanent aspects of taste. Taste-cum-fashion became a leveller in colonial society because of increased access to money and goods, formerly associated with

Old World landed gentry. Pattern book author Rev. George Bowler expressed concern over the transience of public taste:

> We do not claim a greater knowledge, – *more perfect taste*, – better judgement or superior professional skill, to our compeers ... Having made the science of Building a study of some years before entering the ministry, we had gained some knowledge of the principles of *correct taste* in constructing the different styles of private and public buildings, and in common with others we could not fail to notice *the great want of taste and skill* which is so fully manifest in every village and hamlet throughout the land.[9]

Bowler also expressed the desire of most architects and pattern book authors, who wanted to pacify their clients' opinions and distance themselves from builders, as such "it will never do to trust the matter to the *taste and skill* of your builder, for there are very few of those who call themselves practical men and practical carpenters who are competent to design with taste and skill, and to combine all the details of an edifice in the best manner, and in right proportions."[10] The discourses around professionalization and claims of taste were more plainly stated in a book of compiled designs by some of the leading US architects of the day, *A Book of Plans for Churches and Parsonages* (1853): "There are ... those of the plane and the saw who also have an eye for architecture as an art, and such men often build very unexceptional structures. But the majority of carpenters have hardly more sense of what is really involved in Architecture, than is needful to the building of a barn."[11]

Trade and the marketing of goods increased as a result of increased populations, much of which occurred within the developing urban areas. In the Dominion, pattern books that were intended to promote an "elite" social advantage actually provided everyone with the same access to taste, or at least with its claims. The claims were related to the old ideas of value and history as an instrumental force. Thus, the ecclesiastical journal *The Church* engaged in commercialized taste by printing the following account of a new Anglican church in Ontario:

> It was only the other day that a kind friend drove us out in his carriage from Hamilton to see, for the first time, the little Barton church, which is a perfect gem in its way – the model, indeed, for country churches. The architectural correctness of this pretty edifice is due to the good taste of the late incumbent, the Rev. R.N. Merritt ... He was happy in the choice of his architect, Mr Frank Wills, a gentleman who,

we have every reason to believe, is imbued with the religious spirit of his noble profession, as every church architect ought to be. In carrying out the plans furnished by Mr Wills, Mr Merritt's own appreciation of genuine Church architecture and good taste were of service to him. The result has been the erection of a building which affects you with a pleasing interest the moment the eye rests on it; and simple village-church as it is, fills the mind, immediately on entering it, with a quiet and solemn sense of God's presence. We have never entered a church in Canada where the effect of softened light and internal arrangements was so instantaneous and so complete in exciting devotional impressions.[12]

This account was typical of the invented exclusivity that Anglicans seemed to attach to taste.

The growing impact of print media was exemplified by the emergence of public opinion. Greater access to newspapers, magazines, and books spread ideas in social circles and fuelled the diversity of public opinion. The debate focused intently on the issue of architectural style that involved conflicting claims of taste. The church pattern books tended almost exclusively to favour the aesthetics of the neo-Gothic style. British immigrants building a religious infrastructure in the Dominion associated the images of Gothic Revival churches in the pattern books with extended British imperial power. This was particularly important to British rule in the Dominion of Canada because North America had no medieval roots except the ones imposed by the colonial situation. The deployment of British and European medieval-revival motifs lent churches built in the Dominion an appearance of permanence. British-trained architects operating in the Dominion appropriated medieval planning and aesthetics to legitimize the modern cultural claims of their clientele. The church pattern books imported from Britain represented an important transatlantic cultural connection that private money intensified by erecting medieval-style churches in the Dominion of Canada.

Applying taste's social distinctions to the visual and verbal imagery of churches associated the new middle-class consumer with religious institution. The church pattern books spread to, and circulated within, British North America because readerships had been readied by exposure to imported newspapers that prized religious architecture, such as the *Illustrated London News* (1842–1989) and *The Builder* (1843–1966). These British publications spawned equivalent, if short-lived, offshoots in the Dominion: the *Canadian Illustrated News* (1869–83) and the *Canadian Architect and Builder* (1888–1908). The implementation of the visual imagery, in a Canadian and colonial context, was the strength of these magazines. The emerging middle class in the Dominion valued the visual imagery and knowledge in imported books just as pictures from abroad gratified the nineteenth-century viewer's sense of movement and mobility. Thus, the pattern books can be understood to have compressed time and moved architectural fashion across vast distances.

The expansion of print distribution in the Dominion was closely related to the development of infrastructure that included railway lines, a major factor that compressed time and space. Rail connected networks of booksellers, among them, T.N. Hibben and Company of Victoria, British Columbia, which relied heavily on rail for regular delivery of commercial goods. Hibbens also benefited from the lowering of postal rates and tariffs just as architects and builders across the Dominion increased productivity by a timely access to the latest techniques and fashion occurring in Britain and the US. Keeping up with subtle shifts in architectural trends in church-building was as important to the colonial architect as the trends in knowledge was to the bookseller.

Envisioned as boundless and fluid matrices of "libidinal economies," consumers modified, transgressed, and reinterpreted the social order.[13] Through the commercialization of knowledge, Charles Eastlake's book *Hints on Household Taste* (1868, reprinted 1869, 1872, 1878) showed how taste was consolidated around modern lifestyle. Here, he unselfconsciously couples a "commerce of taste" with the growth of arts manufacture, including architecture:

> The faculty of distinguishing good from bad design in the familiar objects of domestic life is a faculty which most educated people – and women especially – conceive that they possess ... that, while a young lady is devoting at school, or under a governess so many hours a day to music, so many to languages and so many to general science, she is all this time unconsciously forming that sense of the beautiful, which we call taste ... to form a correct estimate of the merits of art-manufacture ... We may condemn a lady's opinion on politics – criticise her handwriting – correct her pronunciation of Latin, and disparage her favourite author with a chance of escaping displeasure. But if we venture to question her taste – in the most ordinary sense of the word, we are sure to offend.[14]

Eastlake complained that the transience of fashion, which he associated with "feminine" domestic space, had infringed on the enduring taste associated with "masculine" church architecture. But his complaints were actually indications of what was common practice in the public arena; that is, taste and fashion converged at the point of economy.

The transience of fashion was a problem for pattern book authors selling the idea of enduring taste. In this way, taste and fashion began to be conflated by contemporary pattern book readers. Taste's social superiority and the privilege that went with it were contingent on people's willingness to suspend their disbelief in the transience of fashion.

Case Study: Christ Church Cathedral, Montreal, Quebec (1857)

The British-trained architect Frank Wills (1822–1857) employed an ambitious Gothic Revival design to win the commission to rebuild Christ Church (later promoted to cathedral status) in Montreal in 1857 (fig. 1.6). Fire had destroyed the Anglican church on 10 December the year previous, erasing the earlier Georgian style structure of 1821. The new church galvanized the city, and the commission had the potential to solidify Wills's career in North America. It became an opportunity to reimagine what an Anglican church ought to look like in the Dominion. Wills proposed a cruciform-plan church in the Decorated English style of medieval architecture, specifically recalling the fourteenth-century St Mary's, Snettisham, Norfolk, England (fig. 1.7). The architect invigorated the surface of his church with rich ornamental detail on the buttresses,

Fig. 1.6 Christ Church Anglican Cathedral, Montreal, Quebec.

Fig. 1.7 St Mary's, Snettisham, Norfolk, England, thirteenth century.

spire, windows, and the projecting triple-arched western porch. The roughly textured Montreal greystone added another layer of richness to this building erected, on rue Saint-Catherine, in Montreal's emerging commercial sector.

Bishop Francis Fulford of the Anglican Diocese of Montreal was charged with overseeing the plans for construction. His monumental neo-Gothic cathedral rising 70 metres (230 ft) at the spire became a rallying point for an Anglican, and primarily English-speaking, minority in Lower Canada. Anglicans represented only fourteen percent of the Montreal population. As such, the church expressed in stone the conviction of Lord Durham's famous report of 1839 to the British Monarch that recommended the "French issue" be "settled" through the cultural assimilation and amalgamation of Upper and Lower Canada. This small enclave of the established Church was surrounded by a majority of Roman Catholic neighbourhoods. The architect Frank Wills articulated the tension between Anglican and Roman Catholic sects in Montreal when he wrote about the different styles of architecture adopted in church-building. In his pattern book *Ancient English Ecclesiastical Architecture* (1850) Wills explained:

> There is a catholicity in architecture as well as in the Church, and may be separated from Popery as well in one as the other, the dross removed, the rest is all our own, and let us use it as our inheritance. The wretched Gothic abortions every day witnessed and everyday lauded, have no

more right to the appellation of Christian architecture than the late New England heresy is to be considered as an article in the creed of the Catholic Church; they both have their origin in the vagaries of ignorant men, and ere long, will share an equally ignominious fate.[15]

The reference to "Popery" was a derogatory term used by Anglicans to describe what they believed was an overabundance of ritual in Roman Catholic church service. The implication that Roman Catholic church architecture was impure or "dross" meant that Anglicans claimed the entirety of English medieval architectural history for their own. Indeed, it even appeared unnecessary, or redundant, for Wills to include the term *Anglican* in the title of his pattern book, as was the case with most others written for Anglican use, furthering the Church of England's assertion of exclusive cultural ownership of English medieval architecture and its premiere place in pattern book production.

Frank Wills presented his pattern book in 1856 to the building committee of Christ Church as a matter of advertising. The book was produced with self-promotion in mind because its pages were organized in the fashion of a hybrid of British and US ecclesiastical pattern books (fig. 1.8). For churches in US and Canadian cities, Wills replicated English churches, abbeys, chapels, and cathedrals from the Middle Ages, typical of pattern books printed in London. As a matter of self-promotion, he also included samples of his own church designs in the manner of pattern books produced in New York and Boston. Compared to British books, the US pattern book format allowed for more self-aggrandizement and the general marketing of church-building as an unapologetic commercial endeavour.

Ambivalent to relationships between commerce and religion, the Ecclesiological (formerly, Cambridge Camden) Society in Britain generally applauded the cruciform layout and the exterior ornament at Christ Church, as supervised in construction by Thomas Seaton Scott (1836–1895) after Frank Wills's premature death. Concerning itself very little with economic matters, the society was a learned organization formed by industrious undergraduates at Cambridge University in 1839 to promote and study Gothic Revival architecture. Through the quarterly publication of their *Ecclesiologist* (1841–68) journal, as well as a series of inexpensive pamphlets entitled *A Few Words to Churchbuilders...*, the editors advised their membership of seven hundred architects, clergymen, and enthusiasts on matters of architectural taste. According to its editorial board, comprised mainly of John Mason Neale and Alexander Beresford Hope, Christ Church, Montreal, marked "an epoch in transatlantic ecclesiology."[16] The attention marked an important episode in the ecclesiastical architecture of Canada since the Ecclesiological Society

Fig. 1.8 Specimen page of St Peter's Church, Philadelphia.

acknowledged only two other churches in the Dominion as having worthy Gothic vocabulary: St James' Cathedral in Toronto (1853) and Fredericton Cathedral, New Brunswick (1845).

Another publication that recognized the importance of Montreal's contribution to ecclesiastical architecture in Canada was the *Illustrated London News*, which published an account of the opening ceremony in 1860. A perspective illustration of the cathedral accompanied the description of the building heralded as "the most beautiful specimen of ecclesiastical architecture in Canada, if not on the American Continent."[17] Construction costs were proportionately high, estimated as £35,000, given the inclusion of the elaborate ornamentation of the building. The costs also included a plan to offer a portion of the seats free, or "open," to worshippers unable to pay the fee to lease seats. This meant that the community at Christ Church had been willing to support some portion of the construction costs through donation rather than the lease of every seat in the church. This philanthropic endeavour required the support of donors that had typically made their own fortunes through the new forms of mercantilism made accessible because of Montreal's busy ports. Indeed, Montreal's merchant economy was sustained by the Maritime shipbuilding and shipping industries.

The industrial manufacture that developed in the province of Quebec, and especially at Montreal, after 1850 shaped the political and social debates of the time. Montreal's geographic location on the St Lawrence assisted mercantile, and thus urban, growth. By 1860, Montreal's population growth to 90,323 – supporting 14 foundries employing 427 workers – was sustainable for only a decade. The international economic downturn that started in 1873 weakened Quebec's manufacturing sector, causing the province to lag behind Ontario as an agricultural producer. Quebec failed to develop the wealth and local capital necessary to encourage capital-intensive, high-value-added industry. The economy eventually recovered but permanently brought to a close Montreal's aspirations to erect grand displays of neo-Gothic ecclesiastical architecture.

A SOCIAL LIFE OF CHURCH PATTERN BOOKS

The visual and verbal nuance of church pattern books is divisible into two fundamental formats – specimen books and pattern books – that demonstrate the commercial practices of their places of production. Specimen books were typically produced in Britain and other European countries; the format included the depiction of a series of elevations, perspective views, and architectural details of medieval buildings. There were great numbers of books of churches organized by specific regions in Britain, such as *Churches of Yorkshire* (1844) by G.A. Poole and *A Guide to the Architectural Antiquities in the Neighbourhood of Oxford* (1842). This type of book contained an historical and architectural analysis, depicting church plans, perspectives, and a great many architectural details, including corbels, window tracery, and mouldings worked out in section. They were the architectural guidebooks of their age. Exemplifying the type of book that emphasized its picture content, showing artistic renderings of perspective views, was the book *Specimens of Medieval Architecture Chiefly Selected from Examples of the 12th and 13th Centuries in France and Italy* (1862) by the British architect William Eden Nesfield (fig. 1.9). It depicted the soaring towers, lavish interiors, intricate doorways, and rich foliage popular among architects and enthusiasts. These intricate images promoted Nesfield's skill as a draughtsman, the architect's chief art and mode of communication. The ambitious assertion of history in the service of architecture was matched by the imposing size and weight of Nesfield's book, which meant that a reader had to stand at a table to contemplate the harmony of his large-scale designs and sweeping picturesque exteriors. An authoritative introductory section, typical of specimen and pattern formats, recounted a brief history of medieval architecture and the Gothic Revival. *Specimens of Medieval Architecture* differed substantially from other pattern books emerging out of London's active lithographic presses because it depicted architecture of the Continent rather than Britain. In this way, Nesfield cut against the prevailing belief among many British architects that claimed pre-eminence for English styles from the twelfth century onward.[18] The high degree to which this ascendancy was applauded by British readers, intensified among settlers in the Canadas engaged in instituting religious space, was testament to the power of print and its association with the construction of knowledge. Specimen books that depicted a full suite of views constituted a canon of Britain's architectural and historical achievements, typified by Edmund Sharpe's 1870 publication of *Illustrations of the Conventual Church of the Benedictine Abbey of St Germaine at Selby*. In fact, Sharpe had made a niche business from publishing individual English churches, cathedrals, and abbeys with the aid of colour lithography to enrich the Romantic zest of the limited-edition sets. Raphael and J. Arthur Brandon adopted a similar catalogue format – minus the romantic views – in the publication of *Parish Churches; Being Perspective Views of English Ecclesiastical Structures Accompanied by Plans Drawn to a Uniform Scale* (1849).

By contrast, the type of books referred to as pattern books contained practical plans and workmanlike perspective views of churches that were intended to assist with the actual design, planning, and construction of a building. These books offered uncomplicated drawings of churches in plan, section, elevation, and detail that a capable builder could consult during the construction of a church. This format of book was produced chiefly in New York and Boston in order to promote US architects, a prime example being the 1873 publication of *Church Architecture: Plans, Elevations, and Views of Twenty-One Churches and Two School Houses* by Frederick Withers (fig. 1.10). Withers's book begins to seem quite similar to a catalogue of mail-order goods, showing how closely related was the architectural canon and the catalogue. This becomes apparent when turning the pages of *Examples of Modern Architecture, Ecclesiastical and Domestic* (1873), a haphazard collection of various renderings of well-known architects including contributors Sir George Gilbert Scott, George Edmund Street, and J.P. Seddon.

Fig. 1.9 Specimen pages of Sens Cathedral (left), view of towers at Senlis and Covantres (below).

New York publishers such as Standford and Sword, as well as William T. Comstock, innovated a new format in the pattern book that blended the presentation of medieval specimens with neo-Gothic designs emerging from the drawing tables of contemporary architects. The tactic legitimized new designs by marketing them in close association with the visual history of medieval churches. Frank Wills adopted the approach in the 1850 publication of *Ancient Ecclesiastical Architecture*. Coincident with the appropriation of history to serve modern demands of marketing was Wills's disavowal of being interested in selling designs for monetary profit. His denunciation of history to facilitate contemporary economy (Wills claimed that friends persuaded him to publish a clutch of his own designs in the book) involved a ritual disavowal of making money at the expense of art. Through his disavowal of economic interest Wills asserted a greater respect for the symbolic value of his production, which would indirectly – and thus legitimately – lead to monetary benefit. Wills veiled self-promotion behind humility with an approach not unfamiliar to church missionary movements that spread among settlers. Interestingly, within twenty years this sense of decorum was virtually

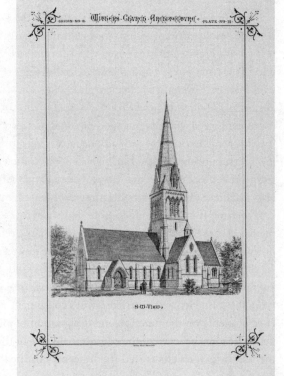

Fig. 1.10 Specimen page of design no. 8, plate 15, from *Church Architecture*.

eroded from the architectural profession in the US, and to some lesser extent in Britain, by architects blatantly marketing their designs for churches in pattern books. By the early 1870s, the US architects Frederick Withers and Henry Hudson Holly produced pattern books that exclusively contained a series of churches they had proposed and built in various US towns and cities. Economy demanded the reduction of the historical introductory narrative, by this time little more than a formality. The formerly heroic quality ascribed to medieval architectural history changed into pithy historical cliché.

Print media helped propel British and European architectural history into the service of modern architectural fashion. Architects in Canada believed that newspapers, journals, and especially books offered accurate representations of architectural fashion abroad. After the 1870s, the centre of public taste for the Gothic Revival, as far as the pattern books were concerned, shifted from Europe to New York. US pattern books appeared to greatly influence the Canadian building trade. The vanguard of this shift was charted by the emigration of Frank Wills from Fredericton, New Brunswick, to New York in 1848. There, he inaugurated the New York Ecclesiological Society, modelled on its namesakes in Britain, and founded a quarterly journal called *The New York Ecclesiologist* that echoed the philosophy and format of the *Ecclesiologist* in Britain.

The spread of pattern books distributed in the Dominion crossed paths with the development of architectural education. In this sense, the encyclopedic volumes of architecture that used small-format diagrammatic pictures supported the commerce of taste marketed in the large-scale illustrations included in the church pattern books. Joseph Gwilt's *Encyclopaedia of Architecture Historical, Theoretical, and Practical* (1842) – with its more than 1,700 inset thumbnail-sized wood engravings – became standard reading for the Ontario Architectural Association and the Quebec Architectural Association long after it was first published in London.[19] Divided into sections of exoticized buildings from ancient Babylon, Persia, Egypt, Greece, and China, the massive volume also included Britain's architecture represented by Gothic or "Pointed" architecture. It is interesting to note that the term "Pointed" in reference to medieval churches, synonymous with "Christian" architecture, came into use during the nineteenth century rather than the fourteenth.

Similar encyclopedic texts taught geometry and proportion using wood engravings inset in the text. *Introduction to the Study of Gothic Architecture* (1849) by John Henry Parker, like Gwilt's continually reprinted book, enlightened students on the function and designation of all facets of architectural detail. Readers believed in the educational value of the material contained in the text, which chiefly traced the trajectory of the Gothic Revival from its roots in England's Saxon heritage to its spread onto the Continent.[20] An earlier reference book on architecture dealing more directly with the notion of taste was *An Attempt to Discriminate the Styles of English Architecture, from the Conquest to the Reformation* (1817), written by the British architect Thomas Rickman. In was in this text that Rickman organized and categorized the architectural histories of the British Isles into terms imbued with geographical and temporal meaning, such as, "Saxon," "Norman," "Early English," "Decorated English," and "Perpendicular." Many of these terms are still in use today. Competing for control of the knowledge market, US stakeholders concerned with the promotion of church architecture enlisted the Rev. George Wolfe Shinn to write *King's Handbook of Notable Episcopal Churches in the United States* (1889, reprinted 1893). Shinn's book could not compete with Britain's rich architectural history. Instead, it presented the deep history of the Episcopal Church in the US and provided data on the architects, builders, patrons, and construction costs. Seeking the most up-to-date technology for illustrations, the publisher engaged the process of photogravure to render a photographic image aided by mechanically etched plates that allowed images to be embedded in the body of text (fig. 1.11). The richness of imagery delivered by the photogravure and other photographic methods merely simulated, in the 1880s, the eighteenth-century's consumption of expensive hand-etched and hardbound books. This progression of imaging technique was neatly encapsulated in James Fergusson's illustrations for *History of the Modern Styles of Architecture* (1862, reprinted 1873, 1891). The book's sequential sections advanced from wood engravings, to steel-plate engravings, to photo-lithographic techniques. In it, one can see the progression in print technologies, brought to market by new economies, of which the "commerce of taste" was an important feature. Fergusson discussed the technical and economic progress of architecture in a manner suited to his status as a wealthy mercantilist from India retired to London to write critical and comparative essays on architecture of the world. Fergusson was critical of progress, as exemplified by the way he contrasted the purity and simplicity of religion against the complicated socioeconomic and technical aspects of modern engineering. Indeed, his introductory section began by stating that the Gothic Revival was "mainly an ecclesiastical movement ... the real hold it has upon the people arises from their religious ... feelings."[21] His volume proceeded through architectural styles used in England, Europe, and the US, concluding with a section on civil and military engineering in which he reinforced the separation of engineering from architecture, hardly a progressive view. Architecture, he argued, was an unparalleled art. It was grounded in nostalgia for the noble edifices of the past while engineering was concerned chiefly with the management of the

Fig. 1.11 Specimen page of a photogravure illustration of Church of the Ascension, Washington, DC.

future. One sees Fergusson clearly infatuated with the exotic architecture of the east and his youth in this criticism of architectural improvements:

> the history of Architecture during the three or four centuries to which the contents of this treatise extend... is sufficiently melancholy and discouraging. For the first time in history the most civilized nations of the world have agreed to forsake the only path that could lead to progress or perfection in the "Master Art," and have been wandering after shadows that constantly elude their grasp. When we consider the extent to which building operations have been carried during that period, the amount of wealth lavished on architectural decoration, and the amount of skill and knowledge available for its direction, it is very sad to think that all should have been comparatively wasted.[22]

It was inevitable that Fergusson turn to the links between commerce, knowledge, and taste, since those three poles were the basis of his lived experience: "we have more wealth, more mechanical skill, more refinement than any nation, except perhaps the Greeks, and taste (even if not innate) may result from the immense extent of our knowledge."[23] From this perspective it is clear how the position of the architect-turned-author was constituted in economy and taste. Church pattern books fed into the commerce of knowledge and taste that both attempted to alleviate and yet often reinforced social disadvantage, in that Hobbesian sense of everyone for himself, in which architects sought out clients from their competitors. On the one hand, church pattern books were caught up in a field of architecture that had its own laws of functioning, as Bourdieu would put it, composed of dominants and dominated. Those within the field, the successful and the struggling alike, tried to hold the field intact by keeping others out and controlling the taste of their clients. On the other hand, church pattern books were akin to the do-it-yourself manual, popularized during the self-help trend of the nineteenth century, which had the appearance of opening up the field of building to virtually anyone. The pattern books provided architectural knowledge and also contributed to the increased demand for it. A general reader's interest in the imagery in the books also enlarged the distance from the building standards that elevated the professional's status. Taste was that other critical and political factor that the church pattern book promised, only to elude the general reader in the assertions of the professional crowd.

During the rise of commercial society, observant Canadian architects recognized the dangerous connection between taste and church architecture in relation to the instrumentality of knowledge. The Vancouver architect Robert M. Fripp noted, "all denominations in the Dominion share guilt in making poor church architecture which is 'history in stone of a nation' ... Perishable as most of our modern buildings are, they will endure long enough to exercise a baneful influence on the habits of *taste* that do duty with most people for education or cultivated taste. Future students of architecture in Canada will be influenced by the junk we build today."[24] Fripp's description of the social and economic mechanisms of taste, a clutch of claims and counter-claims aimed at establishing contested hierarchies, was accurate. In Fripp's words, "cultivated or educational taste" was equated with knowledge only so long as nothing upset the traditional sovereign unity of a subject. Fripp, who owned a copy of James Kellaway Colling's pattern book, *Art Foliage* (1874) (fig. 1.12), understood that church pattern books produced after the 1840s subtly marketed all sorts of new architectural ideas masquerading as traditional building technique. Depicting a series of architectural details, including foliated capitals, tile patterns, and carved ornament, the book marketed history as a dynamic field of representations of knowledge.

Publishers keen to present the full spectrum of progressive-to-conservative church designs as a form of cultivated education created books that appeared to be expensive, bound editions of hand-pulled etchings. In fact the contrary was true; the church pattern books produced after 1840 tended to use cheaper lithographic technology even though the imagery of churches in the books still contained the fine hatch lines associated with hand-pulled etchings.

Colling's books are good examples of this technique. Publishers sold the latest architectural fashions by using pseudo-etched prints marketed as historical authority. The result of the scheme of promoting history to market the latest trends in architecture replaced the mystifying experience of an original work of art with the exhibition value of mechanical reproductions. A later contemplation on the age of mechanical reproduction by Walter Benjamin in the 1930s illustrated how the image's ability to communicate social truths became encumbered by economy.[25]

The attractiveness of the illustrations in the pattern books had a great impact on both professional and non-professional readers. So long as the images were well illustrated, readerships did not seem to mind that lithography had replaced original drawings. Thus, a growing segment of the Anglican Communion was persuaded to support the construction of more complex and expensive churches based on the attractiveness of pattern book illustrations. The structural and architectural analyses in the pattern books eventually diminished. An interesting comparative appears between the plain economic drawing style in Charles Dwyer's *The Economy of Church, Parsonage, and*

Fig. 1.12 Specimen page of Stone Capital, Arum and Hart's Tongue Fern from *Art Foliage*.

School Architecture (1856) and Henry Hudson Holly's picturesque drawings in *Church Architecture* (1871). Dwyer's simplified line drawings that represented two-dimensional elevations of churches did not seem to confirm the reality experienced in the depth of space illustrated in Truefitt's or Holly's perspective renderings. Where Dwyer's drawings seem insipidly instructional, Truefitt's and Holly's appear experiential. The laws of economy were not suspended in architecture and the public accepted it as a fact, intuitively understanding that the architect was courting the social field of his clients, unlike an artist, who was expected to be removed from those concerns.

As a result, the church pattern books were susceptible to shifting economies despite the luxuriousness of specimen books. At a price of £3, *Sketches on the Continent* by the British architect George Truefitt offered a loose collection of medieval churches, towers, windows, and (oddly) door handles in an 1847 publication of the author's European travels. The book's pages were imprinted with a bevelled border around the image, creating the false impression of a copper-plate etching, except that the economical images were actually produced by a high-speed lithographic press. Pricing remained relatively economical even during the major financial downturn of the 1870s. By 1873, Frederick Withers's pattern book *Church Architecture* announced that artistic finery had been replaced by the promotion of photolithographic images, for which US readers gladly paid $12 per copy. The premium on new books was high; used volumes sold for $1.

A central question about pattern book distribution in the Dominion is: who was paying to access the data? Architects kept pattern books in their libraries as reference material and used the books to train apprentices. Inexperienced builders read pattern books when they were commissioned to erect churches, particularly in rural areas where the services of an architect were unavailable. Clergymen read pattern books to stay informed about developments in church architecture, especially when they were considering building or renovating a church. Architecture enthusiasts and other members of the general public read pattern books to gain knowledge of architectural styles, architectural history, and to own images of British and European buildings in lieu of, or in anticipation of, occidental travel.

As knowledge became commercialized within the architectural profession the authors of church pattern books played a complex game of offering and withholding information in order to make themselves indispensable to the building world. In the pattern book market this translated into the architect/author limiting detail in drawings to prevent contractors from edging architects out of commissioned jobs. Pattern book authors and architects like Frederick Withers and A.J. Bicknell warned their readers to avoid using contractors, who they classified as labourers lacking the social access to taste inherent in the architectural profession.

Encyclopedic volumes were used in state-sanctioned architectural education. Architects recognizing the need for professionalization, and the necessity of education in that regard, mandated a national school of architectural training.[26] Leading journals of architecture noted the need for professional training in Ontario and Quebec. "If the public insist on employing men calling themselves architects, but who put up buildings bad in plan, construction, and appearance, then the trained architects, as citizens, should insist upon it that such work is detrimental to the *public taste*."[27]

Missing from the ranks of the selected volumes were the large-format illustrated books, omitted on account of their marketing of visual imagery. Nevertheless, these books had broader appeal and influenced church design more deeply as a result.

On the one hand, pattern books attempted to create a unified method of building a neo-Gothic church. On the other hand, the pattern books actually fuelled public debates about architectural taste. Building committees populated by businessmen who lacked knowledge of architecture, but trusted their own sense of taste, could be swayed by the picturesque presentation drawings that resembled familiar pages from pattern books.

Pattern books prolonged the debates about the way churches should look, not only in opposition to the Classical idiom but also within the depth of the variety of the Gothic Revival. Frank Wills's church pattern book *Ancient English Ecclesiastical Architecture* (1850) conveyed British architectural taste in the context of parish church architecture to the Canadian architects Fred Cumberland and William Storm, who likely consulted it when designing the church of St James-the-Less in Toronto (see chapter 3). Their firm's large collection of pattern books became a legacy to their practice for many years before it was donated to the Thomas Fisher Rare Book Library at the University of Toronto in the twentieth century.

REGIONAL BOOKSELLERS, LOCAL CHURCH-BUILDING, AND NATIONAL IMAGININGS

As businessmen, booksellers consolidated their trade by forming regional associations, such as the Ontario Booksellers' Association (founded 1885). This grew out of casual sales tactics that developed into a network of wholesale and retail operators. At first, temporary collectives of booksellers formed not unlike the brief union of architects in various provinces. Their collective associations responded to regional identities rather than nationalistic ones guided by the federal government. Canadian publishers tried to create the appearance of a nationalized industry while feeding the character of local readerships. J. and A. McMillan of Saint John exemplified this local character in 1867, the year of official Confederation, by exclusively filling book orders for other retailers in New Brunswick. The A.C. Perry Company in Winnipeg, which in 1881 sold books, stationary, and music locally to a limited market, became a specialized trade business in 1889. The W.F. Shaw Booksellers of Toronto only sold to other dealers in the trade, showing the shallowness of the network for distribution.[28]

The professional organizations developed by booksellers claimed national status even if they were regionally based. For instance, the trade journal *Books and Notions*, launched by John Joseph Dyas of Toronto in 1884, claimed to have a national circulation; in fact, it represented only the regional interests of the Booksellers' and Stationers' Association of Ontario. Several changes to the journal's name, including *Canadian Bookseller and Stationer* (1896–97), *Bookseller and Stationer* (1897–1907), *Bookseller and Stationer and Canadian Newsdealer* (1908–10) and *Canadian Bookman* (1909–10), indicated an intent to market nationalism, in theory, if not in fact. The booksellers in Ontario had few alternative agencies to whom they could register a complaint, since there was no national governing body. For instance, the Canadian Booksellers' Association (formed in 1857 by Henry Rowsell, A.H. Armour, and Rev. John Cunningham Geikie, reformed 1876) was national in name only since it represented eighty-seven Ontario booksellers. Their first item of business was to demand an end to the monopoly on selling textbooks used by the Ontario Department of Education. Because of the closeness between the department of education and the provincial government in Ontario, the booksellers' pleas were largely ignored.

Despite the operational verve of regional book markets the anticipation of the railway's completion by the Canadian Pacific Railway Company brought about public imaginings of a national network of book distribution. Newspapers distributed on a national scale significantly contributed to this notion, particularly in the sense that newer nationalisms in the nineteenth century were built upon a national print language.[29] In this scope of things, an architectural visual language held a crucial position in the constitution of national imaginings. Literacy levels were growing alongside commerce, industry, and communications, although pictures, in this case of church architecture, continued to convince people of the existence of architectural correspondence between faraway places. It was quite clear to medievalists that those who controlled the architectural language in things like pattern books had the ability to frame a national architectural image. Whether by conscious design, or more likely by the operations of a capitalist market, architects intent on nationalizing the Gothic Revival in Canada issued book after book in order to infuse their preferred idiom with freshness. All of this was actually problematized by the fact that architectural grammar had a way of crossing national boundaries. Pattern books tried to – but could not completely – control the dissemination and use of architectural vocabulary.

The regional model of book distribution resonated with the way religion and settlement spread across the Dominion. For instance, the same sort of divisional management that represented local markets in the book trade was also instituted in the establishment of the separate dioceses in Saskatchewan (1874), Athabasca (1873), Moosonee (1872), Qu'Appelle (1884), Mackenzie River (1884), Calgary (1888), Yukon (1891), and Kewatin (1901). The fragmentation of Rupert's Land into regional dioceses was an apparatus that geographically divided First Nations and made it more difficult for aboriginals to make unified, and "legitimately enhanced," land claims.[30] The regional distribution of pattern books, like the local importance of church-building, was reflected in organizational terms in the advent of department stores. The advent of department stores, which disrupted the personal relationship between customer and shopkeeper, coincided with the end of books sold by advance subscription. Purchasing books through a bookstore as opposed to a selling agent, not unlike shopping in department stores, made tracking lists of book subscribers obsolete. The earlier publication method of Raphael and J. Arthur Brandon's *An Analysis of Gothick Architecture: Illustrated by a Series of Upwards of Seven Hundred Examples of Doorways, Windows, etc.* (1847), which contained a list of subscribers including British architects Charles Barry, William Burges, and Benjamin Ferry, as well as G.W. Billings, James Kellaway Colling (a pattern book author, himself), and C.R. Cockerell (architect of the Bank of England), was no longer applicable after the 1850s. This is a pity: such lists represented important data for Canadian studies since an earlier subscription list for Brandon's book included people such as the Lord Bishop of Fredericton and the architect Thomas Fuller. Fuller subscribed to the book eleven years before he designed St Stephen's-in-the-Fields in Toronto in 1858. Some architects wrote or stamped their names inside the covers of books they owned, such as the Vancouver architect of Christ Church Cathedral Victoria, British Columbia, J.C.M. Keith did to a copy of James Cubbitt's *Church Design for Congregations: Its Developments and Possibilities (1870)*, but finding these in libraries is fortunate happenstance.

As early as the mid-1850s, the distribution of books in Canada increasingly shifted away from advance subscription sales. Instead, a loose syndicate of booksellers marketed their product by concentrating on volume sales. They dealt in mass sales using the department-store model, based on price, advertising, and increased production. Russell's Bookstore in Winnipeg advertised "$25,000 – most of choice stock to select from with new goods arriving every day by mail, express, and freight from London, New York, and Boston."[31] This situation is not surprising given the increased imports of books from the British Empire creating a "kind of packaged civilization, offered in competition with the local product, and backed by powerful service arrangements."[32] The commercial structure of the Ontario Booksellers Association (OBA) was also imported from Britain, adopted to cope with the complexities of the modern marketplace. At the same time, the OBA provided business opportunities for already established booksellers and impeded newcomers to the trade, which was a mirror of architecture professionalization and a metaphor for the attitudes toward new immigrants.[33]

While the OBA exerted a new level of control over the book trade, individual booksellers tried to establish monopolies through business mergers. The ebb and flow of these mergers was exemplified in 1872, when T.N. Hibben and Company of Victoria purchased the stock of David Spencer's Book Seller and added the services of the bookbinder R.T. Williams to provide "the only complete book bindery north of San Francisco."[34] The bookselling industry was generally characterized as moving from diversification to consolidation. This structure mirrored the collectives forming in other sectors, such as railway, logging, manufacture, and mining. In this manner, the book trade in the Dominion evolved from local merchandising to professionally run commercial concern. The consolidation of booksellers put pressure on the agents for British publishers such as the itinerant bookseller Mr Lawrie, who travelled by rail between Toronto and Winnipeg as an agent for William Collins and Sons of London. Pressures of the consolidating industry caused him to abandon his trade.[35] Sales figures supplied by the Canadian Booksellers' Association demonstrated the situation: in 1876, five hundred booksellers in Ontario sold $750,000 worth of merchandise.[36]

The consolidation of the bookselling businesses gave power to a few privileged corporations, causing concern about rising prices. For instance, the monopoly enjoyed by the railway brought about accusations of price fixing (unidentified as such at the time) for goods travelling east, disadvantaging producers in the west. For that reason, James C. Linton at the Sign of the Big Book in Calgary was able to ship no farther than the foothills of the Rockies.[37]

The regional formation of the book trade within an imagined nationalism in Canada echoed the developing structure of religious institutions in the Dominion. By contrast, the production of pattern books in the US was tightly controlled by a clutch of influential architects and authors including William Comstock and Amos Bicknell. Comstock and Bicknell produced roughly a third of the architectural books published between the 1850s and 1890s. Pattern books like these entered Canada through rail connections located along the Atlantic seaboard, linking traffic from New York and Boston to Montreal and Toronto. By summer 1886, the CPR Company had provided for "no less than 4,135 miles of railway, including the longest continuous line in the world, extending from Quebec and Montreal all the way across the continent to the Pacific Ocean."[38] Another line extended eastward from Montreal across the State of Maine to a connection with the system in the Maritime Provinces and another connected the Great Lakes area with two important US lines leading westward. This vast network of rail eased the traffic of goods, including pattern books, which were a small but significant commodity. Timber, brick, iron, shingles, furniture, and other building supplies were also shipped along these routes, the same ones travelled by settlers establishing new communities and erecting new churches.

EMBEDDING ECCLESIOLOGY IN THE DOMINION

Anglican church-builders and the architects they employed tended to follow a tight set of aesthetic and constructional principles, known as Ecclesiology, which set them apart from other Christian denominations. Ecclesiology referred placidly to the study of medieval church architecture, but its most potent characteristics were moral biases and aesthetic judgments. The promoters of Ecclesiology wanted their species of the Gothic Revival to appear permanent and therefore deserving of wide emulation. The relative ease by which ecclesiology was transmitted to the Dominion illustrated how British-inspired social structures were visibly repeated in the Dominion's architecture. In the Dominion, and especially in the Maritimes, Upper Canada, and English-speaking parts of Montreal, the repetition of British social structures and cultural attitudes helped the Cambridge Camden (later, Ecclesiological) Society become a major power in colonial neo-Gothic architecture. The Society disseminated its objectives, codified as architectural rules, in print by offering advice to architects and church-building committees. This was accomplished via the distribution of the Society's ideas through a series of pamphlets, an architectural church pattern book, and a quarterly journal called the *Ecclesiologist* (1841–68). Anglican readers of the *Ecclesiologist* in the Dominion connected the "correct" antiquarian source with the Society's Christian morals.

During the mid-nineteenth century, Ecclesiological rhetoric intensified. Liturgy, knowledge, science, taste, and fashion came to the fore in debates about the way churches should look in Britain no less than in the Canadas. Yet, Ecclesiology was more ephemeral than its advocates cared to admit, leading a core clutch of supporters to create a continuous stream of claims about its "superiority." The founding members of the Cambridge Camden Society, John Mason Neale and Alexander Beresford Hope, essentially controlled the organization's scholarly output and boasted that its seven hundred members represented the architectural interests of a much larger British population.

The archaeological precedent that underlay Ecclesiology controlled the way that empirical data was used in Gothic Revival churches.[39] Churches built in the nineteenth century were deemed Ecclesiologically "correct" if they obeyed a certain architectural grammar, related to the truthfulness promoted by the architect Augustus Welby Northmore Pugin. Based on the empirical study of medieval churches, Pugin had assembled a set of characteristics to authenticate neo-Gothic churches, which included asymmetrically planned and separately articulated building components, low exterior walls, steep roofs, towers with spires, pointed windows, materials used truthfully, and ornament that served a structural purpose.[40] Pugin had gleaned these principles from the medieval specimens his father, Augustus Charles Pugin, illustrated in pattern books such as *Pugin's Gothic Ornaments, Selected from Various Buildings in England and France* (1831). Ironically, the pattern book authors that followed A.W.N. Pugin tended to reduce his architectural principles to a simplified equation of taste.

Pursuant to the architectural principles advocated by A.W.N. Pugin, the designers of Anglican churches wrote books that reflected the longitudinal axes in his drawings, thus advocating rectangular buildings with aisled naves. Ritual forms of Christian worship were enforced through this type of church design. A series of pattern books, including Raphael and J. Arthur Brandon's *Parish Churches* (1849), Edmund Sharpe's *Architectural Parallels* (1848), Frederick Withers' *Church Architecture* (1873), and George Woodward's *Rural Church Architecture* (1868), described how the Anglican Communion preferred this type of church design. By contrast, other pattern books written for the consumption of nonconformist congregations, including Methodist, Baptist, and even Presbyterian groups, resisted the rectangular plan that facilitated ritual worship. These books illustrated interior spaces organized to create unobstructed sightlines to the pulpit, widened naves, and amphitheatrical seating plans. The British architect George Bidlake, who wrote *Sketches of Churches: Designed for the Use of Nonconformists* (1865), and Joseph Crouch and Edmund Butler, who wrote *Churches, Mission Halls, and Schools for Non-*

conformists (1901), advertised amphitheatrical and centrally planned churches in order to develop effective designs for "experiential" worship and to position Anglicans as conventional, unexciting, and anti-modern.

The Ecclesiological principles of architecture that applied to Anglican churches were transmitted to the Canadas via the immigration of British-trained architects, clergymen, and the importation of neo-Gothic church pattern books, which carried associated rhetorics and imagery. In pattern books, journals, magazines, and historical texts, neo-Gothic was marketed as "Pointed" or "Christian" architecture in reference to its association with a worshipful approach. Based on Romantic ideals of beauty and drama, the Gothic Revival distinguished itself fully from the systematic approach to the Classical vocabulary.

Ecclesiology resonated particularly strongly in the Maritimes among a clutch of bishops newly installed from Britain during the mid-nineteenth century: Bishop John Medley of New Brunswick (1845–92), Bishop Edward Feild of Newfoundland (1846–76), and Bishop Francis Fulford of Montreal (1850–68). They struggled against the local vernacular manner of assembling churches that, for instance, used flat ceilings to hide simple triangular roof trusses. It was more difficult and costly to construct open timber ceilings that exposed the roofing system in the manner of British models. Simple scissor trusses and elaborate hammer-beam systems were described in Raphael and J. Arthur Brandon's *Open Timber Roofs* (1849) (fig. 1.13) and later on in Frank E. Kidder's *Building Construction and Superintendence: Part III, Trussed Roofs and Roof Trusses* (1895). Countering the early Maritime churches that retained the aesthetic of Methodist single-room meeting houses were the Christian overtones about the "correctness" and "tastefulness" of architecture that characterized the open-timber roofs of Ecclesiological churches. This narrative was embedded in the church pattern books. Advocates of Ecclesiology even appealed, in the Dominion, to people's practical logic by arguing that the steeply pointed roofs produced by open-timber systems countered the effects of heavy snowfalls.[41] Eventually, these roofing systems became tradition in the Maritimes, which was known for its high-grade supply of timber, primed by the lumber and shipbuilding industries in New Brunswick and Newfoundland.

Finding the money to build churches in the Maritimes was a challenge for bishops Feild and Medley due to the uneven commercial development in their dioceses. Building Ecclesiologically correct churches was an even larger challenge among a populace that leaned away from the conservative approach represented by the Oxford Movement. Bishop Feild differed fundamentally with his congregants on issues of theology, liturgy, and ritual

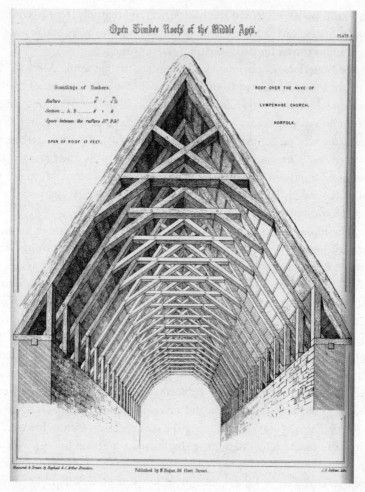

Fig. 1.13 Specimen page showing a scissor truss from *Open Timber Roofs*.

practices. High Churchmen claimed that these differences were visible in steeply pitched roofs, truthful use of materials, separately articulated building components reflecting internal spatial arrangements, and tall steeples that expressed holiness, sanctity, and respect for God and the Body of Christ, essentially Ecclesiology. Asking the populace to give money to build churches was one thing but asking them to fund church buildings that did not represent the ideals of the donor population received a cool reception in Maritime villages. Villagers tended to prefer sermon over ritual, which they believed smacked of Anglo-Catholicism. However, Bishop Feild's commitment to build Ecclesiologically "correct" churches was resolute despite individual and corporate wealth that was thinly spread in a few concentrated pools in lumber, shipbuilding, and shipping and the fact that few of these were available to build the kind of churches the bishop desired. Bishop Feild, among other High Churchmen, used the distinctions between High and Low Church as a type of social classification. Frustrated by the lack of local cooperation from his Anglican congregation, Feild privately referred to them as ignorant "fishmongers" unappreciative of the finer things in life.[42] Strategically, bishop Feild used this classificatory system to his advantage when he travelled back to England to speak with conservative-minded Anglicans officials about raising money for his Newfoundland diocese. It was clear that money to build churches in the Maritimes that looked much like the ones being constructed in an Ecclesiological fashion in Britain was easier to obtain in London. This was because architectural associations and individual Anglican congregations in Britain donated monies to like-minded congregations in the Dominion or, in the case of Bishop Feild, for leaders who claimed architecture was a powerful ideological weapon. Thus, churches in the Maritimes resonated quite strongly with some specific, and some more imagined, counterparts in Britain.

The apparent permanence of medieval buildings legitimized Anglican claims of superior architectural taste, which, in turn, reinforced Anglican self-identification as dominant in colonial society's formation. Church-building was a communal activity heavily involved in the process of identity-making, which chiefly involved classifying one's own group through its dispositions toward other denominations' churches. Thus, church-building bred intradenominational unity while also stirring social tensions in an economically and geopolitically expanding nation-state. At stake was the crafting of a "national" identity for the emerging Dominion. What ought the Dominion look like, and whose social rules would prevail in it? Discourse analysis shows that the equation of privilege and social dominance was complicated because socially and economically dominant Anglican groups in the Dominion did not always welcome the use of Gothic by other religious denominations. Winning the souls of new immigrants to the Dominion, as well as their economic support, was a serious business, and colonial Anglican bishops complained vehemently when non-Anglicans appeared to gain ground. The 1851 census of Lower Canada reported the Roman Catholics only slightly ahead of Protestant church-builders, the former having built 385 churches versus 275 for the latter.

Though the Anglican communion perceived itself pre-eminent, the Dominion's democratic society encouraged other denominations to express architectural choice and variety within the general confines of a neo-Gothic grammar. Local debates about the way churches should look and the variations of neo-Gothic in pattern books were shot through with the question about whether aesthetic variety was equated with taste or fashion. The politics of pattern books presented a unified look for Anglican churches, but a variety of church designs ensued across the Maritimes and Lower Canada (not to mention British North America) partly in response to the variety of church designs exemplified in the variations of "styles" in pattern books. In essence, local debates about the way churches should look were a microcosm for the larger negotiations over the way the formation of the nation should unfold. The debates about the variety of neo-Gothic architecture in churches were not limited to a local phenomenon. Britain negotiated land settlements with the US by directing the Dominion in ways that were not always beneficial to the colony.[43] The dispute over logging the Columbia basin, in an area between New Brunswick and Maine, was indirectly related to church-building and pattern books because timber was the chief material component of each product.

Maritime business interests became disadvantaged on account of the wealth accruing in adjacent regions. As a result, donations to church-building enterprises in Montreal were more frequent after that city assumed the benefits of fishing, farming, and sometimes logging and shipbuilding once enjoyed by the Maritimes. Consequently, Bishop Fulford in Montreal did not have to appeal to the British public for money to complete his cathedral.

Money was an important factor in building churches, but the advocates of Ecclesiology publicly expressed its architectural principles in doctrinal terms. They saw Ecclesiology as an architectural science with religious overtones. This perspective on Ecclesiology mirrored a description of an imagined confederated Canada in a remark made in 1866 by the New Brunswick politician Francis Hibbard. He noted that a unified Canada "would advance more rapidly in science, and literature, in railroads and telegraphs, in civilization and religion, than we do at present."[44] As instruments of knowledge, taste, architectural principles, and communal enterprise, church pattern books were significant markers of the intersection of science, governance, efficiency, and technique. Just as the combination of these factors was involved in the process of identity-making, so, too, were they part of the negotiations for Confederation. In the Dominion, as in Britain, the Ecclesiological movement became an instrument of religious and social politics: architectural taste and archaeological "correctness" became synonymous with liturgy and worship.[45] "Correctness" legitimated class division and conservative politics. The architectural aspirations of the Anglican communions became encapsulated in pattern books responding to:

a taste for the study of Ecclesiology [which] has been of late rapidly increasing. Volume after volume superbly illustrated has been issued from the English press, but most of these have been adapted for the use of professional architects, or of those who have devoted their leisure to the study of numerous examples around them. A mere glossary ... is not sufficient to show the American student what an Ancient English Parish Church is ... The present book is intended to meet this want.[46]

Linking taste with Ecclesiology, and science with art, introduced new concepts to group identification. The conceptualization of identity was complicated by the bifurcating structure of national and regional political powers.

2

ECONOMY AND RELIGION FROM THE MARITIMES TO UPPER CANADA

AN INTERSECTION OF CHURCH, STATE, AND BIG MONEY

> Our scheme is to establish a government that will seek to turn the tide of European emigration into this northern half of the American continent – that will strive to develop its great natural resources – and that will endeavour to maintain liberty, and justice, and Christianity throughout the land ... I go heartily for the union, because it will throw down the barriers of trade and give us control of a market of four millions of people.[1]

George Brown was a member of the Legislative Assembly of Upper Canada and an elder statesman of Reform politics when, on 8 February 1865, he conceptualized the Canadas as a place where the accumulated forces of freedom, fairness, and religion met natural resources exploited for profit. Brown was likely recounting personal experience as founder of the Globe newspaper, Liberal member of Parliament, and advocate of the Free Church of Scotland (a branch of the Presbyterian Church), showing that the embodiment of commerce, politics, and religion was more than philosophical musing. Previously, in the 1850s, he had used print media and political clout to support the abolition of the Clergy Reserves (a one-seventh share of all Crown Land in Upper and Lower Canada endowed to the "Protestant" clergy in the Constitutional Act of 1791) that had been interpreted by the first lieutenant governor, John Graves Simcoe, as belonging solely to the Church of England. Brown envisioned that the accrual of monies from the sale of the Clergy Reserves ought to be spread equitably among the leading religious organizations in Canada. Disputes over the Clergy Reserves erupted periodically as old arguments were rehashed in the public domain. Bishop Stranchan of the diocese of Toronto held particularly strong views over a prolonged period that the Clergy Reserves belonged rightfully to the Church of England, pressuring the British Government to block the transfer of land to the Canada Company in 1827 and, instead, allow the Church of England to sell not more than 100,000 acres each year. In 1824, the Church of Scotland (Presbyterian) persuaded the legislature to allow the reserves to be shared, although fresh arguments erupted in 1854–55: the Provincial Parliament wanted to secularize the Clergy Reserves altogether. A lump sum payment of £188,342 was eventually agreed upon, which was shared among several Christian denominations. Nevertheless, Bishop Strachan continued to make public his objections to limitations of the Church of England's power until his death at the age of ninety in 1867.

Bishop Strachan and others in the religious field continued to make general assumptions that money invested in church-building would consequently solve social problems, a relationship emphasized by those in control of religious institutions. Church-building was envisioned as an important part of the forming society on par with economy, self-governance, freedom, and progress in the Dominion, but the costs were downloaded to individual communities of worshippers. Church pattern books drew these factors together in the constitution of modern lifestyle and collective identity because the books marketed church-building as a legitimate and viable solution to social problems. As envisioned by the Church of England, the Gothic Revival was predominantly the favourite style of the church pattern books because it had already been associated with a symbolic return to Britain's preindustrial and uncomplicated era. The dramatic quality of pointed windows with elaborate tracery, the verticality of spires and finials, as well as asymmetrical massing of building components harmonized with the image of Canada as untamed wilderness. On this account, the architecture of Anglican churches in Canada had a particularly strong relationship with the Gothic Revival. Indeed, nineteenth-century Anglican identities in the Canadas were wrapped determinedly in a British aesthetic and ideological packaging, a metaphor likened to the oilcloths protecting book shipments that routinely crossed the Atlantic.

The rise of a new commercial society in the Canadas, exemplified by the increased amount of books and periodicals entering port cities and customs houses, underwrote new responsibilities for individual and collective social action. *The Illustrated London News* not only connected the colony with its homeland but it also created a collection of likeminded readers in Canada. Individuals were beginning to be understood as belonging to various consortiums of consumers, demonstrated by advertisements for Minton's tiles in the pattern books. The idea of national progress as the sum of individual industry and uprightness was mirrored by a paradigm shift in religious institution that valued individual souls as the foundation for collective growth. Thus, missionaries were directed to amass souls on Earth as much as they were to spread gospel.

Churches mattered in the constitution of individual and collective identity but were also the focal point of tensions between individual and collective interests. Within a single congregation that was building a church there were often pockets of dissent objecting to the way building funds were collected and spent. So much controversy erupted around the practice of leasing seats in Anglican churches to wealthy congregants that an increasing number of new churches advertised large portions of "free" seats for the use of less fortunate people. This was the cause of considerable tensions within congregations, sometimes played out in the general public arena, owing to some moral objections about the wealthy patrons influencing their churches. The situation was problematic since financing strategies used to construct churches often relied on large donations from wealthy land and business owners in tandem with smaller sums of money collected through group activities such as social teas and bazaars. Equalizing the power relationships between clergymen and community leaders privileged by wealth and profession put significant pressure on Anglican liturgical practice. Traditionally, High Anglican clergy were isolated during church services behind choir screens; individual communicants were able to see salvation but not partake of it in this life. Under these new social conditions personal religious development became the overall goal.

In the Maritimes, church-building had the potential to galvanize religious and secular demographics alike, as shown in the frequency of church-construction projects appearing in the *Illustrated London News* (1842–1971) and the *Canadian Illustrated News* (1869–83). The connection between religious and secular interests was given architectural expression by leading British architect George Edmund Street (1824–1881), who remarked, "it is unhappy that [the revival of gothic architecture] should ever wish to divorce religious and secular art; as if religion were a thing for Sundays only, and not for every moment of every life."[2] Street had articulated the tensions between religious and secular lifestyles that were constituted in new commercial society. To that end, a reciprocal marketing relationship connected church pattern books and church-building with everyday social and commercial structure.

A contingent of architecturally minded bishops of the Anglican Church, including John Medley of New Brunswick, Edward Feild of Newfoundland, and Francis Fulford of Montreal, were charged with ministering to the expanding networks of settlers and new immigrants in remote communities. Broadly speaking, their purpose was to make the colonies a better place, something akin to the way England was imagined in their minds. Their appointments marked the interface of the force of religious institution, the "commerce of taste," and politics, especially evident in the manner of new cathedrals erected by the individual bishops. The transatlantic transmission of architectural taste-cum-fashion was exposed particularly by the way in which each of the bishops requested drawings and pattern book illustrations from British architectural and ecclesiastical associations, such as the Oxford Architectural Society and the Society for the Propagation of the Gospel in Foreign Parts.[3]

The small number of Anglican clergy in the Maritimes and Upper Canada was ill equipped to service the immense and remote geographical area. Missionaries were funded through the Church Mission Society in Britain, but that money was not extended to facilitate architectural projects. Nevertheless, bishops and missionaries pressed on because religious faith tended to resist economic realities. For this reason, remote communities built churches without having a clergyman appointed. In short, the belief in social progress rallied church-builders in the Maritime colonies despite economic realities to the contrary. Despite the complicated nature of the situation, some of these communities forged ahead with the construction of churches on the assumption that a "proper" neo-Gothic building would help attract a larger congregation and a permanent minister. These early efforts at church-building in the Maritimes, especially during the 1840s and 50s, required the bishops to make frequent trips to England in search of funding. The colonial Bishop John Medley of Fredericton, New Brunswick, did just that. He was the first to sanction a model/copy relationship for a neo-Gothic cathedral in Canada, connecting architectural style and offshore funding with churches built in the Canadas. Having studied a number of pattern books and church designs before leaving England, Bishop Medley spread the knowledge of church-building that was marketed by the plans, sections, elevations, perspective drawings, and related discourses found in the pattern books that included the Ecclesiological principles advocated by the Cambridge Camden (later Ecclesiological) Society.

Case Study: Fredericton Cathedral and St Anne's Chapel, New Brunswick

Bishop Medley's cathedral in Fredericton (fig. 2.1) was both an imperial and an Anglican architectural statement in its adoption of British Ecclesiology. Prior to the commission of Bishop Fulford's cathedral in Montreal, the association between the Bishop of New Brunswick and his architect, Frank Wills (later replaced by William Butterfield), was a decidedly British affair in the Canadas, reflecting the Maritimes' moderate and Loyalist politics.[4] Cultural

Fig. 2.1 West entrance of Christ Church (Anglican), the cathedral of Fredericton, New Brunswick.

affinity with Britain was expressed architecturally when the fourteenth-century fabric of St Mary's, Snettisham, Norfolk, England, was chosen as the model for the Fredericton Cathedral. Bishop Medley and Frank Wills had left England together with the plans for the new cathedral packed away in their baggage. The flowing window tracery in the west window of Fredericton cathedral is a recreation of the stone tracery in the west window at Snettisham, as is the triple arch west entrance porch (fig. 2.2). The decision to use the Snettisham church as the model was initiated by the Right Rev. Bishop Coleridge of Exeter, who presided over Bishop Medley's consecration and supplied a donation of £1,500.[5]

The layout for Fredericton's cathedral was also modelled on another well-known British church: St Mary's, Shottesbrooke, Berkshire (figs. 2.3 and 2.4). In December 1844, Bishop Medley had written to the OAS asking if St Mary's church in Shottesbrooke would "be a good model for a small cathedral?"[6] He claimed to have heard from the famous British architect Thomas Rickman in the affirmative. Medley remarked that "Shottesbrooke church is published by the Society [and] if so I should be greatly obliged if that could be among the number" of books to be shipped to New Brunswick.[7] Medley received the shipment of books on or before 26 February 1845. Shottesbrooke was a cruciform fourteenth-century church that had undergone extensive restoration in 1844 by British architect William Butterfield. Butterfield had produced a set of

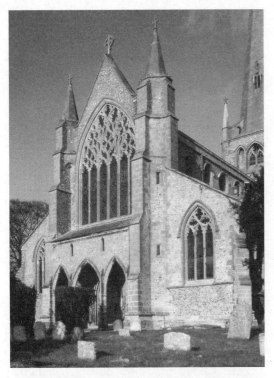

Fig. 2.2 West entrance of St Mary's Snettisham, Norfolk, England.

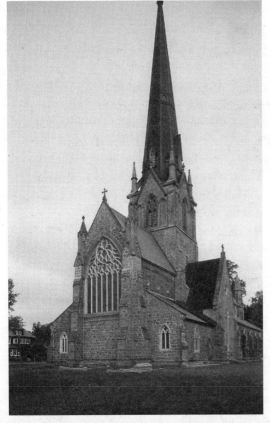

Fig. 2.3 East end of Christ Church (Anglican), the cathedral of Fredericton, New Brunswick.

Fig. 2.4 St Mary's, Shottesbrooke (thirteenth century), Berkshire, England.

drawings based on his restoration published by the Oxford Architectural Society. The layout of Shottesbrooke included north and south double-bay transept arms and a three-bay chancel in the east end. Wills's perspective drawing for Fredericton shows a similar cruciform plan, though cruciform churches ran counter to architectural tradition in New Brunswick. Clearly Bishop Medley and his architect, Frank Wills, envisioned a cruciform plan for the cathedral, although congregants following the slow progress of construction would not likely have imagined the same.

In the spirit of interchange, Bishop Medley also asked for models from the Ecclesiological Society, claiming that "they might also aid me much by small plain wooden models for wooden churches in the country."[8] Asking after models of timber churches was a concession to the unwanted expense of an architect in rural economies. But more importantly the differing positions in architecture pattern books sent by rival British architectural societies solicited much debate about the way churches should look in the Maritimes. The books' instigation of aesthetic debates was a metaphor for the debates around geopolitical unification in the Dominion. Notwithstanding a British colonial transatlantic push toward federation for the Canadas beginning around the mid-1850s, some sectors of New Brunswick, for instance, remained stringently opposed to Confederation during the Tilley government's term.[9]

In November 1848, the journal of the Cambridge Camden Society reported "favourable accounts of the progress of Fredericton cathedral," the new seat of Anglican Bishop John Medley.[10] Fredericton's positive attention from the *Ecclesiologist* was somewhat unusual for the journal, which generally expended ink on negative criticisms. Canadian church-building factored rarely into the journal's approximate ten-year long coverage of colonial church architecture, but Fredericton's cathedral was mentioned on at least four occasions. Churches in the Empire's more prominent colonial holdings were more notably covered in the *Ecclesiologist*, and it was clear that the editors greatly hoped that Medley's architectural prowess would spread to other clergymen.[11] Fredericton's cathedral was the first archaeologically "correct" Anglican cathedral established in the Canadas in its scale, proportion, layout, and details. Medley's architectural experience was not slight, having founded the Exeter diocesan Architectural Society in 1841. The society was a kindred spirit to the Cambridge Camden Society, a group of which Medley was a proud member. On 14 December 1844, he wrote to the OAS asking, "to take out a stock of architectural books and drawings" that the Society deemed useful.[12] The OAS "agreed to give a set of the Society's publications to the Bishop Elect of New Brunswick."[13] Bishop Medley responded by letter with his thanks for the architectural books and made a further request for some decorated tiles "for a new chapel I am building."[14] Floor tiles provided by Minton's of London, the famous manufacture of porcelain products adorned the Chapel of St Anne's, which served as temporary worship hall until the nave of the cathedral was completed.

Availing himself of the opportunity for public speaking on architecture and taste, Medley gave a lecture in 1857 to the Church of England Young Men's Society in Saint John on the subject of "good taste." In the talk he remarked:

> In our household arrangements, in our dress, in the social festivities, we shall eschew the extremes of extravagance and meanness, and look upon all things, great and small, as given us that we may discharge the duties belonging to them in the best possible manner ... Thus, while we carefully guard the sacred deposit of truth from all adulteration, and found our religion strictly and soberly on God's most holy word, good taste will preserve that religion from sourness and self-complacency,

and will make it gracious and acceptable to all who have sufficient candour to appreciate our intentions, and generally useful to the world.[15]

Strategically equating "truth" with "good taste," Bishop Medley also adopted a medieval model for Christ Church Fredericton in order to avoid the "extremes of extravagance and meanness."

Indeed, ecclesiology equated beauty with economy, truth, and taste. For instance, the *New York Ecclesiologist* (1848–53) expressed the matter succinctly: "beauty and economy will be the result of our working upon true principles."[16] The architect Frank Wills was a founding member of the New York Ecclesiological Society, which introduced the "new" mode of neo-Gothic to the US. 1,500 copies of the magazine's inaugural edition was printed and given gratis in the prospect of developing a readership. Wills understood the claims and distinctions underlying a "commerce of taste." In an article for the second installment of the *New York Ecclesiologist* he wrote, "finery, everywhere, takes the place of dignity; and if, by accident, anything is good at first, it is afterward spoiled by a Committee of Taste, who stick a little lump of unmeaning putty here, and a dab of the same convenient material there; and, in the end, to quote the language of a friend, 'more is expended to make the Church look *fine*, than would have been sufficient to make it *beautiful*.'"[17]

References to taste considered, the decision to model Fredericton Cathedral on St Mary's, Snettisham, still proved unexpectedly controversial for Bishop Medley. The Ecclesiological Society objected to modelling a cathedral on Snettisham's parochial church design. To the sensibilities of the Oxford Society, Frank Wills's plan to have a lower chancel roofline than that of the nave was particularly unsuited to the grandeur warranted by a cathedral. Could Bishop Medley have left neglected a fundamental "building principle" of ecclesiology: that cathedral rooflines were uniform across the nave and chancel? Quite the contrary, since Medley exhibited historical and architectural knowledge of ecclesiology in his published pamphlet *Elementary Remarks on Church Architecture* (1841). In essence, economy resolved the differences between the Bishop's and his architect's vision for the cathedral; that is, the Bishop knew he need not have worried over a complete structure that he could as yet afford to build. Bishop Medley had the time to change components of the cathedral before each was begun.

Besides, Bishop Medley had other things to worry about. In New Brunswick, Anglicans were few in number and among them there was distaste for the bishop's High Church or Tractarian ideals. Resistance to the High Church position was marked among the general populace of New Brunswick. Perhaps Bishop Medley viewed the slow construction process advantageously, giving him time to sway the local population toward his High Church ideals before the architectural reflection of those ideals became visible in his cathedral. At some point Medley's ideals became overt, even to a leading nonconformist who was heard to observe, "so we went towards Rome."[18]

Construction of Bishop Medley's cathedral began in May 1845 with £3,000 raised from congregants in the Bishop's new diocese. By the following October Lieutenant Governor Sir William Colebrooke laid the cornerstone, attracting local prestige and illustrating the established Church's imperial connections. The nave and aisles were built by November 1847, which depleted building funds. Frank Wills moved to New York in order to continue his architectural practice there, and Medley returned to England in search of more financing.[19] Upon his return from England the diocese's coffers had grown to £20,000. In his possession was also a new set of drawings by the well-known British architect William Butterfield, which altered the cathedral's roofline to reflect a form prescribed by the Ecclesiological Society.

Though Bishop Medley agreed in principle that the design needed changes, the act of realizing those changes was a complicated affair. Bishop Medley's address to the Ecclesiological Society at its annual meeting, held on 9 May 1848, shows that there was some discrepancy between the new drawings by Butterfield and the private thoughts of the bishop. The bishop described the current dimensions of the nave, noting that construction of the tower and choir were not yet begun. Bishop Medley was careful to specify the size of the choir he anticipated building: "a choir, 40 feet in length, with aisles, would be sufficient for our purpose. It remains to be seen how this might be connected with a tower."[20]

However, the bishop's private thoughts about the way the cathedral should look deviated from Butterfield's drawings of the proposed cathedral, which were printed alongside the address to the Ecclesiological Society. Butterfield's illustration of the chancel was clearly not the forty-foot length that Bishop Medley anticipated. Furthermore, Butterfield's drawing explicitly showed how the choir was to be connected to the tower, leaving no question of its arrangement except in the mind of Bishop Medley. The bishop's verbal address indicated that he did not anticipate using Butterfield's drawing as presented, knowing that much negotiation about the way the cathedral would look still lay ahead in New Brunswick. What was on the bishop's mind was the expense and pragmatics of church-building in the colonies, to which he noted, "had thought of two towers, as at Ottery and Exeter, but shall be content with one, if a cathedral-like appearance can be produced at less expense; for I am desirous to do whatever is most thoroughly practical, provided it be correct and church-like."[21]

The inclusion of a tower and spire in Bishop Medley's vision for his cathedral signified the Anglican image of power: the cathedral is still visible from a distance across the river. Medley's cathedral was intended to take its place at the apogee of Canada's architectural taste, presumably legitimizing the bishop's complaint that "there is a strong feeling in favour of Pointed architecture, though there is little knowledge of the subject, and great difficulties arise from having no positive standard before men's eyes. It must be expected that many eagerly cling to old forms, however unsightly they may appear to others, and one must honour their feeling, though one cannot admire their taste."[22] Interestingly, the Bishop had to adjust his own taste to comply with the Ecclesiological Society's judgment. The *Ecclesiologist* noted that Bishop Medley had modified the design for the tower drawn by Butterfield to give the tower windows greater simplicity while preserving the general effect. Indeed, by the time the cathedral was completed in 1853, much had changed from Butterfield's published drawing. The bishop got his choir, which was placed under the crossing tower, and he got a two-bay chancel area much more generously laid out than in Butterfield's plan – though the chancel was built with a roofline at the height of the nave. Twin north and south vestries adjacent to the chancel replaced Butterfield's cozy little vestry that would have been complete with its own fireplace. Butterfield's drawing of the vestry indicated it was essentially a stand-alone structure linked through the south aisle to the main body of the church. The bishop's image of himself reading by the fire in that vestry must have appeared excessive in light of the freezing winter nights that the poor in Fredericton had to endure.

The construction process of Christ Church Cathedral, once again, illustrates the interface of religion, economy, taste, and politics at the theoretical and actual point of social formation. Part of the project to construct a new cathedral involved building a "temporary" chapel to house the congregation. The architecture of the chapel, dedicated St Anne's (Frank Wills, 1847) (fig. 2.5), was inspired by the thirteenth-century fabric of St Michael's, Long Stanton, Cambridgeshire (fig. 2.6). St Michael's was advocated for emulation in Empire colonies because its simple design, steep roof, low walls, and plain western bellcote were an inexpensive and manageable way to achieve Ecclesiological principles. Illustrations of Long Stanton were published in Raphael and J. Arthur Brandon's *Parish Churches, or Perspective Views of English Ecclesiastical Structures Accompanied by Plans Drawn to a Uniform Scale* (1848) and the same authors' *Open Timber Roofs of the Middle Ages* (1849). Wills designed several such churches in the US, which he published in his pattern book *Ancient English Ecclesiastical Architecture; and Its Principles Applied to the Wants of the Present Day* (1850). Wills also built a version of St Michael's, Long

Stanton, that was essentially a model/copy for the Anglicans at St Michael's in Sillery (1856) outside of Quebec City (fig. 2.7). St Michael's, Sillery, makes an excellent contrast to the Roman Catholic church of Saint-Michel, Sillery (1852), built to the plans of architect Goodlatte Richardson Browne (fig. 2.8). The Roman Catholic church has a central western tower partially integrated into the main body of the nave, tall walls, shallow roof, polygonal east end, and vaulted interior using plaster in imitation of the richer stone material. The English-speaking Irish Roman Catholics at Saint-Michel did not follow the same ecclesiological principles of architecture as the English-speaking Anglicans at St Michael's. The Roman Catholics intentionally recalled what they considered to be the beauty of Roman gothic architecture; in this case, the source was likely Santa Maria Sopra Minerva in Rome (1280–1370). By contrast, the Anglicans believed in the superiority of the "truthfulness" of ecclesiological architecture. The cultural differences reflected in these distinct positions on architecture exemplified the interdenominational divisiveness that continued for the next fifty years.

Bishop Medley decorated St Anne's chapel in the most fashionable manner, importing stained glass produced by the companies of Beer and Warrington and floor tiles gifted from Minton's of London. Medley's vision of ecclesiastical taste, published in *Elementary Remarks on Church Architecture* (1841), connected architecture and morality: "there is a higher ground on which we may rest the argument for the necessity of some knowledge of Church Architecture, and it is this: – *A deficiency in taste where the object is to pay religious reverence to the Almighty, implies a deficiency in moral perception, and a deficiency in moral perception cannot exist without injury to the moral and religious character.*"[23] That the Bishop believed himself possessed of architectural taste and knowledge gave credence to his blunt remark to a leading parishioner: "Mr R., when you build a church, build a church, and when you build a barn build a barn."[24] Debasing an iconic building associated with agrarian workers, such as a barn, to assert the high moral fibre of Anglicanism was a typical ploy among the conservative churchmen. Barns were not considered architecture by churchmen and conservatives whose definition of the term did not include things built by mere intent.

Despite the added expense of building the chapel with hammer-dressed grey sandstone, Bishop Medley especially noted that the chapel was intended for the poor with all seats free from the expense of pew rental.[25] Leaving all of the seats free was a controversial decision, since pew rental was a significant source of church income; therefore, construction costs had to be offset entirely by donation. This was no surprise since Bishop Medley was an ardent supporter of free seats, having published a paper on the subject in the inaugural

Fig. 2.5
St Anne's Chapel, Fredericton,
New Brunswick.

Below
Fig. 2.6 Specimen page of St Michael's,
Long Stanton, Cambridgeshire (thirteenth
century) from *Parish Churches*.

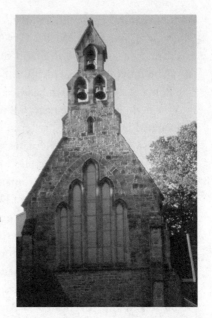

edition of the *Exeter Diocesan Architectural Society Transactions*, repeating 3 Phillim 16: "there shall be no property in pews."[26]

Nevertheless, he used the opportunity to advertise the chapel's free seats to a British audience in order to solicit donations to complete Fredericton's cathedral. The case was one of religious politics in which the sale of church seats to the "highest bidder" was a sign of progressive economy. Medley argued

Fig. 2.7 St Michael's Anglican Church, Sillery, Quebec.

Fig. 2.8 Roman Catholic Church of Saint Michel, Sillery, Quebec.

in a reform manner conservatively against the closed pew system, noting it was "not only contrary to all sound principles of Architecture, and fatal to all excellence in the interior arrangement of a Church, but that it is alike inconvenient, illegal, and unchristian, and that the arguments in its favour, and the objections against the system of open seats, properly understood, are fallacious and untenable."[27]

Comparative Case Study: St Simon and St Jude, Tignish, PEI

In 1857, the year that Bishop Medley gave his lecture on "good taste" to the Church of England Young Men's Society in Saint John, a small building committee formed in Tignish, PEI, in order to consider the construction of a new Catholic church for the congregation at St Simon and St Jude (fig. 2.9). As chair of the building committee Father Peter MacIntyre (1818–1891), later bishop of Charlottetown, personally hired the Brooklyn, New York, architect Patrick Keely (1816–1896), whose Irish heritage may have influenced the award. In any event, there was clearly some cachet in having one's architect hail from a major metropolitan area, given credence to the type of design chosen in a

Fig. 2.9 St Simon and St Jude, Tignish, Prince Edward Island.

growing town. In this manner, the people of Tignish could imagine themselves exchanging economic capital for the symbolic capital of a church enhanced by the cultural capital associated with a cosmopolitan city. Further solidifying the commission was Keely's adoption of fellow Irishman A.W.N. Pugin's architectural ideals, limiting ornament to its constructional purposes.[28] The central placement of the tower partially embedded in the western facade and the symmetrically arranged window and stair turrets were not based on Pugin's ideals but represented the type of geometrical references approved of by Catholic advocates of Classicism. The church clearly articulates Gothic vocabulary – pointed windows and window tracery, stepped buttresses, and separately articulated side entrance – although the strong symmetrical features cannot overlook the link with Classicism and Rome.

Practicing in New York would have put Keely in close proximity to the pattern books written by the architect Richard Upjohn. Published in 1852, only five years prior to the Tignish award, *Upjohn's Rural Architecture* depicted two remarkable models for St Simon and St Jude: Christ Church, Brooklyn (1841–42) and Dr Pott's Presbyterian Church, New York (1844). The church was structurally similar to one published by George Woodward in 1868 in *Rural Church Architecture* (fig. 2.10). Though we are not dealing with a model/copy relationship, it is nevertheless clear that there is a certain compositional expediency in the basic arrangement of structural and aesthetic components. A centrally placed tower flanked by windows, which appeared to articulate side aisles, was a common feature in pattern books, due to its easy replication from drawing to three-dimensional building.

The spare profile of Upjohn's drawings were easy for architects to transpose and difficult for amateurs who needed greater detail to carry out the job on their own. Though not particularly written for the use of Roman Catholic church-builders, Upjohn's frugal designs satisfied the Tignish congregation's desire to appear modest in a location where they were not socially dominant. As late as 1885, the *Charlottetown Herald* continued to describe Father MacIntyre's situation in PEI as having "a Catholic population – scattered over a country where to be a Catholic was to be intellectually, socially, and commercially at a disadvantage. There were no Catholic schools outside of Charlottetown, there was no Catholic filling a public office of any importance – indeed to be a Catholic was to be regarded with suspicion and distrust by one half of the population of the colony."[29]

Though the construction of St Simon and St Jude's church was the effort of a closed community of Irish-Catholics, they nonetheless took the opportunity to disrupt the power of the local Anglican Church by building the town's

Fig. 2.10 Specimen page of design no.5, plate 12, from *Rural Church Architecture*.

first brick structure. Brick was considered a building material for towns and not villages and the distinction was an important one. The community that built St Simon and St Jude consciously asserted its position within the social structure of the village of Tignish clothing the church in a richer fabric, brick, in anticipation of the village's productive future that never materialized.

TARIFFS ON IMPORTED BOOKS AND PATTERN BOOK CONSUMPTION

Britain's repeal of the Corn Laws in 1846 resulted in tariffs periodically placed on the importation of a large variety of goods, including books. Despite temporary reciprocity agreements between Canada and the US that ebbed and flowed between 1854 and 1866, tariffs on books were eventually lowered to make imports desirable in the Dominion. This effectively shut down the local production of pattern books and cemented the notion that the Dominion imported taste from Britain and the US. Ontario's printing presses continued to print all manner of textbooks, newspapers, and travel journals, but serious forms of knowledge came from what were considered to be reliable publishing houses in Britain and Europe.

The libraries of Ontario's architects and builders were lined with imported architectural reference material and treatises no less than pattern books. In the 1840s, the Kingston, Ontario, builder-turned-architect William Coverdale (1828–1884) had owned sixty-three pattern book publications on subjects covering civic, religious, and domestic building.[30] Thirty years later, architects working in Ontario were still collecting pattern books. The architectural partnership of William Storm and Fred Cumberland continued to place new pattern books on their shelves from the 1840s to 70s. Their extensive collection included the Ecclesiological Society's *Instrumenta Ecclesiastica* (1847), Frank Wills's *Ancient English Ecclesiastical Architecture* (1850), Raphael and J. Arthur Brandon's *Open Timber Roofs* (1849) and *An Analysis of Gothick Architecture: Illustrated by a Series of Upwards of Seven Hundred Examples of Doorways, Etc.* (1873), William Butterfield's *Elevations, Sections, and Details, of Saint John Baptist Church, at Shottesbrooke, Berkshire* (1844), and James Fergusson's *Illustrated Handbook of Architecture* (1855).

When the fashion for pattern books shifted from British to US volumes, William Storm invested in volumes from New York publishers. These included *Bicknell's Victorian Village* (1873) and Edward Jenkins's *The Architect's Legal*

Handbook (1880). The US pattern books provided concrete design ideas, technical knowledge, and a connection to a large market for ecclesiastical architecture developing south of the Dominion's border.

These church pattern books collectively established a repository of neo-Gothic church designs that served the various needs of Cumberland, Storm, and their students. As commercial products, the books trafficked in practical construction solutions, appealing designs, and the logic of adapting construction to local building materials and labour markets. Pattern books were often consulted in varying extents before the construction process began since patrons wanted to see preliminary drawings before committing funds to a project.

3

SELLING ECCLESIOLOGY AS IDENTITY IN THE DOMINION OF CANADA

THE ANGLICAN CHURCH JOSTLES FOR SOCIAL POSITION

The newly appointed Anglican bishop of Newfoundland, Edward Feild, arrived in the port of St John's, Newfoundland, in 1846 to find his flock outnumbered by Roman Catholics more than four to one. Feild quickly discovered that his church was in a "crisis" of demographics visibly expressed in architecture.[1] A massive Roman Catholic basilica built in the neo-Classical tradition of round-headed arches and Greek style columns surveyed the town from the highest geographical point. When Feild beheld the Roman Catholic cathedral compared to what he termed a "wooden shed" of a church he inherited from his predecessor, Bishop Spencer, immediate plans for a monumental cathedral in the Gothic Revival vocabulary of the Church of England ensued. The massive scale of the project, intended to equalize the social and religious terrain, required the bishop to draw on monies earmarked for the expansion of the colonial diocese.

Feild's bold stroke of building a costly cathedral in St John's appeared to take money away from missionary work in his diocese, further isolating fishing communities stretched out along the Newfoundland and Labrador coasts. In fact, the bishop was the most isolated of all, a High Churchman aligned to the Tractarian form of Christian worship focused on the ritual Eucharist in a land of Low Church ideals. The fishing communities that comprised the Anglican diocese in Newfoundland and Labrador preferred a rousing Sunday sermon and the shoulder of a local minister in times of family crisis. The local residents cared more about survival in the harsh Maritime climate than their Anglican bishop's status-conscious aspirations. Yet, the bishop insisted that architectural rivalry was one of the most effective ways to expand his colonial diocese and delegitimize the Roman Catholic population derogatorily termed Hiberno Romanists. Using architecture to express elite status was an old strategy, employed by Anglican colonial bishops even in towns where the established Church was not dominant. The audacity of Bishop Feild's plan to broadcast the superiority of the established Church in St John's was characteristic of the acerbic clergyman. Finding little financial support among the Low Church fishermen, Feild succeeded in raising funds from England to complete the project.

Bishop Feild's counterpart in New Brunswick was Bishop John Medley, who constructed the first cathedral to employ a Gothic vocabulary that was archaeologically "correct" and up to date with architectural fashion in Britain. Bishop Medley also believed in the importance of High Church ritual, expressing it through his architectural training in Britain prior to the colonial appointment. Feild's cathedral of St John the Baptist (begun 1846) in St John's, Newfoundland, and Medley's cathedral in Fredericton, New Brunswick, were the visible result of the established Church's economic strategies and social reforms, in which architectural fashions reinforced unsustainable claims of social superiority. They were also products of cross-denominational rivalries transplanted across the Atlantic to colonial settlements. Bishop Feild rebroadcast this rivalry familiar to members of the Church of England in London in order to raise significant amounts of money to finish his own colonial cathedral project, which enjoyed little local support.

Case Study: Anglican Cathedral of St John's, Newfoundland

Bishop Feild's monumental cathedral in St John's (nave completed 1850, transepts 1880–85, fire-damaged 1892, restored 1893) (fig. 3.1) capitalized on the reputation and taste of its architect, George Gilbert Scott (knighted 1872 for his service to architecture). Having never set foot on Canadian soil, Scott shipped the drawings from his London offices in the care of his assistant William Hay, who acted as clerk-of-works for the project.[2] The transmittal of the full suite of drawings to Bishop Feild's home in St John's, Newfoundland, represented trade in economic and artistic capital around the symbolic capital of the established Church. Scott's drawings show how the architect adopted the proportion and ornament of English medieval models of the thirteenth century for the cruciform plan with crossing tower. The graduated lancet windows of the east end recall Lincoln Cathedral and York Minster in England, and the small scale of the west entrance appeared in English cathedrals at Wells, Ripon, and York Minster.[3]

Initially, Bishop Feild had set his sights on a modest construction project modelled on a drawing he had seen in a book by the renowned neo-Gothic

Fig. 3.1 St John the Baptist (Anglican Cathedral), St John's, Newfoundland.

architect A.W.N. Pugin. *The Present State of Ecclesiastical Architecture in England* had published three church drawings, one of which was the Church of St Wilfrid, composed of nave, aisles, clerestory, chancel, and tower in the simplified Early English style.[4] What appealed to the bishop most was that Pugin had estimated the construction costs at a reasonable £5,000.[5]

However, Feild and his architect held far grander aspirations for the project, which necessitated significant fundraising schemes. As a result, the events surrounding the cathedral project were as rocky and crestfallen as the Newfoundland landscape. Newfoundland's main industries of fishing and shipbuilding were in decline in the mid-nineteenth century, creating challenges for local fundraising. To maintain total control over the project he embarked on a complex "game" of taste and social conventions. His claim that Newfoundlanders' lack of sophistication required to produce a "correct" sense of taste meant that, in the words of his associate William Grey (principal of Queen's College at St John's), they were susceptible to:

> fashions are palmed off on the credulous fashion-hunters as new which really are stale enough in England. Church-building is in the same predicament; the revival, which began with you in 1839, can scarcely be said to have begun here, although there have certainly been more enquiries what Gothic architecture is within the last two years

than ever there were before in Newfoundland. You wonder perhaps that, under these circumstances, Newfoundland can boast of our noblest colonial cathedral. But this is the doing of our noble-hearted Bishop alone. The building is quite unappreciated by the majority of persons here ... they see no beauty in it, because it is not finished.[6]

Grey's letter reveals a paternalistic attitude, presenting Newfoundlanders as impatient children lacking the knowledge requisite to project the cathedral's image into the future. The letter also presents the local Communion as having insufficient faith in their bishop.

Bishop Feild charged that Newfoundlanders were as deficient in their appreciation of ecclesiological architecture as they were of the sacraments and rites of the Anglican Church. He complained privately about a previously abandoned cathedral project composed of a flat roof and no pillars, no chancel, no font, and no tracery in any of the windows. Still, Bishop Feild skillfully manipulated his claims to knowledge and taste in order to avoid awaking the ire of his congregation of "fishmongers." His chief worry: that the congregation would misinterpret the Cambridge Camden Society's strict principles of Ecclesiology as High Church doctrine. The bishop feared that such attacks would have scuttled financial support in England.

Feild knew he was not going to get enough local money to complete his project. He wrote to his colleague and fellow clergyman William Scott in England in 1844, bemoaning that "the fact is there are no more means to complete or proceed with [the cathedral] and I can see no disposition on the part of the people to come forward with additional subscriptions at all adequate to the object."[7] All he required of the local communion was lack of interference with his wishes. Casting his fundraising net across the Atlantic, he wrote to the Society for the Propagation of the Gospel, the leading British financier of Anglican missionary activity. To obtain England's financial support Feild reported that Newfoundland's financial crisis had caused "our projected Cathedral to have died a natural or unnatural death through want of funds, and of love. The subject now is never raised even in talk."[8] The "crisis" had taken on an economic and architectural dimension. Nonetheless, money was not easily forthcoming and it appeared that Feild had to rely on divine intervention.

Providentially, a fire that destroyed large parts of St John's, leaving hundreds of people homeless, became the rallying point for the established Church in Newfoundland. A civic committee for the relief of the sufferers of the fire at St John's succeeded in obtaining a Royal letter from Queen Victoria authorizing the Archbishops of Canterbury and York to adopt measures for providing relief.⁹ Anglican Church officials in St John's opportunistically positioned themselves to intercede in the delivery of the funds in order to get financial control for their cathedral project. The Anglican Archdeacon of St John's Thomas Bridge wrote to the Society for the Propagation of the Gospel in Foreign Parts asking for it to be:

> possible to make some arrangements for the disposal of the Collections under [the Queen's letter], by which a portion of them may be applied to the restoration of the church. That, I would think, would be right and just, seeing that the great bulk of those who will share in the Relief supplied for those who have suffered temporal loss by the late fire, will not belong to our Communion, whilst all the contributions under a Queen's letter will, of course, come from members of it.¹⁰

The established Church in England raised the money and the Church of England in Canada wanted to keep a significant portion of the money away from the Roman Catholic contingent. Archdeacon Bridge's letter also shows that sentiments had not changed toward the Roman Catholics on the island in a decade since Bridge's predecessor, Archdeacon Edward Wix (1802–1866), had written in his journal in 1836 that "you were living in a town, which, for the lawlessness of a large portion of its inhabitants, who are excited to breaches of the peace by a most seditious Romish priesthood, is as little desirable a place of residence as many of the disturbed townships of Ireland."¹¹

With money in hand, the process of building a large stone cathedral, even on an island composed chiefly of rock, turned out to be a formidable enterprise. To begin with, suitable masonry had to be shipped to St John's, which exasperated British authorities, who criticized Bishop Feild's seemingly spendthrift ways. Arthur Blackwood, senior clerk to Under-Secretary of State for the Colonies H. Merivale, attacked Feild's project on economic grounds: "it would seem that the £16,000 which has been spent on the Cathedral is insufficient to complete the Building, & that the Bishop does not know where the rest of the money is to be found to finish the interior & make it serviceable. Two good stone churches might have been built for that money."¹² The St John's cathedral project was clearly under the microscope of British authorities, who were conducting a rather loose cost-benefit analysis, although no one seems to have objected to the way emergency relief funds were spent in Newfoundland.

CAPITALIZING ON VISUAL IDENTITY IN THE MARITIMES

Church architecture was recognized for establishing community and denominational identities. Church pattern books broadcast them on a scale limited only by the places where books could travel, and that spread as far as the railway's transcontinental achievement and core branch-line enterprise. European and British-trained architects arriving with architectural drawings packed into steamer trunks discovered that their source material became stale relatively quickly. Pattern books regularly arriving from Britain, and later the US, kept architects apprised of the latest fashions abroad. In essence, pattern books were perpetual fashion and identity machines. They provided the continuous source of data that helped market identity alongside taste.

In the mid-nineteenth century, the cultural and political link with Britain maintained a strong transatlantic identity. Architecturally, the Gothic Revival was viewed in the Dominion as quintessentially British. Maintaining that link meant architects needed to be aware of the latest fashions. In the 1840s and 50s, British-trained architects working in the Maritimes, Ontario, and Anglophone Quebec subscribed to pattern books, journals, and magazines from London in order to keep apprised of subtle changes to neo-Gothic fashion at home. Pattern books became the architectural substance that referred back to British society, something that increasingly needed to be verified by the printed page.

Canadian audiences identified with the imagery found in church pattern books illustrating British churches in English landscapes. *Designs for Country Churches* (1850) produced by the British architect George Truefitt served as an example of a church pattern book depicting religious architecture in idyllic English scenery. The manicured landscape of mature trees and rolling hills harmonized with spires, turrets, and the asymmetrical massing of nave, chancel, porch, and tower. These scenes struck a chord with church-builders in the Dominion who were trying to craft the Canadian wilderness into the pastures and meadows they imagined still existed in England.

Looking closely at the designs in Truefitt's book, one finds within its twenty-two full-page perspective illustrations several solutions to single-elevation churches that employ tapered buttresses (fig. 3.2). Clearly, no one would suggest that an architectural powerhouse of the calibre of Sir George Gilbert Scott would require the use of a pattern book. Yet, tapered buttresses were a common feature in pattern books printed before Gilbert Scott was a marketable name in architecture. Rather than look for model/copy relationships, it is important to note that pattern books were part of a complex network that transmitted architectural motifs, contributing to the incredible amount of design possibilities available to people constructing chapels, parish

Fig. 3.2 Specimen page from *Designs for Country Churches*.

churches, and cathedrals. The churches illustrated in the hardbound volume adhered to Ecclesiological principles and were meant to facilitate, in Truefitt's words, the "rise and progress of the revival of the taste for Pointed Architecture." The term "Pointed" was synonymous with "Christian" architecture to describe the Gothic Revival style.[13] Though the book lacked a long historical introduction and was chiefly a picture book, Truefitt wrote a short preface in which he outlined the reason for producing the pattern book. This is a rare example of a pattern book author writing about the motivating factors and of the future that he envisioned for the Gothic Revival.[14] He referred to the shift in fashion from neo-Classical church designs to poor imitations of medieval buildings that lacked authenticity, noting:

> public taste, however, in due time improving, the worthlessness of these first productions, became evident, and the members of the profession then began to perceive, that while utter ignorance prevailed as to the principles of the style in which they were called upon to design, and their only chance of avoiding failure lay in a servile repetition of examples already in existence: this plan was accordingly introduced and by degrees adopted as a general rule. Books of examples appeared in rapid succession and "Authority" having taken the place of "Originality," Church Architecture and "Copyism" became synonymous terms.[15]

He then noted how the nineteenth-century invention of classifying "various gradations of style," by the separate achievements of the architects/authors Thomas Rickman and Matthew Bloxam, created a core of knowledge needed to decipher the mystery of medieval architectural beauty. As did nearly all of the Gothic Revival architects of the day, Truefitt believed that dividing medieval architecture into chronological periods conforming to certain visual characteristics that included the terms "Norman," "Early English," "Decorated," and "Perpendicular" amounted to an above-ground archaeology revealing hidden secrets of medieval master masons. The final obstacle, he remarked, was overcome through "the publication of the excellent practical rules and correct advice of the Ecclesiological Society, and of the 'True Principles of Christian Architecture,' by Mr A.W. Pugin, that we are chiefly indebted for its removal. These works at once gave the clue to the real spirit of the style, and in a great measure cleared up by the mystery that had so long attended it."[16]

Truefitt stated that the purpose of his book of drawings, which were not copies of medieval churches but rather renderings envisioned in the spirit of them, would inspire other architects and students to remove the stigma of "copyist" from their profession. He credited Pugin's book *True Principles* and the practical rules and advice of the Ecclesiological Society with giving a clue to the "real spirit" of the style. He also positioned himself as a moderate-conservative in terms of the High Church issue by citing both Pugin and the Ecclesiologists as his influences. There was no mistaking his designs for Anglican church-building purposes with their emphasis on the articulation of the tower and versions of an aisled nave suitable for processions. It was the notion of "spirit" that Truefitt claimed legitimated his church designs and protected them from accusations of pure fantasy. Architects protected themselves from accusations of creating flights of fancy by anchoring their designs in the authority of the past and, at the same time, wrapped themselves in unassailable cloaks of taste.

In the Maritimes during the 1840s and 50s, taste was essentially consolidated around British examples. During that same period, the construction of neo-Gothic churches in the Maritimes and Lower Canada expressed the economy, politics, and patterns of public taste that were indicated in the pattern books. At the same time, these same factors did not constitute a singular Dominion identity but rather a network or tapestry of multiple identities consolidated around geographic and temporal power structures (provincial, urban, religious, social) as concentrated settlement expanded west, north, and even inward from the coasts. Denominational differences were reflected in the aesthetics and plan of churches, meaning that Roman Catholic, Anglican, Presbyterian, Baptist, and Methodist groups each manipulated the neo-Gothic style in subtly different ways. Cultural differences were also reflected in ecclesiastical architecture. Predictably, Acadian churches in PEI had a French neo-Gothic flavour.

Temporal differences displayed significant changes to the elevations of neo-Gothic churches. The growth of consumer society influenced the demand for variety in church aesthetics, and the pattern books were symptoms of the new commercial practices. The potency of Ecclesiology in print media, and the pattern books in particular, developed a raft of architectural principles marketed in terms of taste. Pugin's principles of neo-Gothic that favoured the association of religion and architecture legitimized and reified those architectural rules as though they were positive implements of the social order. The business of church-building and the consumption of the pattern books in Lower Canada and the Maritimes were constituted by an already established British identity that drew its power from the Anglican Church and association with the British monarch. An important point to be made in the way that the Anglican Church asserted Royal connections speaks to the commercialization of religion in the sense that monarchy trumped claims of legitimacy by all other denominations. The Canadas' description as a "Dominion" was a compelling image because of the combination of religious and secular elements of society. Neo-Gothic doctrines conscripted history into commercialized modern lifestyle and pushed forward the renewal of production and consumption. Spurred on by the pattern books' commerciality, religion itself appeared to have been packaged for commercial consumption.

BRITAIN'S PARISH CHURCH MODEL IN RURAL TOWNS AND EMERGING CITIES

During the 1860s and 70s British rural parish churches acted as models for a variety of ecclesiastical buildings in the Dominion. Among the several reasons for advocating parish churches as models for the colonies were economic and practical considerations, which included lowering the cost of materials and the amount of skilled labour needed to complete the job.

A popular parish church model was St Michael's, Long Stanton, Cambridgeshire, which was shown in Raphael and J. Arthur Brandon's pattern book, *Parish Churches* (1848), in a manner that highlighted its relationship with the landscape and the picturesque (see fig. 2.6, p. 60). Frank Wills seemed to have played with the same notion of the picturesque when he depicted St Anne's Chapel, Fredericton, New Brunswick, in his pattern book *Ancient Ecclesiastical Architecture* (1850) (fig. 3.3). Typically, these designs included a west-end gable surmounted by a bellcote that was flush with the western facade. Usually, a round window flanked by a group of simple lancets was housed in the western gable. The repetition of subtle variations in different pattern books and its adoption across Canada was a powerful combination.

Fig. 3.3 Specimen page of St Anne's Chapel, Fredericton, New Brunswick.

Fig. 3.4 St John the Evangelist (Anglican), Oxford Mills, Ontario, 1869.

As already noted, St Anne's Chapel, Fredericton, New Brunswick, by Franks Wills was aesthetically related to a collection of other parish churches in Canada that had been marketed in the pattern books. Included in the grouping of parish churches that have low walls, steep-pitched roofs, and a single, double, or triple bellcote integrated into the west wall are the Anglican Church of the Messiah (c. 1855), rang du Bord de l'eau, Sabrevois, Quebec, and St John the Evangelist (1869), Oxford Mills, Ontario (fig. 3.4). The arrangement was repeated in timber at St Mary's Church (1865), New Westminster, BC, built by the architect J.C. White. St Stephen's-in-the-Fields (1856) at the corner of College and Bellevue, Toronto, by Thomas Fuller combined the silhouette with rich constructional polychrome in brick and stone.

The parish model-type used at St Anne's appeared in a variety of pattern books that included a design for an iron church published in the second series of *Instrumenta Ecclesiastica* (1856), this one authorized by the Ecclesiological Society (fig. 3.5). It also appeared at the west end of a generic church design in Frederick Withers's *Church Architecture* (1873) (fig. 3.6). The bellcote silhouette was still popular in 1880 when Amos Bicknell's company published a compilation book of other architects' designs entitled *Specimen Book of One Hundred Architectural Designs, Showing Plans, Elevations, and Views of Suburban Houses, Villas, Sea-Side and Campground Cottages, Homesteads, Churches and Public Buildings* (1880), which included another of Frederick Withers's renditions of the distinctive gable. The Rev. F.J. Jobson published a scaled-down version minus the bellcote in a design for a village chapel to be used by Wesleyan Methodists in *Chapel and School Architecture as Appropriate to the Buildings of Nonconformists* (1850).

Fig. 3.5 Specimen page of a timber church from *Instrumenta Ecclesiastica*.

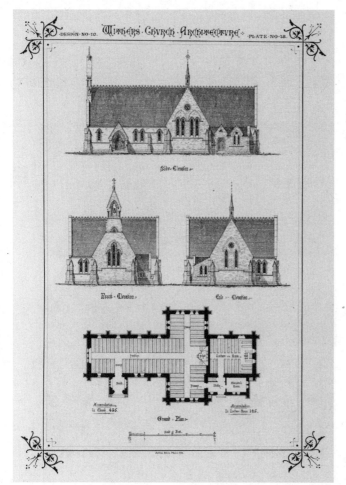

Fig. 3.6 Specimen page from *Church Architecture*.

*Case Study: The Burial Chapels of St James-the-Less
and the Toronto Necropolis*

The burial chapels of St James-the-Less (1857–61) and the Toronto Necropolis (1872) served identical purposes and exhibited strikingly similar neo-Gothic characteristics. Both chapels were characterized as High Victorian Gothic, an architectural fashion that displayed a new kind of structural logic omitting external buttressing in favour of smooth wall space. It reignited public excitement for neo-Gothic architecture by departing from the archaeological precedent adhered to by Pugin and the Ecclesiologists. The well-known British architect George Street referred to the progressiveness of High Victorian Gothic as "development," describing a complicated suite of new ideas in proportion, simple ornament, European source material, and massing.[17]

Fig. 3.7 St James-the-Less (Anglican), Toronto.

Fred Cumberland, in partnership with William George Storm, adopted the polychromy and simple wall articulation of High Victorian at the Anglican cemetery chapel of St James-the-Less (fig. 3.7). The freshness of Cumberland's vocabulary, in Canadian terms, was less likely to attract criticism in a chapel dedicated to funerary use as opposed to regular Sunday services. Visitors came sporadically. Indeed, the low walling at St James-the-Less harmonized with the gentle rolling hills of the surrounding cemetery. Inside the chapel, mechanical innovation allowed a coffin to be lowered through the floor of the chancel at the east end to an awaiting horse-drawn hearse.

Cognizant of the dangers of what the British architectural critic John Ruskin called machine-made modes of deception, Cumberland and Storm laboured to infuse unornamented brick with medieval spirit. The carvings on a series of small corbels that project from the interior wall posts exhibit the requisite amount of variety for a medieval church. Strong comparisons exist between the St James chapel and the parish church models contained in Raphael and J. Arthur Brandon's *Parish Churches* (1848) and George Truefitt's *Designs for Country Churches* (1850) (fig. 3.8). The muscular corner tower arrangement prominently displayed in the pattern books was echoed in the husky corner tower of St James-the-Less. Henry Langley applied a similar method to the Toronto Necropolis. Following George Street's advice, Langley used brick to achieve a symbiosis with neighbouring domestic and commercial buildings, refraining at the last minute from the vigorous red and black waves of constructional polychromy, a multicoloured brick patterning popular in late 1850s Britain.

Fig. 3.8 Specimen page from *Designs for Country Churches*.

To sustain a notional image of rustic English burial in a crematorium these cemetery chapels utilized the picturesque in ways similar to its marketing in the church pattern books. The urban public did not want to think about the high cost of burial except in a bucolic sense of the serene. Images of pastoral churches in pattern books extended the image of a simple country burial beside a "handsome little sanctuary, enshrined in a grove of low-growing oaks and maples and flowering shrubs."[18] In reality, the overcrowded burial grounds of the non-sectarian Necropolis came free of charge, although the undertaker required remittance.

Crematoria also caught the public's attention. Albert C. Freeman's book *Crematoria in Great Britain and Abroad* (1906) used English, European, and American neo-Gothic church designs to veil a thoroughly modern convention. Crematoria employed medieval artistic and architectural knowledge to assuage contemporary fears of disease associated with urban burial. The sanitary motive of modern cremation still had to be hidden behind an acceptable historical facade. Thus, cemetery chapels became a new form, arising with the establishment of large burial grounds located on the outskirts of cities.

The shift toward larger cemeteries in the post-Confederation era signifies the cultural importance of property, expressed in section 91 of the British North America Act of 1867. In establishing legislative authority over "the Public Debt and Property" as its primary concern, property became prioritized as second only to "the Regulation of Trade and Commerce." The advice in church pattern books about securing land free of debt before building a church held new value in the Dominion. Congregations were advised to go into debt only for the purposes of constructing a church, rather than for the purchase of land. This notion demonstrated that the public understood quite well that the land underneath a church in the Canadas was sacred by agreement, or construction, rather than by a divine and otherworldly force. As the disposal of the Clergy Reserves demonstrated, the relationship between land and religion in the Canadas was constituted in economic practice and susceptible to criticism in the public domain. An important case study of the construction of St James Cathedral in Toronto demonstrates how the idea of sacred land was put to the test in the public domain.

4

PROPERTY OWNERSHIP AND CHURCH-BUILDING: THE FINANCIAL STRUCTURE OF CHURCHES IN ONTARIO

STRUCTURING LAND ACQUISITIONS FOR CHURCHES IN ONTARIO

The connection between property ownership and church-building provides an avenue for studying the assertion of religion in the spectrum of Canadian economy, politics, and social systems. The Anglican Church in the Dominion attempted to use the mechanics of property ownership to leverage its privilege and prestige. Whenever possible, agents acting for the established Church tried to procure land for free or at reduced cost. When purchasing land, building committees employed a fixed-rate mortgage amortized over many years with the intention of discharging it through donations accumulated over the years. Finding the money to construct the church building was a different matter, usually involving the sale of subscriptions or shares that translated into the leasing of pews in the church. Alternatively, short-term credit was used to pay contractors and builders in cases where seats were anticipated to be let "free" to the communion. In either scenario, businessmen sitting on building committees and church advisory councils were indispensable because of their access to pools of wealth.

The acquisition of land for religious expansion required a system of ecclesiastical governance as much as it did monetary and property donations. The structure of religious councils was similar to corporate boards owing to the prevalence of businessmen and industrialists occupying those voluntary posts. The Church Society of the Diocese of Toronto, which shaped much of the financial operations of Anglican churches throughout Ontario, was an ecclesiastical corporation. Modelled on Britain's Society for the Propagation of the Gospel in Foreign Parts, the Church Society's board was composed of leading members of the community and men of industry. They were prepared, after the union of Upper and Lower Canada in 1840, to capitalize on the loosened restrictions governing the use of land as capital against borrowed money. The small Anglican congregation building St Peter's church on Carlton Avenue in Toronto procured a mortgage of $3,700 in 1864 on property that cost them $700. Their borrowed capital exceeded the value of the property acting as collateral, since churches were considered excellent credit risks and banks were bullish on the future value of land in Ontario. Yet, the reality of religious finance was that many churches became insolvent, particularly during economic downturns. During the major economic slump of the 1870s, the Central Presbyterian Church in Toronto accumulated such large debt, amounting to $30,000 from building its church and schoolhouse, that the congregation was faced with ruin. Nearly a decade later, Central Presbyterian still had a "debt on the church in the shape of a mortgage held by the Star Life Assurance Company, London, England, amounting to £5,000 sterling," which drew interest of 6 percent and necessitated the congregation to raise $110 per week in order to meet its expenses.[1]

The structure of Anglican church-building and land-acquisition committees mitigated financial problems by attracting powerful board members with business experience, political clout, and access to land. The chair of the building committee at St James' Cathedral in Toronto was John Beverley Robinson (1791–1863), a former judge and "unofficial figure-head" of the Family Compact who had close ties with Lieutenant Governor Sir Peregrine Maitland (1777–1854). Robinson invited Frederick Widder (1801–1865) onto the committee because he was an official with the Canada Company, an influential British land and colonizing venture. Rounding out the building committee were successful businessmen Thomas Helliwell (1795–1862), Peter Paterson (1807–1883), and Charles Albert Berczy (1794–1858). Each of them, respectively, owned interests in local breweries, milling, and dry goods. Patterson cast a long shadow over Ontario's economic development by founding the British American Fire and Life Assurance Co., the Consumer's Gas Co., and the Canada Permanent Building and Savings Society (later the Canada Permanent Mortgage Co.). Patterson and Berczy had each been directors of the Bank of Upper Canada, which had impacted mercantilism in the Dominion through short-term loans for railway but succumbed to reckless land speculation in the 1840s. The Anglican Church's employment of a corporate strategy indicated how finance was the "door through which the laity entered the inner courts of the church."[2] Wealthy settlers donated land to their church, thereby exchanging economic capital for cultural, social, and spiritual capital. D'Arcy Boulton (1759–1834), the leader of Upper Canada's affluent Family Compact, gave land on John Street in Toronto to establish St George's Anglican Church (1845). However, the proximity of the gifted land to the family's estate effectively made the church into a private chapel, cementing the connection between religion, property, and privilege. The architect was Henry Bowyer Lane, a close family friend who appreciated that the Boulton's would attend no church, on land donated by them, lest it be endowed according their social standing. The cost of the small chapel was $24,000, and it represented one of the last uncomplicated land transactions between the social elite and religious institution.

Land speculation and rising property values had become problematic for the Church of England in the Dominion, even before Confederation. The situation altered the distribution of the Clergy Reserves, which represented approximately 1.3 million acres of land interspersed throughout the Dominion and initially promised to the Protestant Church in the Constitutional Act of 1791.[3] Despite decades of legislative and public battles over the Clergy Reserves, the situation had been settled by 1854, largely in the government's favour. The lands were sold through the government's agent, the Canada Company, but only a small portion of its revenue, £245,000, accrued to the combined coffers of the leading religious institutions in the Dominion, and not the Anglican Church alone. An editorial in *The Church* lamented that the Church of England in Canada had been "deprived of her unquestionable rights. What ecclesiastical property in the empire is anywhere safe? Should her revenues be sacrificed in Canada, because a real or presumed majority demand it, can they, with some weight of argument and high moral influence be preserved in Ireland?"[4] The enforced sharing of the proceeds from the sale of the Clergy Reserves paralleled the negotiated unification of Confederation. The government's political power enforced a settlement on the Anglican Church's potential ability to serve its members by arguing in favour of the "common interest" of the general population in the Dominion.

When the Clergy Reserves were rescinded, the material expansion of the Anglican Church began to depend more fully on funds received from specialized Anglican organizations in Britain, including the Society for the Promotion of Christian Knowledge and the Society for the Propagation of the Gospel in Foreign Parts. However, these institutions eventually withdrew financial support, causing the Anglican Bishop of Toronto John Strachan (1778–1867), for instance, to ask for money from local businesspeople to finish the construction of St James' Cathedral. On a local scale, individuals came forward to help financially. Strachan was searching for supporters similar to Mrs Proudfoot at St Paul's Anglican Church, who organized a bazaar that netted $4,000, and W.A. Baldwin, who mortgaged his farm for $8,000 to complete the project on Bloor Street in Toronto in 1873.[5] Interestingly, the church bazaars run by women's auxiliaries raised significant funds on par with commercial enterprise, though the bazaars were tainted with frivolity, seen as nothing more than "ice-cream socials." A robust structure of religious governance combined with local support was required in the Dominion in order to counter the government's withdrawal of lands initially promised for religious expansion.

Case Study: Selling Church Land to Rebuild St James' Cathedral, Toronto

During Toronto's Great Fire of 1849, a burning ember ignited the wooden spire of St James' Church, causing the entire tower to fall into the body of the ten-years old Georgian-Style structure. In place of the boxlike church, built in 1839 at a cost of £5,100 and £1,075 for the spire, a large neo-Gothic cathedral was planned in 1850 at an anticipated cost of £12,000. The estimate did not include the completion of a tower and spire (fig. 4.1). The reconstruction of St James' was envisioned by the Anglican cohort in Toronto as part of the city's architectural regrowth following the Great Fire, which destroyed fifteen acres of the business district. The reconstruction of a large portion of the city was imagined to place Toronto in league with a notional suite of European and US cities, including London, Chicago, and Seattle. The reconstruction of St James coincided with Toronto's fashioning itself as both an Imperial and even Continental European city; and efforts initially involved protracted debates on the way the new St James should look, as well as the sources of income needed to support its completion.

Within two weeks of the fire, the congregation organized a new building committee to discuss plans and costs, as well as search for a suitable architect. Sporadic but intense negotiations took place from 1851 to 1853 between Bishop John Strachan and members of the vestry building committee about the choice of architect and the cathedral's design. A competition to choose the best design, representing one of the first of its kind in Canada, was initiated and attracted eleven entries. Meanwhile the vestry committee identified a significant financial problem: the church's coffers lacked the money to construct the elaborate building desired by the bishop. With $5,000 insurance money from the fire there was insufficient funds to construct a cathedral. The shortfall seemed insurmountable. The mortgage on the previous building had yet to be discharged, and so the bishop was reluctant to ask congregants to lease seats in the new church. It had been only a decade since their last subscriptions. Thus, the bishop hatched a scheme that involved selling church land comprised of eight city lots on King Street to commercial developers in order to raise the balance of the funds necessary, representing a good portion of the amount not covered by the insurance.[6] It was a divisive proposal that enraged the building committee and congregants who did not want to see storefronts

Fig. 4.1 St James' Anglican Cathedral, Toronto photographed in 1852 before the completion of the tower in 1874.

lining their cathedral property. In their opinion, the cathedral had already given up too much land, reducing four acres to one and a half.[7] Controversy escalated when the public learned that the bishop intended to sell church lands presumed to contain old graves.

The land auction was blocked by a collection of incensed citizens, many of which had no religious affiliation aside from the belief in the sanctity of burial in churchyards. The vestry building committee proposed an alternate plan that involved reusing the old foundation and some of the Georgian cathedral's burnt but intact exterior walls. Bishop Strachan rejected this plan outright on the grounds that it was impossible to harmonize the longitudinal axis of a Gothic Revival church with the square proportions of a Georgian building. A battle ensued that was periodically broadcast in the public domain. To counter the bishop the building committee hired the respected Toronto architect William Thomas, who pronounced the soundness of the Georgian foundation. In response, Bishop Strachan wrote pamphlets stating that he had the authority to deconsecrate church lands if doing so saved the Church from financial ruin. The bishop was undeterred by the prospect that he might undermine religious principles for the immediate interests of his cathedral and architectural proclivity. His logic, which placed a high value on economy, serves to underline what might be termed religious real estate, meanwhile chastising his detractors for caring only about the cost and appointment of leasing their pews.

Religious faith and economic optimism, tempered by practical concerns, and interdenominational rivalry contributed to decisions regarding the scale of the cathedral project. Strachan was trying to do more than simply rebuild, he was actively seeking to mark the Anglican faith as the dominant religion in this new, burgeoning metropolis of Toronto. Monumental church architecture like St James' Cathedral satisfied the city's ambition to assure a leading role in regional politics. The scale of the cathedral, though small by European standards, was designed to fulfill Toronto's growing need to identify itself with the larger European cities and proved to be a substantial economic burden for both the congregation and its bishop. Nevertheless, the cathedral – and its expression of current fashion in transatlantic ecclesiastical architecture – was a potent symbol of Bishop Strachan's belief that prestige ought to accrue to the established Church. This position, one shared by a range of Anglican groups, saw the economic development of Canada as an outcome of Anglican effort and accomplishment. Thus, multiple layers of Toronto's new, fashion conscious civic self-image were linked together in the building of a single cathedral.

Preventing the "legitimate" sale of the churchyard, in Bishop Strachan's mind, was the public's interpretation of the term "consecration." Believing that public opinion was strongly influenced by journalism, rumour, and erroneous tradition he argued that the preservation of consecrated land was less important than the funding of a new, prominent cathedral worthy of the prestige of the Anglican Church in Canada. In his printed pamphlets distributed to the public at large the Bishop disputed burial practice within the city limits by noting "public opinion, as well as, the law were against burying in churches or cities; and, being injurious to health." He noted in particular that urban burial was a modern invention unsupported by either theology or hygiene, attempting to legitimize his position. Troubling his logic was the virtual impossibility of determining the limits of a city in the midst of rapid expansion. The pamphlet showed that Bishop Strachan expected religious rank and privilege to induce public acceptance of his economic scheme; but its distribution in the public sphere was a matter he misjudged.

The pamphlet prompted responses from Strachan's opposition within St James' building committee. In a newspaper editorial, Mr Bramhill, a committee member, warned that consecrated ground could not be deconsecrated for commercial purposes. "If consecration is not a fiction then will no good churchman wish or dare to alienate one inch of ground consecrated not alone by this service of the Church, but consecrated and endeared by the dust of those who died in the faith."[8] A letter to the editor of the *Globe* newspaper noted that the "Church ground in strictly parochial property, vested, not alone in the district of St James, but in which the whole members of the Church ... will claim a voice." The author advised building a parish church and school for the betterment of Toronto society rather than the "vain and dangerous childish yearning for the pomp of a cathedral" at the risk of disturbing the "ashes of the founders of the church and the city itself." He prayed that the bishop "refuse to forget that the dead are sacred."[9]

With only a handful of supporters, Bishop Strachan pushed ahead with his plan, even disrupting the design competition. After having reviewed the eleven entries from leading architects, including Frank Wills, William Thomas, Kivas and John Tully, John Ostell, and US resident Gervase Wheeler, and settling on the proposal by the architect Fred Cumberland, "the building committee was induced to enter into communication with the author of a design which had not received a single vote when the prizes were awarded, and Mr Smith of Montreal was invited to attend the committee." George H. Smith of Montreal was Bishop Strachan's preferred architect. Smith provided drawings for a grand neo-Gothic cathedral to exceed the old church's 2,000-seat capacity. Its cost would have outstripped Cumberland's proposal. Strachan was adamant that he and his supporters could afford this monumental building if the congregation compromised on the sale of some church land. Pushing his point further, the bishop insisted that the vestry building committee meet privately with Smith. They were induced to provide the architect with unprecedented access to all of the competition entries, consider his final design, and pay him £25. When the building committee finally rejected Smith's proposal, the bishop was able to persuade them to spend £5,000 more than they originally contemplated by providing transepts of thirty-four feet.[10] To create a grander west view Cumberland was asked to reposition the tower to a central location, over the processional entrance. Cumberland's final plan involved a more than moderate use of British and European models in addition to US patterns where the silhouette was dependent on a strong western tower.

While the bishop was arguing points of planning with his building committee, the rescission of the Clergy Reserve lands threatened the fiscal condition of the Anglican Church in Canada. By 1850, the Colonial Government of Canada was revisiting the abolition of the Clergy Reserves. Bishop Strachan became the chief opponent of the elimination of the Clergy Reserves. In frustration and disbelief, he wrote to the Right Hon. Lord John Russell, member of British Parliament and Reform advocate, that, "we [Anglicans] have fallen into a state so extraordinary and humbling in a British colony where the Romish Church has increased in efficiency, wealth, and importance."[11] By the mid-1850s, the British Foreign Office had determined even to rescind the offer of monies accruing from the sale of the Clergy Reserves, divesting the Anglican Church in Canada from sizeable property and money. The ire in Bishop Strachan's letter to the colonial government was resoundingly clear:

> I was favoured with a copy of your bill, providing for the confiscation of the Clergy Reserves, and I declare, without hesitation, that it is the most atrocious specimen of oppressive legislation, that has appeared since the days of the French Convention. Can members of the United Church of England and Ireland be expected to summit calmly to this monstrous robbery?... Are you not rejoicing in the hope that the voice of prayer, and praise, and the preaching of the Gospel, will soon cease to be heard in Upper Canada?"[12]

His words left no doubt that the he believed that that property ought to accrue to the Anglican Church in Canada as a right of its social status in colonial expansion.

Problems persisted that threatened to derail the entire rebuilding process. The rescission of the Clergy Reserves stymied the bishop's hope for an architectural legacy in his diocese, feeling that he needed the monies accrued from that land to finish his cathedral. Tenders from builders advertised in *The British Colonist*, *The Church*, and *The Patriot* returned bids that were 50 percent higher than expected. The contracting firm of Metcalfe, Wilson, and Forbes supplied the lowest bid at £16,500. In actuality, costs overran to £18,803.17.7, leaving the bishop with a £9,335.17.7 deficit in exchange for what he deemed was an unimpressive building very unlike a cathedral. Increasing the level of insult, the English religious press pronounced St James' inferior to the design for Montreal's Christ Church by the late architect Frank Wills:

"altogether Montreal Cathedral will, when completed, mark an epoch in transatlantic ecclesiology. It will be the largest completed cathedral in America of our communion; for though the new one at Toronto would, if completed, be larger, it is as yet unfinished, and on (we believe) a much inferior and less correct plan."[13] The reference to a "much inferior and less correct plan" was clearly pointed at St James' layout. If the British religious press was correct in its judgment, then Bishop Strachan had indeed been right to demand that St James' not use the footprint of the former Georgian style building. He knew that the heavy proportions of a Georgian design would ruin the aesthetic of a Gothic Revival church meant to demonstrate weightlessness and verticality. However, he failed to fully consider that printed notices distributed in the public domain had the tendency to amplify scandal.

THE SOCIAL STRUCTURE OF FINANCING CHURCHES IN ONTARIO CITIES

The rescission of the Clergy Reserves galvanized the social structure of urban religious communities. Lawyers, businessmen, and builders were called upon to sit on the boards of church-building committees, providing their professional service free of charge. The service became a status symbol demonstrating the wealth and social connections of these people willing to donate their time. Their efforts were aided by the large payments made by entrepreneurs who had profited from land speculation, mining, or lumber. Religion received a lion's share of these donations because people invested in it the hope of ordering society and winning salvation.

The risk for church-builders holding a mortgage on their church was eased by their ability to use urban plots of land as loan collateral. A business-like etiquette, showing a "club" mentality, existed around land transactions in Ontario cities that benefited the wealthy, as it had traditionally done in Britain. Thus, mortgage foreclosures were less frequent among the privileged classes; Anglican groups felt they belonged to this group.[14] Rising land prices released any residual tensions associated with holding a mortgage. The value of the property at the corner of Bloor and Avenue Road in Toronto, which had been acquired for the Anglican Church of the Redeemer (architects Smith and Gemmell, 1878), nearly doubled from its $10,000 purchase price only a decade prior. The increase was attributed to the "rapid enlargement and improvement of the city."[15]

The placement of churches in urban settings was a factor of land values not overlooked by public scrutiny. With a keen eye for religious architecture, cities attracted spectators who recorded the social life of church buildings. John Ross Roberston, editor of the *Toronto Telegram*, serialized his observations of church architecture in compelling chronicles about taste, lifestyle, and religious society. He combined a description of St Peter's Anglican Church on Carlton Street with its social context decades before art historians became interested in the social history of objects, noting that the building was:

> a modern English Gothic church with such proportions and offsets that is rather picturesque in appearance. It partakes of the cleanliness and neatness of that section of the city in which it is located. There is an assimilation of property and people ... that determines the architectural condition of living. Neat cleanly and cultured people will have homes and surroundings correspondingly superior. The same rule applies to churches, to that even the outside appearance of a church edifice is ... indicative of the kind of people who attend it or support it.[16]

Roberston's narrative refocused on a tranquil depiction of daily urban life in close proximity to religious activity:

> A walk through Rosedale glen, through the cemeteries, over the Don [River] and along its banks will reveal ... many persons that had discharged their religious duty by going to church in the morning and leaving their pews vacant for the common people in the evening. But it was a pleasant and refreshing sight to see little children merrily skipping over the beautiful lawns in innocent play, while the contented mother luxuriously enjoyed the picture from the open window of a richly furnished drawing-room.[17] With all this loveliness of nature attuning the spirit to worship the Power that created it, nothing is lost by entering a beautiful church where the classic surroundings complement the outside natural beauty. And St Paul's is an attractive one.[18]

This idyllic social circle that Robertson described was metaphorically the portrayal of an English town demonstrated by the "Gothic stone structure that conveys an impression of massiveness and solidity, though not a large building; its outline is well proportioned and it is an ideal structure, such a one as is frequently met with in the land across the sea – the real home of the Church of England."[19]

Other correspondents agreed that the "beauty of the principal streets [of Toronto] had been very greatly increased because St James Church had been completed."[20] Its renewal in 1854, minus the tower, began a period of Anglican self-reflection in Toronto. However, by the late 1860s other Christian denominations had outstripped the Anglican sect in architectural expression. St Michael's Roman Catholic Cathedral had completed its tower under the direction of architect Henry Langley in 1867. In that same year Langley also completed the monumental Metropolitan Methodist Church. Both buildings surpassed the architectonics at St James', as each temporarily exceeded the towerless Anglican cathedral in height. This rivalry permanently ended in the 1870s as a new building committee at St James' undertook plans to construct the cathedral's tower and spire.

Case Study: Raising Canada's Tallest Church Steeple at St James' Cathedral, Toronto

St James' Cathedral in Toronto aspired to an unprecedented height at the date of its consecration in 1854, which was not realized until the tower and spire were completed two decades afterward (fig. 4.2). In 1874, workmen installing the weathervane atop the spire of St James' neo-Gothic spire could easily look down on a series of other churches in the neighbourhood and on the horizon. At 309 feet in height, and the tallest spire in North America, an eye of faith

Fig. 4.2 St James' Anglican Cathedral, Toronto.

may have given one grounds to believe that Britain's cathedrals were visible across the Atlantic, so close was the tower design to English models. Indeed, a sense of "imagined community" continued to link Canada with Britain well beyond official Confederation in 1867. The phenomenon was particularly strong among Toronto's churches that paralleled Britain's developments in neo-Gothic architecture. Britain's adherence to archaeological precedent and empirical study of medieval buildings in the architecture of A.W.N. Pugin in the early 1840s fully emerged in Canada within a few years and spread across the Dominion within a decade. Even the subsequent departure for using medieval precedents as models – pioneered by George Edmund Street at All Saints, Margaret Street, London (1849–59) – was transported to Canada in quick succession.

Church spires in Canada such as the one at St James' received visual enticement and social prestige through association with British social distinction. The church spire held the glamour allied with civic power; it was an important social icon made all the more potent because many church projects failed to ever complete the spire when financial support and community interest flagged. The original tender to architects at St James' did not call for the inclusion of a tower for economy's sake. However, the interdenominational rivalry with the Roman Catholic Cathedral of St Michael's (fig. 4.3) a few blocks to the north signalled the rise of the tallest church spire ever built in Canada and, for a short time in the 1870s, North America. In 1865 Henry Langley and Thomas Gundry completed the bell tower at St Michael's, and it dwarfed St James' until Langley, then assisted by his nephew Edmund Burke, was called upon to remedy the situation with a spire fifty-six feet taller. Langley and Burke based their design on drawings by William George Storm rejected in 1863 to arrive at the slim spire with delicate finials and crockets.

Undeterred by the global recession of 1873, Torontonians believed in the robustness of local economies. At the moment of completion in 1874, the tower and spire marked a significant point in Torontonians' identification with the economies in major European and American cities. The metaphoric "view" from St James's tower allowed Torontonians to see their city, and themselves, in the cosmopolitan manner they imagined. On 7 August 1874, a letter to editor of the *Globe* newspaper expressed admiration for the tower and spire of St James's Cathedral, by making positive comparisons with British and European church architecture. The writer produced a table illustrating the various heights of European cathedral spires, among which St James ranked sixteenth behind the leading example – Strasbourg cathedral's 466-foot spire. Toronto's Anglican cathedral was given the pride of exceeding, by one foot,

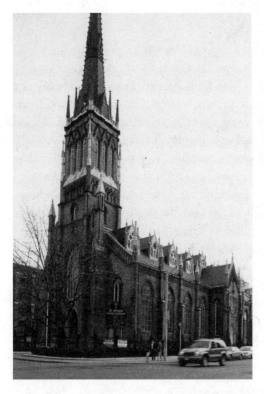

Fig. 4.3 St Michael's Roman Catholic Church, Toronto.

Britain's Norwich cathedral. In a further expression of civic pride, the report stated that:

> although the spire of St James Cathedral in this city is not so high as quite a number in Europe, it is sixteen feet higher than any structure in North America, ninety-six feet higher than the highest in Montreal, and seventy feet higher than any in Toronto. Let us hope that an edifice so lofty, and so much admired already, will in due time, with its expected illuminated clock, be brought to a thorough completion, and that no loss of life or serious harm will be sustained therewith.[21]

The rivalry with other Toronto churches was not slight. Then, Anglicans had only slightly outnumbered the Roman Catholics in the 1860s in Toronto with census records showing 14,125 Anglicans, 12,135 Roman Catholics, 1,288 Baptists, 525 Methodists, and 1,231 Presbyterians.[22] Despite the reality of the population figures, Anglicans believed in a "chain of being" that placed themselves at the top, and therefore worthiest of accruing social and economic benefits.

The tower and spire at St James' pronounced Toronto's civic and economic rivalry with Montreal permanently closed. It showed that Toronto had edged ahead in economic growth due to the joint US and Canadian initiative in 1895 to deep-dredge the St Lawrence, opening up the Great Lakes to transatlantic shipping. St James' was situated a few blocks north of a sector of the city that religious authorities thought needed supervision: Toronto's first wharf. In the 1850s, the Grand Trunk Railway expansion brought immigration and commercial goods traffic to Toronto, but it also brought smuggled goods and what proper society termed "undesirable" people. Low-cost dwellings and drab merchant shops (whose landlord was none other than the Anglican Church) extended north of the wharf and surrounded the broad, manicured church grounds. The affluent residences stretched further north of the cathedral along tree-lined Jarvis and Sherbourne Streets. The cathedral's space appeared to be encroached upon by this "undesirable" element, which the church benefited from financially. The cathedral was, thus, situated between affluent, established Torontonians and many poor immigrants, especially those from Ireland, travelling in steerage on ships arriving in the wharf. The poor became the cheap labour manufacturing, in some cases, the expensive goods that collectively helped to maintain the affluence of many Anglican families for several generations. The spire of St James' Cathedral rose in tandem with the conflicted economic and social expansion of Toronto and served as a marker of the enduring presence of the Anglican Church in Ontario and Canada's newly expanding confederation.

An image of St James Cathedral, published by the Canadian Pacific Railway in 1890, provides a fascinating view of the cathedral, its tower, and the surrounding buildings (fig. 4.4).[23] St James Cathedral dwarfs the neighbouring structures as well as those depicted far in the distance. Toward the horizon line, on the left-hand side of the engraving, are the towers of Metropolitan Methodist and St Michael's Catholic Cathedral, shown in diminished perspective. The square tower of Metropolitan Methodist with its corner turrets and finials is clearly shown. Other towers shown include Little Trinity Anglican Church. The viewer's focus, however, is the unprecedented height of the St James tower and completed spire. The subject of the image is spectacle. The purpose of the image printed in the CPR guidebook was to attract travellers to tour Canada by rail. However, there is a great deal else going on in the image. The neighbouring two- and three-storey commercial buildings stretched along King Street indicate the robust economy of Toronto in the 1890s. Horse-drawn carriages and trams parade along the street while residents promenade beneath the canopies, sampling the wares of local merchants. To tourists, Toronto was shown in a favourable cosmopolitan perspective. The cathedral was at the centre of it all, the symbolic capital of religion apparently legitimizing the commercial intent of the city. Looking more closely, one also

97 • PROPERTY OWNERSHIP AND CHURCH-BUILDING

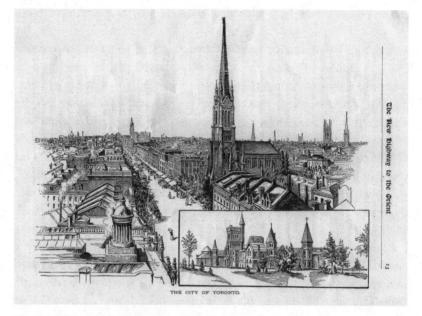

Fig. 4.4 St James Cathedral and environs, Toronto.

notices a collection of rudimentary buildings adjacent to the east side of the cathedral and just behind the multi-storey buildings on the left of the picture, in the foreground. One of these small structures has a chimney flanked by two small windows and the roof shows two small dormers. This is likely one of the tenement houses that was owned by the Church of England, a poorly kept low-rent facility that Church officials preferred remain invisible. It was for this reason that the eastern transept door, depicted immediately behind this tenement, was bricked up. The east transept doorway would have connected the congregation with the largest part of the churchyards, except that the low-rent housing was also visible to people exiting the doorway. Thus, to keep up appearances of gentility the doorway was permanently blocked.

CHARITY, OWNERSHIP, AND ADVERTISING IN RELIGIOUS INSTITUTION

In the nineteenth century, the erection of a church tower was the most visible manifestation of charitable giving. A monumental architectural afterthought like a tower, completed years after its church was consecrated, attracted considerable excess personal capital. Donations were pooled in a church's bank account, compounding for years, until its sum translated into the vertical architectonic aspiration of its sponsors. The harsh reality of materialism was countered primarily by individual, rather than corporate, charity. Claiming to be beacons of social responsibility, church towers were advertisements for faith and hope in a world increasingly dominated by corporate power. The construction of church towers was also the last significantly visible effort by charities to benefit from the personal wealth accumulated under mercantilism. It represented a significant shift as many affluent Toronto neighbourhoods relocated closer to the centre of commerce, constructing new churches in new suburban districts.

Churchgoers had to reconcile the idea that organized religion had a price tag while salvation was freely given. The material growth of the Anglican Church in Toronto, no less than in other parts of the Dominion, had a financial component that was objectionable in principle to some of its worshippers. Nevertheless, the practice was chiefly condoned because churches needed money to survive. Anglican worshippers complained about the economic costs but accepted the rough balance of benefits and concessions. The cost of religion manifested in the controversy over pew rental, which equated economic capital with preferential seating, social status, and superior sightlines to the altar. This was especially true in large churches with longitudinal axes that seated upward of eight hundred worshippers. Wealthy individuals visibly expressed their social status by paying for visibly better seating arrangements closer to the High Altar. The practice was normalized in society to the extent that the poorer classes sitting in the rear of St James' Anglican Cathedral in Toronto dare not whisper their discontent for fear of reprisal. At the time of its construction, St James' Cathedral was outfitted with box-pews that were expected to bring a collective income of £2,250. These personal spaces of worship were cordoned off from adjacent boxes and accessed from a small gate. A growing counter-movement in the Anglican Communion offered "free" seats, and numerous small churches across Canada were built without pew rents. The church of Holy Trinity, Toronto, was built with a donation of $5,000 from an anonymous woman in England under the proviso that the seats continue to be "free and un-appropriated forever."[24]

With the expansion of general consumer markets, church-builders became captivated by greater amounts of design choices available for ecclesiastical architecture. The phenomenon was related to the growth of personal wealth and the depth of economies, since increased consumer demand stimulated new production. In the sense that one could browse through a pattern book for a suitable church design, building a church became associated with "buying" a church. Small communities lacking immediate access to architects benefited greatly from increased consumer choice. At the same time it had the effect of commercializing ecclesiastical design. A continual distribution stream of new church pattern books supplied the reading public with a virtual unlimited amount of church designs. With so much variety, users of the pattern books became highly selective. The elite sense of taste marketed in the pattern books, under the guise of education, encouraged users to pick from parts of plans and drawings that they believed most applied to their individual needs. This meant that churches built in the Canadas were not only reflections of British antecedents – even direct copies – but they were also a medley of the aesthetic and structural components seen in the pattern books. A remarkable thing about the church pattern books, setting them apart from newspapers and magazines specializing in architecture, was the equalization of the unified method of building churches with the variety of designs.

New forms of advertising, assisted by the commercial expansion of business in Ontario and adjacent regions, caught the attention of church-builders. Advertising conflated fashion's visual and verbal data with something proffered as knowledge. Self-promotion in US pattern books was common. In his publication *Ancient English Ecclesiastical Architecture* (1850), the architect Frank Wills advertised that he was "prepared to furnish designs and working drawings of churches, schools, and other buildings." Frederick Withers's *Church Architecture* (1873) raised advertisements to the highest level of craft, using chromolithographic (colour) plates to illustrate an advertisement for Minton's Tiles. Indeed, it appeared as though advertisements in US church pattern books, much like their counterparts in residential architecture, were acceptable. A variety of products and services were hocked in the front and rear sections of these books, highlighting the business savvy of publishers if not also authors. Seemingly nepotistic, publications by the US architect George Woodward, such as *Woodward's Architecture and Rural Art* (1868), contained advertisements for the architect's numerous other books, including *Woodward's National Architect* (1869, reprinted) and *Rural Church Architecture* (1868, reprinted). Woodward was more than an architect and pattern book author, he developed a publishing and distribution empire by retailing the books written by his colleagues and competitors. To that end, he printed a catalogue entitled *Architectural and Mechanical Books* (c. 1868). The popularity of mail-order pattern books is illustrated by Woodward's catalogue, which explained in painstakingly clear language "How to Remit Money." Woodward's commercial aspirations did not stop with book retailing. An advertisement in *Woodward's National Architect* signalled how he also acted as sales agent for Dixon's Low Down Philadelphia Grate, a home-heating device that claimed there was not a "single educated Physician in Philadelphia who owns the home he lives in, who is not supplied with one or more of these delightful luxuries" (fig. 4.5).[25] The advertisement's text is significant because it drew together education, medicine, the social respectability of doctors, and the necessity of luxury. Dixon's heating device was not cheap at $35 to $60 each. The inclusion of the advertisement for Dixon's heating device in Woodward's pattern books "objectively" discussing the merits of modern heating and ventilation illustrates the blurred borders between commerce and "knowledge."

As consumers, Canadians exerted no influence on the plans, aesthetics, and even the advertising offered in the church pattern books they imported. Their consumer power lay in customer selectivity that they had yet to fully realize. Anglican church-builders in Canada appeared satisfied with the sort

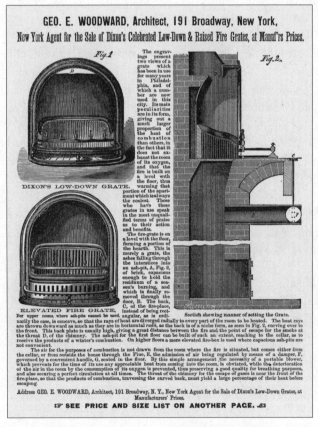

Fig. 4.5 Specimen page of advertisement for "Dixon's Low Down Philadelphia Grate," for which the architect served as commercial agent.

of material emanating from Britain and the US, without feeling the need to encourage the production of Canadian church pattern books.

The sole pattern book produced in Canada during this period came from the Presbyterian Church. Looking for an architectural voice of its own, the Presbyterian Church felt compelled to issue a church pattern book specifically tailored to its form of worship. Developed through a contest held during 1891, the General Assembly of the Presbyterian Church in Canada produced a slim pamphlet of church patterns, entitled *Designs for Village, Town, and City Churches* (1893). Practical and ideological, the pamphlet was intended to "be of some service to those congregations about to build churches, more especially in rural districts."[26] The General Assembly favoured a democratic approach to the pamphlet's production by holding a nationwide competition conducted in conjunction with the Ontario Association of Architects (OAA). Junior and seasoned architects and draughtsmen were induced into the competition through small cash prizes and the opportunity to publish their designs. Unfortunately, the contest was met with ambivalence. Few submissions were received even a year after the competition was announced in 1891, resulting in further calls for entry. By May 1892 the competition was threatened with cancellation. The OAA registrar, W.A. Langton, received a letter from the "Committee of Experts" that noted, "we have examined the competitive designs ... and with much regret we beg to say that in our opinion there is not a sufficiently large number of suitable designs among them to warrant the committee in publishing a pamphlet."[27] They complained that few of the entries could actually be utilized as Presbyterian churches. The designs submitted appeared eerily reminiscent of Anglican church designs. Perhaps, Canadian architects had too long been accustomed to passively reading church architecture books.

Undeterred, the architecture committee pressed ahead by publishing the small number of designs submitted to competition. A variety of church types were illustrated since the call for entries had been vague. Few architects and church-builders agreed upon a layout and aesthetics plan. W.A. Langton submitted a presentation drawing and plan from a commission to build a small stone parish church in Assiniboia (fig. 4.6), modelled on the thirteenth-century fabric of St Michael's, Long Stanton. Daniel J. Creighton of Montreal, James Russell of Toronto, and E. Lowery and Son supplied a variety of churches with amphitheatrical seating plans that improved visibility of the pulpit and overall acoustics. W.L. Munroe, G.F. Stalker, and the partnership of Greg and Greg offered plans with longitudinal axes typified by Anglican churches. All of these designs ranged from neo-Gothic to Scottish Baronial to Renaissance Revival. None opted to employ the arts and crafts popular at the

Fig. 4.6 Specimen page of W.A. Langton submission from *Designs for Country, Town, and City Churches*, 1893.

Fig. 4.7 Specimen page of Arthur E. Wells's winning entry for design of Presbyterian Church from *Designs for Village, Town and City Churches*, 1893.

time, except Arthur E. Wells, winner of the competition, whose drawing was highlighted in the pamphlet. The progressive nature of his design received due reward (fig. 4.7). The creation of an equivalence of fashion and taste with regard to building churches in Ontario was demonstrated most clearly in Langton's design. The integrated raking roofs and scheme of porches created a new sense of the bucolic.

The Presbyterian pattern book was reminiscent of the arrangement of US pattern books, which contained advertisements in their front and back pages. R.J. McDowall's piano and organ retailer of Kingston paid for a full-page advertisement. Other sponsors included the Owen Sound Stone Company, the Rathburn Co. Door and Moulding Manufacturers, Castle and Son providers of stained glass, and the Globe Furniture Co. of Walkerville, Ontario, makers of pews, pulpits, and chairs. A US church-bell manufacturer was listed, the Clinton H. Meneely Bell Co. of Troy, New York, which showed the close relationship between US manufacture and Canadian consumption. W. Drysdale & Co., Booksellers and Stationers of Montreal were also advertisers. Presumably the Drysdale Booksellers carried copies of the pamphlet *Designs for Village, Town, and City Churches*. These advertisements were naturally related to church-building, but they also demonstrated the close relationship between religion, manufacture, new commercial practices, and the book trade.

The Presbyterian Church (previously the Church of Scotland) had historically attempted to distinguish itself from the Church of England in architectural terms. As such, the fortified aesthetic of the Scottish Baronial style and the monastic impression of neo-Gothic resonated in the drawings included in *Designs for Village, Town and City Churches* (fig. 4.8). The importance of such a distinction was demonstrated during an acrimonious rift that split the congregation of St Andrew's Presbyterian Church in Toronto. The opposing factions each chose a deliberately different architectural language once it was formally decided to divide the congregation. The seceding camp led by Rev. G.M. Milligan of Detroit built a church using the vocabulary of the Decorated phase of thirteenth-century medieval churches, with its broad window proportions and elaborate tracery. At the expense of $57,000 to the leading architectural firm of Langley, Langley, and Burke the design, lacking "especial ornamentation and elaboration but ample in the symmetry and harmony," was complete in 1877.[28]

The elder group associated with the congregation's founding in 1821 awarded construction of their new church to William George Storm, formerly of Cumberland and Storm, soliciting a design modelled on the "famous Kirkwall Cathedral in the Orkney Islands, and the style of architecture described

Fig. 4.8 Specimen page of "Design for a Large Town Church in the Scottish Baronial Style," by D.J. Creighton from *Designs for Country, Town and City Churches*, 1893.

as Norman Scottish."[29] They were located on King Street West near the growing commercial sector of the city. Using innovations in floor plan and seating arrangements, the congregation opted for a wraparound gallery that distinguished them as a community from their former group. The interior has been remodelled, but it was originally similar to the layout at St David's Presbyterian Church (fig. 4.9) (David Stirling, 1866: now Grafton Street Methodist). The floor plan of the elder group's church – known colloquially as "New St Andrew's" – also recalled the attempts at an amphitheatrical arrangement with improved sightlines as published in George Bidlake's pattern book *Sketches for Churches Designed for the Use of Non-Conformists* (1865) (fig. 4.10).[30] Nearly bankrupted through a fatal expansion of St Mark's Church, the congregation at New St Andrew's lost its minister, Rev. W.J. McCaughan of Belfast, Ireland, who resigned because the congregation was $2,100 in debt. With the intent to publicly ridicule the congregation, McCaughan wrote a letter to the *Toronto Telegram* remarking, "we are behind financially solely on account of our own congregation, which should pay its own debts." Embattled by the vacating reverend, New St Andrew's Church published a

Fig. 4.9 St David's Presbyterian Church. Architect: David Stirling, 1866 (now Grafton Street Methodist).

full account of its finances in the *Toronto Telegram*, tabulating the costs of financing St Mark's, pew rental incomes, and envelope donations, in order to refute "these injurious reflections on the church finances, whether emanating from the press or the pulpit." The audit noted land acquisition costs since 1876 amounted to $167,752.17 combined with $163,000 in missionary expenses.[31]

As patterns of social behaviour, the construction of churches involved significant personal investment that raised the stakes of success and brought about interpersonal dispute. Building a church in the nineteenth century was inextricably connected to modern economy. The canonization of medieval motifs in church pattern books was one robust example of the business of building churches because church-builders purchased the books. Unlike an architect providing a set of drawings at reduced price to a church on humanitarian grounds, the pattern books commodified aesthetics. The advent of pattern books in the milieu of church-builders was not very different from commercial railway travel, since each promised to modernize the Dominion of Canada. The rhetorics of land and spirituality were equally prevalent in church pattern books as they were in CPR guidebooks, which prompted travellers west to "see this world before the next."

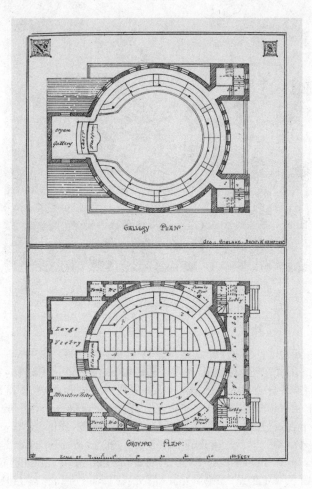

Fig. 4.10 Specimen page of a plan showing a precursor to the amphitheatrical layout from *Sketches of Churches: Designed for the Use of Nonconformists*.

5

THE SPREAD OF EMPIRE IN WESTERN CANADA: RAILWAY, RELIGION, AND CHURCH-BUILDING

THE MOBILITY OF CHURCH PATTERN BOOKS IN THE CONTEXT OF ERECTING CHURCHES IN THE WEST

Post-Confederation settlement, ventures into independent business, and organized religion were characterized by rapid expansion, as though growth ensured survival. In this respect, immigration patterns and new railway lines seemed intimately intertwined. People migrated west for opportunity that developed in growing towns located along rail lines, receiving a wide variety of their goods by steam train. These items included staple goods, books, and specialized supplies for church-building: floor tiles, stained glass, and heating units. Even vestments and church plate were more easily and cheaply shipped great distances by rail than shorter routes by horse and cart.

Mobilizing the flow of people and capital westward, the CPR was marketed as an apparatus of Canadian nationalism and an unprecedented economic opportunity for individuals. As is well known, the political importance of extending the railway into British Columbia revolved around drawing the province into Confederation in 1871. The feeling was protectionist rather than nationalist since the Government of Canada believed the rail would protect the Prairies from the threat of annexation by the US. The rule of law held the government and the CPR to their promise to complete the railway, although neither group truly understood the expense and difficulty of the project at the outset. Those involved with the project understood that profits were dependent on the mobility of goods and people. The control of land was an integral part of that equation. The Canada North-West Land Company, which was given the responsibility to sell building lots in forty-seven townsites on the main CPR line between Brandon, Manitoba and coastal British Columbia, placed quarter-page advertisements in local newspapers promising land at $2 per acre located near "schools, churches and municipal organizations."[1] The situation was captured in Anne Mercier's 1903 novella, *A Home in the Northwest* (1903), describing the fictional adventures of a family of British settlers to Canada, whose "everlasting" contribution to the Dominion's social formation was the construction of an Anglican church in the rural northwest. The fictionalized social space of the novella included free and equal association between domestic servants and their employers, an encounter with the "noble savage," and a community rallying around crises. According to the story's protagonist Ada, the family needed to build a church for:

> the lonely ones, the young men who have no sisters, no women to make a home of their log shacks, and no church to go to near enough without an amount of exertion and arrangement for which real zeal is necessary ... If there were but a church at the Creek, only three miles away, what a blessing it would be. And to have a clergyman ... who could help Rupert now of an age for confirmation, but by no means growing more inclined towards it, the rough outdoor life seeming to raise his boyish animal spirits to a dangerous extent.[2]

A brief appearance by the visiting bishop certifies that the greatest deprivation is the distance from the church, a centre of spiritual life and civilization. Ada's story embodied the loneliness of Prairie life countered in only two known ways: religion and the productive family unit. Her plea to build a church for the general welfare of the sparsely distributed population is doubly a myth since the true motivating factor for building the church is to find a husband for Ada. To approve its architecture the bishop was petitioned for a design, which he gladly provided when the family raised £50 to prove their sincerity. "He drew out a pencil and notebook, and at once began to sketch both groundplan and elevation of a simple and neat wooden structure, with a bell-turret and a chancel."[3] The church therein described was the Ecclesiologist's model, St Michael's, Longstanton, with its western bellcote and separately articulated east end.

The reality of moving settlers to the Prairies and beyond was a complicated and expensive matter. The success of settling the west depended on advertising the benefits of migration to vast numbers of Canadians and immigrants. In response, a government sponsored document was produced, *Colonists' Handbook No.1* (1882), highlighting the benefits of migration, although its authors were accused of exaggerating and falsifying data about the productivity of some of the Prairie farmlands and the number of churches accessible to newly arriving settlers.[4] No mention was made of the vast distances between homesteads in the Prairies as well as the distressing deficiency of clergy in remote areas. The handbook questionably advertised Canada's advanced state of government, militia, and education. The mobilization of people westward, enticed by offers of cheap farmland, "ready-made-farms," and free livestock feed occurred in a burst of activity. It was an aggressive expansion campaign, according to Henry Youle Hind's accusations presented to the archbishop of Canterbury claiming that opportunist Canadian bureaucrats falsely described the fertility of the land west of Manitoba and the state of completion of the Canadian Pacific Railway. He complained that the Society for the Preservation of Christian Knowledge, which had sponsored the handbook, had been defrauded by inaccurate trade returns that abused the poor and deceived immigrants and the English investing public under the cloak of religion and knowledge. More accurately, Canada was described as a net trade exporter of raw goods to the United Kingdom. Residents of Canada were described as enjoying superior communications in railway, postal, and telegraph services. In reality, little of this infrastructure had been officially or satisfactorily completed at the time. The handbook advertised that "Improved farms" available for purchase for £1 per acre in Manitoba and the Northwest Territories had three or four feet of rich black loam top soil. Some purchasers discovered a different truth upon arrival. In other cases, in Ontario, 200 acres of free farm land was advertised to anyone over the age of eighteen provided they clear fifteen acres and construct a permanent dwelling. The commonly used ploy to attract settlers to these areas was to convince people that opportunities were fast disappearing in the west. To soothe anxieties about moving to a distant and unknown place the handbook promised that Canada's infrastructure was sufficiently developed. Virtually nothing was mentioned about the displacement of First Nations and Métis living on much of the same land.

Land ownership and organized religion, and even the CPR, became devices to enhance social controls. First Nations were routinely encouraged to give up hunting and fishing in exchange for a more sedentary agrarian lifestyle, the intent being to restrict free movement across lands being settled by immigrants. The federal government both excluded the Métis from the new social order and ignored the looming problem about land claims. Disputed land title with the Government of Canada over property around the Saskatchewan River contributed to the agitation of the Métis that sparked Louis Riel into open rebellion in 1885. The CPR proved invaluable in the quelling the second rebellion when it transported more than one thousand men of the 90th Battalion of Winnipeg Rifles by rail to confront the outnumbered Riel in front of the Gothicized single-cell clapboard church of St Antione de Padoue, Batoche, Saskatchewan (built in 1883). The small church became a strategic but ineffective set piece in Riel's defense. It was almost predictable that Riel's arrest occurred at the church, which was associated with an imperial strategy designed to keep First Nations and the Métis from moving about the land.[5] Thus, the westward mobility of desirable settlers was achieved at the expense and displacement of less desirable people.

Religion was clearly a component of the settlement of the west, a trump card masking the economic strategy behind settlement expansion that displaced, and attempted to erase, aboriginal peoples and Métis. Commercial enterprises that owned massive tracts of land, like the CPR and the Hudson's Bay Company, assisted the spread of religion by parcelling off plots for churches at reduced prices. On New Year's Day 1844, the *Winnipeg Free Press* noted that the Presbyterian Church had made "satisfactory progress" by erecting churches in numerous towns in the Northwest, including Broadview, Cadurois, Calgary, Turtle Mountain, Gladstone, Greenwood, Indian Head, Moosejaw, Prince Albert, Rat Portage, Regina, Stonewall, Virden, Dominion City, and Humesville, on land they purchased at a discount from the CPR. Company President William Cornelius Van Horne and Vice-President Thomas Shaughnessy could afford to be generous since the railway concern had received gratis an incentive of 25 million acres from the Government of Canada. In Vancouver, the CPR provided five lots (cost $500 each) at the crossing of Georgia and Burrard Streets to the Anglican diocese of New Westminster for the purpose of building Christ Church Cathedral. Unable to meet its financial obligations to the CPR, much less build a church, the congregation was left to worship in a half-built basement, locally known as the "root cellar." The building committee resigned in 1892, whereupon the project was rescued by J.W. Weart, a Toronto bookkeeper living in British Columbia, who suggested they leverage the value of their leased land against a mortgage provided by the Sun Life Insurance Company. Devising a scheme to incorporate the Christ Church Building Company, Weart issued shares worth half as much as the land itself, providing collateral at minimal risk. The deal generated enough cash to begin a building campaign despite there being negligible paid up capital on the shares. All that mattered was that the value of the land exceeded the amount of the mortgage. In 1894, Charles Osborne Wickenden, a local Vancouver architect, was awarded the $25,000 contract to complete his distinct Gothic Revival design consisting of a wide, aisle-less floorplan and elaborate hammer-beam roof evoking Raphael and J. Arthur Brandon's pattern book *Open Timber Roofs*.

Settling the Prairies and the west was a logistical balancing act among regulatory bodies of government, the unevenness of capitalism, and the potency of religion. Homesteaders setting up farms, labourers in mining camps, and opportunists searching the gold fields moved alongside missionaries attracted to congregations of people and capital. Connecting people in an unbroken chain across two coasts was also a scheme to ship freight as well as unsettle First Nations from traditional lands. The CPR project was often cast in the guise of a national project when in reality it was a commercial endeavour. In fact, the CPR Company had to be supplemented by a host of other business ventures to remain solvent financially, which included the development of its own sleeping and parlour cars, which competed for equal mileage with the Pullman Company of sleeping cars on international runs. The company also set up the Canadian Pacific Telegraph, warehouse operations, and a steamship and hotel line as adjunct businesses. Hotels were deemed a necessity in 1886: dining cars could not be used on the steep western side of the Rockies because the cars were too heavy. Hotels provided places for travellers to eat.

Anticipating a positive social effect through the erection of pastoral Gothic Revival churches across the Dominion, missionaries spread west especially to convert First Nations to Christianity. Church pattern books, as exemplars of taste, science, and knowledge, were co-opted into the process of appropriating First Nations and Métis lands by showing the idyllic relationship between religion and the land. The pattern books even expressed the so-called superiority of western building techniques that were taught to First Nations carpenters as a way of acculturating them and making them feel inferior at the same time. The Anglican missionaries used these building techniques to create schools adjacent to churches within close proximity of the Métis in the Red River and Saskatchewan River areas. One example was the Anglican Archdeacon J.A. Mackay, who took over the responsibility of First Nations mission schools on the Cree Reserves at Eagle Hills, Moosomin, and Thunderchild in anticipation of building churches there.[6]

Case Study: A High Victorian Gothic Revival Church at Stanley Mission, Saskatchewan

On a tiny island accessible only by riverboat, on the Lac La Ronge Reserve in northern Saskatchewan, the Rev. Robert Hunt built a Gothic Revival church in 1850 (Holy Trinity, Stanley Mission) (fig. 5.1) whose architecture was unusual for being exceptionally up to date with High Victorian Gothic in London, England. The Rev. Hunt's diary illustrates how pattern books and the influence of local churches transferred British architectural fashion to this remote area of the Prairies. Prior to arriving with his wife, Georgianna, at the Hudson's Bay trading post from England and moving into an area close to the Woodland Cree, Rev. Hunt had "studied views & descriptions of more than 50 Churches & Chapels."[7] So far advanced were his plans for building a

Fig. 5.1 Holy Trinity Church, Stanley Mission. 1853–56.

church in the remote parts of Saskatchewan that he had arranged to ship nails, hinges, and stained glass before leaving England. Rev. Hunt's diary indicated his interest in Christ Church, Cumberland House (The Pas) (1847), a monumental neo-Gothic timber frame structure that measured 63' by 27' surmounted by a 70' tower built by the Rev. James Hunter. However, this does not fully account for its similar articulation of plain, unbuttressed exterior walling in the High Victorian Style that emerged from William Butterfield's design of London's All Saints Margaret Street (1849–59) (fig. 5.2). It is unclear how Hunt's design might have had some connection with Butterfield's.

Construction difficulties delayed the completion of Rev. Hunt's church for seven years. A shortage of timber was the chief cause. By March 1856, the "frame of the Church Spire was set up on the ground, which completed the skeleton of the building."[8] Thereafter, consecration was delayed until 1860 because of the sporadic delivery of boarding for the exterior finish. The Rev. Hunt's frustration over irregular shipments of goods to Saskatchewan's more remote areas was illustrated by the five-year delivery period for roofing felt required for insulation. Inept shippers had damaged the large rolls of felt sent from Britain just as all of the stained glass arrived shattered.[9] Atypical of the experience of more heavily travelled routes, Hunt waited another six months for a second shipment of coloured glass.

The Rev. Hunt's ideas for Stanley Mission were comparable with the influential writing and High Victorian architecture produced by the British

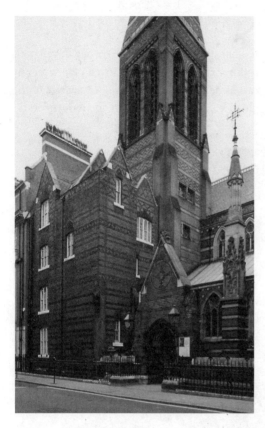

Fig. 5.2 All Saint's Margaret Street (Anglican), London.

architect George Edmund Street.[10] For this reason, the "considerable space of wall un-pierced" by windows was adopted at Holy Trinity because it was believed to admit a greater amount of play in the coloured light on the interior. Street's notion of the "right management of light" was related directly to the system of window fenestration at Stanley Mission. Without claiming a direct link, Holy Trinity was related to other High Victorian churches published during the mid nineteenth century. For instance, the aisled nave with clerestory at Holy Trinity, except for the placement of the tower, bears a remarkable resemblance to the published image of J. Roger Smith's the New Independent Chapel, Abergele, North Wales included in Davey James Brooks's *Examples of Modern Architecture Ecclesiastical and Domestic* (1873), showing how Hunt drew on a stock neo-Gothic vocabulary (fig. 5.3).

The monumental size of the church at Stanley Mission, built almost entirely by Cree and Chipewyan workers, challenges commonly held beliefs that First Nations craftsmanship was second rate. At the time, it was believed that First Nations would be able to complete only modest architectural projects. It must also be borne in mind that the term "volunteering" carried different connotations for First Nations than White settlers. Free service to religious institutions was expected of White settlers as a sign of social belonging. By contrast, First Nations were cast as being conscripted into the service of the church as a strategy to make them acculturated, but permanent outsiders.

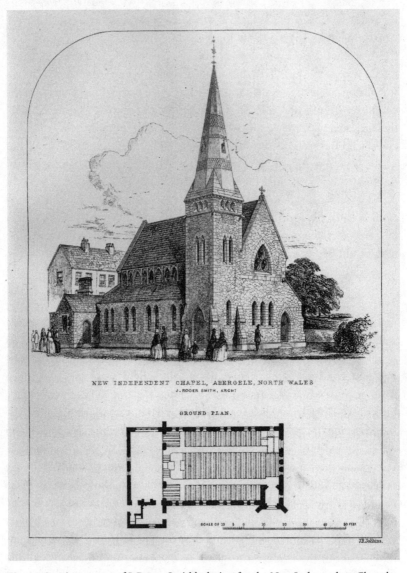

Fig. 5.3 Specimen page of J. Roger Smith's design for the New Independent Chapel, Abergele, North Wales.

Comparative Case Study: Riel and St Antoine de Padoue, Batoche, Saskatchewan

The Métis had settled in the Red River area since the 1820s, although they had become politically separated over the issue of farming by the 1870s.[11] The 1869 Manitoba Rebellion arose because of disruptions to Métis participation in the fur trade, which disrupted their economic and social structures.[12] After the situation had been defused by John A. Macdonald's concessions made for the release of hostages, and as part of the agreement, Riel went into exile in the US for five years. During this period, much of it spent in Montana, he began to style himself as an Abrahamic prophet. His diary contains references to the establishment of a new religion, an offshoot of the Roman Catholic Church, in which Riel had studied unsuccessfully to become a priest in his youth. He envisioned the Métis as the chosen people and himself as a priest-king and infallible pontiff. As a result of his return to the Métis people, initially to help deal with land claims and the grain market crash, Riel established a provisional government on 19 March 1885 and a "Catholic, Apostolic, and Living Church of the New World." Riel returned to his old strategy of taking hostages in the hope of negotiating a settlement with the government, but he failed to understand that the railway could dispatch troops to the field within weeks. He was captured near the church of St Antoine de Padoue on 12 May 1885, after three days of skirmishes with British Regulars.

The prelude to this situation had only been exacerbated by the Hudson's Bay Company, who advertised "Farming, Grazing, Coal and Mineral Lands for Sale"[13] to a predominantly White settler readership. Similar strategies were employed by the government, intent on controlling the First Nation and Métis movements by encouraging them to farm instead of hunt. Church pattern books fed into this strategy by emphasizing the importance of building European-style communities. Some members of the print media recognized the problematics of the situation. For instance, the *Saskatchewan Herald* (1878–87), which usually assumed a conservative position, identified farming as a scheme to "pauperize the half-breeds."[14] Though, still showing its cultural bias, the *Herald* discredited "Indian farmers" as a warrior race, thereby endorsing the privileges of White settlers and farmers.[15]

The construction of churches like St Antoine de Padoue was associated with an imperial strategy designed to keep First Nations and the Métis from moving about the land, much of which was being sold to settlers by the Canada Company and agents of the CPR. The Northwest Rebellion of 1885 revisited the earlier and unresolved problems of the Manitoba Rebellion of 1869, in which Louis Riel led a combined force of Métis, First Nations, and groups of disenfranchised European settlers and extracted federal government concessions regarding the establishment of Manitoba. The 1885 Rebellion resulted when Riel discovered that the lands his people customarily held along the Saskatchewan River were about to be surveyed, a prelude to appropriation.[16]

The timber-framed, clapboard church of St Antoine de Padoue (1883), Batoche, Saskatchewan, was completed less than two years before it became a strategic component in the failed defense of Riel at Batoche. The Gothicized single-cell church with segmented western tower was typical of the simple churches built in rural areas from Manitoba to Vancouver Island. The simple clapboard church evoked chapels-of-ease, which were small single-cell structures. It was significant that the battle and Riel's subsequent arrest were played out in front of the church building because religion had been an instrument of social control that encouraged the Métis to become "industrious farmers."

DISTRIBUTING PATTERN BOOKS THROUGH A MATRIX OF BOOK DEALERS ON A NATIONAL SCALE

The architectural ideas communicated in print to church-builders lacking formal artistic training, like Rev. Hunt of Stanley Mission, Saskatchewan, was conveyed along distribution routes laid out by a community of booksellers. A loose collection of booksellers operating independently across the country, many of them largely unaware of each other, imported and distributed books from Britain and the US. This occurred largely because a small clutch of regional book agents travelled around Canada selling their wares. For this reason, the appearance of a national community of readers, whether real or imagined, was constituted economically on a regional scale. The owners of various booksellers – including Robert Dicks (Sign of the Book) in St Johns, New Brunswick; James C. Linton (Sign of the Big Book) in Calgary; and T.H. Hibben (Hibbens Books) in Victoria – sold imported goods to a regional customer base (fig. 5.4). Even though the booksellers were supplied by shipments that travelled across country by rail – a new commercial venture in itself – the regional flavour of their customers was significant.

During the 1870s book shipments from the US increased in tandem with the expansion of branch rail lines extending from the US into Canada. Thus, New York and Philadelphia publishers were able to ship directly to markets in Toronto, Winnipeg, and even Vancouver, expanding the regional aspect of the book trade. The growth in cheap books imported from the US also influenced

Fig. 5.4 Interior of T.N. Hibben and Company Bookseller, Victoria.

the growth of regional book markets in Canada. These regional business patterns were consistent with the regional patterns of identification and settlement growth reflected in church-building.

The structure of the book trade in Canada demonstrated that there was neither a unifying culture of the "nation" nor a straightforward expansion of settlement in an undisrupted state. In reality, the spread of the book trade occurred by a series of energetic expansions accompanied by equally sharp consolidations. The formation of the book trade comprised an opportunistic collection of parts while projecting official images of a unified whole. Thus, the rhetoric of "national unification," which was more imagined than material, was not entirely consistent with booksellers' actual commercial practices. Booksellers operated through a network of regional agents.

The movements of the pattern books among the buying public sold the idea that history was something familiar. Neo-Gothic churches built in the Dominion, inducing a medieval connection with Britain, still required verification by the printed page. In reality, pattern books marketed church designs while covering the tracks of their commercial purposes, notably the economic control of public taste. The church pattern books marketed history and the picturesque as reactions to institutional controls on daily life. The pattern books combined bucolic images of an open landscape with references to the medieval past, even though reality was reflected in the invention of standard time and the rigidity of railway schedules, both of which organized the workday schedule. People looked forward to Sunday as a respite from modern life by retreating to the pastoral setting of their church. Illustrations in Holly's *Church Architecture* (1871) accentuated picturesque qualities. Design number 13, plate 28 illustrated a church surrounded by mature but manicured tree, symbolizing God's communion with nature and religion's self-described custodial care for society (fig. 5.5). Note the close correspondence of the triple western entrance porch with Christ Church, Montreal, and Fredericton Cathedral. The pretension of the elaborate tower illustrated both the latest architectural fashion and technology. The book marketed the latest scientific construction methods in tandem with the conventional and picturesque landscape because the combination held large public appeal. The appeal of the uncomplicated medieval past was so strong that people disregarded the modern fact of the pattern books' technical reproduction – lithography.

Fig. 5.5 Specimen page of design 13, plate 28, from *Church Architecture*.

The appeal of new images of church architecture had a causal relationship with the renewal and improvement of religious buildings. In 1890, the Anglican congregation at St Paul's, Regina, built a new church to replace one constructed only seven years earlier, which had been described as a "neat ecclesiastical edifice" designed by the local architect Mr Sproat.[17] The church-building committee at St Paul's decided their congregation deserved a stone and brick edifice costing roughly $15,000. The commission was awarded to the architect Frank H. Peters even though only $3,300 had been raised through subscriptions. He designed a neo-Gothic parish church with a wide nave, low-slung slopping roof, and a bold quasi-detached corner tower similar to the muscular varieties found in George Truefitt's *Designs for Country Churches* (1850) and Raphael and J. Arthur Brandon's *Parish Churches* (1849).

Case Study: Holy Trinity Anglican Church, Winnipeg, Manitoba

Charles H. Wheeler (1838–1917) was an ascending Winnipeg architect in 1883 when he was awarded the commission to build Holy Trinity Anglican Church in his hometown. Like many architects lacking the pedigree of an apprenticeship in the office of an architect's offices, Wheeler's drawing skills and familiarity with architectural styles were gleaned from books. His humble roots in the building world began as a carpenter, bricklayer, and stonemason. Schools of architecture had not been established until the mid 1890s, leaving those without prior advantage of family and financial connections to contend over less lucrative and inconsequential contracts. Thus, it must have been a personal and professional triumph in Wheeler's mid-life to be awarded the commission to build a new Anglican church, dedicated Holy Trinity, in the city of Winnipeg, gateway to the west (fig. 5.6). He had fought particularly hard to win the design competition, succeeding after the second round of tenders. As with many competitions, an entry more ambitious than its modest budget would allow was awarded first prize.

With a moderate budget of $60,000, Wheeler's cruciform design was a bold statement of the later phase of the Gothic Revival, with heavily tacked-on buttresses rising to finials and an equally lavish tower. A diminutive, octagonal vestry set off of the generous chancel appeared unnaturally tall. The tower was never completed, due either to a shortfall of building funds or, more likely, to an overambitious building committee. Without the tower in place, the dormer windows in the roof that allowed additional height in a single-storey building appear emboldened. Dormer windows fully integrated into the roof became popular in the late nineteenth century. The device was illustrated in 1873 in Frederick Withers's pattern book *Twenty-One*

Fig. 5.6 Holy Trinity, Winnipeg. Presentation drawing of design by Charles H. Wheeler, 1883.

Churches (fig. 5.7). Wheeler experimented with an elaborate hammer-beam roofing system similar to ones illustrated in Raphael and J. Arthur Brandon's pattern book *Open Timber Roofs* and also shown in a cross-section in Withers's volume.[18]

The commission of Holy Trinity accelerated Wheeler's professional career; he subsequently assumed the vice-presidency of the newly formed Manitoba Association of Architects (MAA) in 1906. It was mainly an administrative post concerned with maintaining fee schedules, but in his official capacity Wheeler also published articles advocating for a national style of architecture. "Increasing knowledge will add to the number of those who appreciate and desire good work, and their sensitiveness in matters of good taste will incite the producers to higher efforts. We may feel confident that our national architecture will not fail under the test."[19] An astute observer of the professional development in architecture, Wheeler chronicled the attempts to create a national standard of practice. To that end he championed balloon-framing, a process of building timber frames with nails rather than complicated dovetail joints,

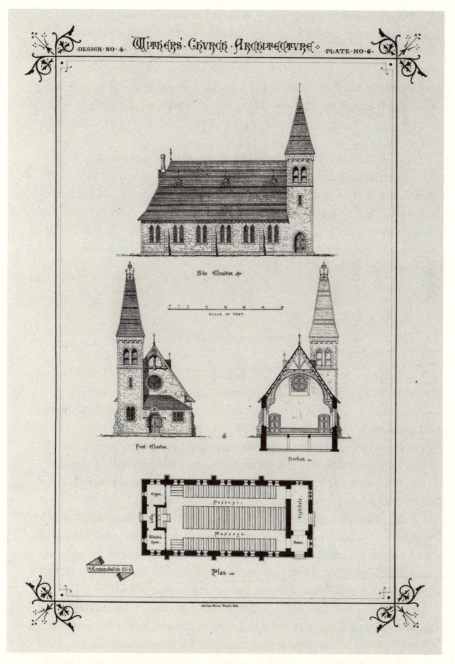

Fig. 5.7 Specimen page of design of a church with corner tower and roof dormers detailing a hammerbeam roof in cross section.

speeding construction and saving money. The method could be applied to timber churches, assisting the rapid establishment of Prairie communities. Seeking to elevate the importance of architecture and technical achievement in its cause, Wheeler deemed the advent of construction to exist on par with the merits of the Canadian Pacific Railway. Subsequently, his vision of an urban infrastructure included technical advances in planning, sanitary plumbing and heating and ventilation for public buildings, churches, schools, stores, and residences.[20]

A complicated individual, Wheeler's nationalist sentiment inevitably surfaced in official colonialist remarks negating the rights of First Nations. "Thirty or thirty-five years ago Winnipeg was an aggregation of log houses surrounding Fort Garry, an Hudson's Bay Company post on the plains of Manitoba and the territories stretching away for nearly a thousand miles westward to the foot hills of the Rocky Mountains, uninhabited, except by Indians and half-breeds."[21]

REAPPRAISING A "NATIONAL STYLE OF ARCHITECTURE" ALONGSIDE THE SPREAD OF BOOKSELLERS

The CPR promoted – but could not live up to – the objective of establishing national unity simply by transporting goods and promoting tourism. CPR officials attempted to create a national architecture by consistently using the Baronial Style in their stations and line of hotels built before 1900. However, the variety and sheer number of neo-Gothic churches built across the Dominion vied for – and complicated – the national identity. A satisfactory compromise was never achieved because the heterogeneous viewing public did not champion a single style for Canada. In addition, architects did not help the situation because they had difficulty organizing even regional self-regulatory bodies based on a standard set of principles. Many regional professional organizations formed, but they quickly disbanded due to internal squabbling. The architect William George Storm described the lack of cooperation as the "modern system of competition and the rivalries of private practice which bring into undue prominence individual interest, until the members of the profession may be described as a number of fortuitous atoms."[22] It was not an easy matter for architects to build a profession, since this necessitated putting aside their personal differences in favour of creating a self-regulating organization. The architectural historian Kelly Crossman has shown how uneasy collectives formed among Ontario's architects in the last decades of the nineteenth century.[23]

By the 1880s, several regional and municipal architectural organizations had formed, not long after earlier failures to "restore the profession in the eyes of the public."[24] They were spurred into action because of the increasing amount of competition from US architects who were winning prominent commissions in Canadian towns. Thus, magazine trade in Canada competed with US pattern books' self-proclaimed authority in an attempt to sway public taste away from architectural styles deemed American. Thus, it was no accident that the seemingly casual formation of the Architectural Guild of Toronto in 1887 preceded the establishment of the professional journal *The Canadian Architect and Builder* (1888–1909). The journal exemplified the problems of establishing a national voice in Canada because its editors and narratives were chiefly focused on Ontario and Quebec. Nevertheless, the journal aspired to galvanize architects around the formation of legislation that eventually brought into existence the Ontario Architects' Act (1890). These events coincided with the formation of the Ontario Association of Architects (1890) and the standardization of architectural education in that province, all modelled, more or less, on similar developments in the architectural profession in Britain, Australia, and the US.

The ongoing importation of British and US pattern books undercut the nationalist and regional professionalizations of architecture in the Dominion. For this reason, the loose syndication of booksellers that profited from importing their wares were unwittingly playing into the hands of US taste when they tried to establish self-regulatory bodies.

When the question of a national style of architecture arose periodically in Canada, there was division between using a British or US model. The *Canadian Architect and Builder* tried to settle the question, not by advocating a unique style for Canada but by pointing out that England had "a knowledge of architecture and cultivated taste – the natural consequence of a leisure class of educated men and a country stocked with examples of good architecture."[25] Toward the pursuit of sustaining an imagined "little Britain" in parts of Canada, the journal reprinted a speech made in London by John Belcher, the newly elected president of the Royal Institute of British Architects, which concluded:

> Increasing knowledge will add to the number of those who appreciate and desire good work, and their sensitiveness in matters of good taste will incite the producers to higher efforts ... It will not be long, I venture to prophecy, before public opinion will declare itself definitely and decidedly, insisting upon grace and refinement both in our public buildings and in our important thoroughfares. Given such an

opportunity, we may feel confident that our national architecture will not fail under the test, but will reflect the highest and noblest qualities of our race.[26]

Belcher was referring to neo-Gothic as Britain's national style, even though the battle with neo-Classicists continued.

Illustrating the public's ambivalence toward developing a national architectural style, the *Canadian Architect and Builder* had reprinted the Boston architect J.R. Putnam's nationalist rhetoric as though it had robust meaning for Canada. He claimed that US society "will develop a national style of architecture which will surpass in splendour anything hitherto known in the history of art."[27] Putnam's idea of national architecture was decidedly neo-Classicist, following the broad fabrication of a US civil society effected through its public architecture. His position was meant to influence the formation of an Ontario-centric image of Canadian identity.

The complex economic negotiations behind Confederation and the unstable political unity it represented were not extended to aboriginals. Instead, Canada projected an image of unity during the expansion of the religious and commercial components of colonialism. A significant concern to settlers was the pacification of the indigenous peoples. It was generally believed that pacification could be achieved through engaging aboriginal people in farming, an activity that would also limit their geographical mobility. This was the method by which First Nations were acculturated and imagined as settlers in their own land. For this reason, Archbishop Robert Machray of Rupert's Land remarked on the massive region as a whole, noting that all of its First Nations had been converted to Christianity, when he circumnavigated the Red River, Lake Superior, and James Bay area in 1868.

Archbishop Machray's preferred form of travel was the rail, which showed that modernity had already visited Canada west before the last spike of the CPR was hammered in at Craigallachie in 1885. During his visits, the Archbishop toured sawmills, fisheries, and farming operations employing First Nations. His mobility via the railway, something the pattern books were already doing, showed how Christianity and commerce had effectively paved the way for European ways of life. Modern European lifestyle involved the appropriation of whatever lands and people were deemed expendable, exploitable, and otherwise outside of the new social order. The important factor was that Aboriginal catechists, working with the Anglican Church, had already converted to Christianity the Cree and Chipewyan bands in the immediate area of Stanley Mission before the arrival of the Church of England missionaries.

Case Study: St George's-in-the-Pines and the Banff Springs Hotel, Banff, Alberta

It must have been apparent to Anglicans touring the Rocky Mountains that the town of Banff needed an Anglican church (fig. 5.8). Communing with nature gave tourists a spiritual appetite that initiated the erection of the church of St George's-in-the-Pines in 1889, a year after the inauguration of the Banff Springs Hotel. The church was built to the specifications of British architect F.P. Oakley, with additions until 1897. Oakley's output was middling

Fig. 5.8 St George's-in-the-Pines (Anglican), Banff, Alberta.

by British standards – his only significant contribution was the Children's Hospital and Dispensary, Manchester (1905) – though his status as a British architect was a saleable commodity.

The commission for the luxury hotel was another affair altogether. The CPR president William Van Horne personally selected his architect, the American Bruce Price, whose daughter was Emily (Price) Post, the famous authority on American etiquette. Prestige, monumentality, and solitude were the requisite characteristics for the architect's design, which Price achieved through the application of Scottish Baronial, Chateau Style, and arts and crafts elements. A spacious lobby and octagonal rotunda, overhanging balconies, parlours, dining rooms, smoking rooms, reading rooms, and bars comprised the luxury offered. Visitors' main access point to nature, and by extension the Divine, was the vista viewpoints built into the hotel's design, offering stunning panoramic views. Even those visitors too timid to venture into the Old Growth Forests and towering mountain peaks were inspired by a view from a window seat, a tea service within easy reach. The Banff Springs Hotel was marketed as one of company's crowning achievements.

After the Hotel's inaugural year, a steadily decreasing number of Canadian patrons were replaced by a growing number of US and international guests. In 1888, Canadian tourists represented 53 percent of the 1,503 guests compared with 26 percent for US tourists. By 1891, the situation was reversed, with Canadians representing 25 percent of the 3,389 guests, compared with 56 percent Americans. Thus, US tourists assisted the creation of a western social economy and a locus of identification framed around religion and representations of nature. Between 1902 and 1911, the CPR's hotel guests at Banff increased steadily from 3,890 to 22,000. The Banff Springs Hotel turned away roughly 5,000 guests each summer, coinciding with rumours that the nearby Mount Stephen House booked three or four guests to a room by sending three on excursions while the fourth occupied the room *pro tem*.[28] The increased international tourist traffic necessitated the building of a new Banff Springs Hotel in 1910, a commission awarded to Bruce Price's disciple the US, architect Walter Painter. Twelve years after tourism started in Banff, the CPR's old frame hotel was a crown jewel that needed "improvement" and was replaced with an eleven-storey concrete structure faced with Mount Rundle Limestone.

Tourists were expected to believe in the compatibility of the massive hotel project and the intimate town church, each in diametrically opposed architectural vocabulary. St George's-in-the-Pines was built during the expansion of the tourist trade in Banff. Built of local limestone, the small parish church's appearance contrasted with the forests surrounding the town of

Banff. Limestone was chosen to evoke permanency, richness, and an aesthetic corresponding to rural English churches. Similarly proportioned churches were marketed in George Truefitt's *Designs for Country Churches* (1850) and Raphael Brandon's *Parish Churches* (1849). A scissor truss used to support the church's open timber roof recalls illustrations in Raphael and J. Arthur Brandon's *Open Timber Roofs* (1849) and represented the building's sole expression of the limitless forested mountains beyond.

6

AN UNFINISHED BUSINESS
OF WESTERN EXPANSION

MISREPRESENTING OPPORTUNITY AND OPENNESS
IN BRITISH COLUMBIA

The westward expansion of settlement to its terminus in British Columbia after the 1880s was an economic enterprise in the guise of a nationalist program. Settlement expansion would have been an ephemeral government strategy without miners, loggers, railway workers, merchants, and financiers searching for profit. The combination of physical labour and investment capital aided the rapid development and exploitation of natural resources. The rumour of immeasurable wealth in the Cariboo gold fields attracted men of fortune, just as trade with Asia was an equally enticing draw for migrants. Trading partners in California and along the Pacific Rim during the 1880s and 90s later subsided once British Columbia developed a more robust economy in the 1910s, nurtured by a sharp increase in population, the price of wheat, and entrepreneurial finance capital. Regional issues dominated political and economic initiatives even after British Columbia signed the British North America Act of 1871, a proviso being the completion of the CPR. The railway's ability to compress travel time between and within the coasts became synonymous with forming a Canadian identity, though British Columbia's signature on the BNA Act of 1871 did not complete the nation.

In British Columbia, this strategy was enhanced by an immigrants' handbook: *The Province of British Columbia, Canada: Its Resources, Commercial Position, and Climate* (1890). The handbook was associated with Britain's plan to connect Europe with Asia through an uninterrupted flow of trade across British North America. Its publisher was not a government bureau but the Canadian Pacific Railway. From the opening phrase, it brazenly claimed that the CPR had given birth to western economy, "suddenly transforming BC into an easily accessible and profitable field for commercial enterprise from earlier mere dabbling on the shores of the ocean of commerce."[1] Canada's contribution to the effort was nothing more than the fuel and food resources needed to drive the train from coast to coast. In furtherance of the grand vision, the Canadian Pacific Company had created steamship routes between Vancouver and Asia, demonstrating that the city's future lay in speculative endeavour. The handbooks demonstrated the combined importance of space and commerce in the era of new settlement.

In declaring British Columbia's sudden expansion, the handbook took little notice of the moderate populations in the region's towns according to the 1881 census.[2] An interconnected but dangerously short supply of money translated into unpretentious churches, built mainly of timber, as though congregations anticipated future, guaranteed wealth translating into lavish and larger churches. The actual growth was typically reserved for Vancouver and Victoria, though a host of other towns, such as Port Moody, only briefly flirted with expansion.

The handbook inaccurately portrayed the city of Victoria, outstripped in population and trade by nascent Vancouver, claiming the latter as the economic centre of the west coast. Despite their equivalent populations at 15,000 apiece, the CPR had a vested interest in marketing their terminus city, Vancouver, as a city without equal.[3] A description of Vancouver's economic development privileged that city with allusions to the value of new building constructions, the mileage of paved roadways, and increased property values. A proliferation of "grand edifices of stone, brick, and iron" that replaced the wooden buildings burned in the fire of 1886 advertised Vancouver's prominence.[4] Victoria's architectural achievements in brick and iron merited barely a mention. The "real" state of affairs in Vancouver appeared in a letter written by the Anglican Priest Henry Glynne Fiennes-Clinton, the rector of St James' Church (1885–1912). Clinton's High Anglican inclinations stressed pastoral leadership and social consciousness. These were apparent in a letter about Vancouver:

> all the swagger in the world will not build houses, and if they don't mend soon they will have this place a city of shanties, without water, roads or drains ... The roads are quite impassable from the mud holes ... Some new roads they have been making are worse as they cross boggy land and therefore there is no bottom to the roads at all, and if you once get stuck you might reckon on taking forthwith a journey to the centre of the earth.[5]

In the 1890s, eager to construct an appearance of "empty" land awaiting the industriousness of migrant settlers, the handbook disregarded the traditional lands of First Nations and their nascent claims on that territory.[6] Since the Treaty of Oregon in 1846 between British and US military might eventually stabilize the international border, regional and federal authorities operated under the impression that official treaty with First Nations in BC was unnecessary. James Douglas, factor of the Hudson's Bay Company (later governor of British Columbia), negotiated fourteen treaties with the Coast Salish people on Vancouver's Island – abruptly cancelled by his successor, Joseph Trutch.[7] Consequently, land was appropriated in BC without treaty.[8] The Douglas Treaties were used as binding legal and social contracts, achieving compliance from First Nations, who were convinced into believing that the two cultures' continued friendship depended on adhering to printed contracts and the Divine right of English law. The idea of Divine right was reiterated through clergymen and missionaries engaging in the enterprise of converting First Nations to Christianity.

Aboriginal people on the west coast were invisible in the handbook, reflecting the perceived irrelevance of Native Peoples and any land claims they might bring forth. First Nations who built neo-Gothic churches using features found in pattern books inadvertently reinforced their own invisibility because the buildings appeared as though they accommodated European settlers. The Englishness of neo-Gothic church architecture became associated with colonial violence against First Nations, although clergymen and missionaries believed they were improving the lives of aboriginal people. Indeed, this relationship showed how religion was the socially pacifying arm of colonization, and the pattern books its architectural and moral connection. The plan of action involved the provision of religious-based re-education for First Nations in segregated reserves, which had the effect of making aboriginal people appear to be immigrants in their own land.

The constitution of group and individual identities relative to national imaginings was particularly expressed in the rhetoric around the construction of railway conglomeration. The railways spread the pattern books, and thus indirectly disseminated knowledge, and all three impacted the lives of First Nations by attempting to replace their traditional beliefs with European and Positivist knowledge systems. Understanding the mobility of the pattern books in light of the marketing of knowledge and science, as well as that of fashion and taste, involves examining colonial strategies, policies, and procedures of trade. The central feature of colonial expansion positioned some groups, especially indigenous peoples and the Métis, as social others.

Settler handbooks were a locus of identity-creation subtly bringing religion into the dialogue, with repeated references to the availability of churches in the west. Religion was a major component of Canadian identity during settlement expansion inasmuch as churches represented the most significant, nongovernmental social support network available to settlers. In this sense, interdenominational rivalries expressed in architectural terms as grand churches was not the only sign of these group's struggles. Religious conversions, group baptisms, revival camps, charity activities, the observance of Sunday Sabbath were, no less than the clergy's custodial role in residential schools and support of the ban on potlatch, signs of religion's influence in the new social formation. Settlement expansion represented the combination of economic, political, cultural, and religious forces used by groups and individuals in power relationships. The development of business conglomerates that limited the unrestricted expansion of western Canada around 1900 was virtually assured by the major recessions of 1874 and 1884, which restricted the profitability of farms and independent business concerns. All this translated into generally poor financial support for rural Anglican parishes. A significant aspect of these relationships involved the myth of the west being a place for opportunity when in reality a small group of privileged people controlled industry and commerce. Closed social constructs had devastating effects on the lifeways of First Nations peoples along the west coast and throughout the territory. White missionaries' and settlers' preconceived ideas about aboriginal cultures expressed the rigidity of closed systems.

Case Study: Religious Industry at the Mission Church of St Paul's, Metlakatla

A massive timber church, the largest north of San Francisco and west of Chicago, was erected at the Anglican missionary town of Metlakatla, BC, in 1874. As a social experiment intended to acculturate, "improve," and "save" eight hundred Tsimshian First Nation from Fort Simpson, the town of Metlakatla had been founded near the Alaskan border by the lay missionary William Duncan (1832–1918). He had partnered with the Tsimshian intending to create an idyllic English village complete with single-family dwellings surrounded by white picket fences. The prevailing theory was that adapting British social behaviours and engaging in a Calvinist work ethic would absolve the stigma of being aboriginal.[9] Their church at Metlakatla, dedicated St Paul, was the centrepiece of the faith-based development project. For this reason, virtually all of the photographic images of the town depict the church located at its centre (fig. 6.1). The faux-Englishness of the town was a paternalistic

Fig. 6.1 St Paul's Anglican Church, Metlakatla, British Columbia, c. 1874.

strategy intended to acculturate the Tsimshian as though they were immigrants to Canada.

The Tsimshian of Metlakatla were led astray to believe that adopting British mores, visibly reflected in neo-Gothic architecture, would raise their social status in Canada. Their collective goal of owning the land that the town stood upon was never realized. Instead, the Tsimshian of Metlakatla were seen as Victorian curiosities even though Canadian politicians and British aristocracy publicly applauded the efforts to "civilize" this particular First Nation band.

It remains unclear whether William Duncan or the Metlakatlans devised the plan to adopt Carpenter's Gothic, a simple timber style known for multiple gabled roofs and decorative gingerbread bargeboard cut-outs, on a monumental scale. St Paul's in Metlakatla had all of the markings of a cathedral, except name. Its massive nave accommodated 1,100 seats, unprecedented in churches built for the purpose of converting First Nations to Christianity. However, Metlakatla was a unique project since all of the town's inhabitants were expected to attend church services with regularity; in essence, a "company town" whose product was salvation.

St Paul's is an example of using patterns of living familiar to Aboriginal culture in the conversions of Native Peoples since the nave of the church was planned like a First Nations longhouse. In fact, the layout of the church was a large rectangular box, typical of churches used by First Nations, embellished architecturally on the exterior west end. It had asymmetrical crenellated west twin towers that framed a cathedral-like triple-gabled entrance, evoking the Carpenter's Gothic style. An eclectic use of pointed and round-headed windows appeared related to the transoms of houses. The overlarge buttresses, built more for show than support, appear to be massive spur-walls protruding from the exterior as if carved members. The overall design, though eclectic, owes something to arrangements found in *Woodward's Rural Church Architecture* (1876) (fig. 6.2), particularly with respect to the round-headed triplet in the west end situated above a projecting gabled entrance. The side tower offset by a gabled aisle and the positioning of the corner buttresses with weatherings completes the comparison.

The open timber roofing system at St Paul's follows Frank Kidder's advice in his pattern book *Trussed Roofs and Roof Trusses*, which demonstrated how

Fig. 6.2 Specimen page from *Woodward's Rural Church Architecture*. George Woodward, 1876.

to use horizontal tie beams in spans wider than thirty-five feet. This roofing technology was slightly different from "Howe," or Bridge, trusses used in homes that had angled supports to resist compression. Instead, the rafters of St Paul's Church rested directly on top of the timbers of the top chord of the truss. In Kidder's view, rafters "greatly enhanced" in their dimensions and "special calculations" were needed for cutting the timbers.[10] The roofing system at St Paul's used a hybrid of the domestic truss and the hammer-beam variety typical of neo-Gothic churches built after the 1870s in Canada.

St Paul's Metlakatla radiated industriousness. Indeed, the church reflected how life in the northern village was structured around the combination of religion and industry. Photographs of life in Metlakatla, shown in aristocratic circles in England to prove the successes with "civilizing" aboriginals, illustrated the Tsimshian's daily working life in their sawmill, soap factory, fish cannery, and general store as well as partaking of religious education. Beneath the layer of civility displayed in the photographs was a complex and dark relationship. Duncan's complex "paternal" bond with the Tsimshian strained beneath layers of his authoritarian rule. He was unwilling to provide education above the first two years of primary school, kept a list of grievances against the Tsimshian concerning their "superstitious trust in signs," and noted their "excitability to rebellion" and "unwillingness to engage in public duty."[11] Duncan believed that these social failures could be overcome by the combined civilizing capacity of religion and commerce. Though the village's various businesses were unprofitable, it was his view that the important part of its commerce was the potential to instill a Christian work ethic. This attitude has had to be reconciled against the size of Duncan's personal estate, valued at the time of his death in 1918 at nearly $140,000; he had been accumulating and selling Tsimshian artwork and cultural artefacts. Duncan's view of Christian religion and morals as the antidote to the problems of technocratic society has not been satisfactorily reconciled against his large personal treasury.

The image of industrious Tsimshian in Metlakatla was a monolithic sign of civility promoted by Duncan to veil internal discord. Town residents regularly engaged in activities deemed illegal by White authorities, such as hiding ceremonial masks inside the walls of their houses, thus resisting the ban on the potlatch. They continued to live communally in the English-style houses Duncan built as single-family dwellings. Tsimshian elders insisted that church services be held in their own language rather than English. Architecturally, their chapel contained two interior support beams carved to represent the four phratries of the Coast Tsimshian.[12]

The renown of the church at Metlakatla attracted the attention of the bishop of Caledonia, William Ridley, who attempted to appropriate two acres of land on Mission Point in Metlakatla, where the church stood. The bishop's attempts to assume control of the church were met with strong opposition because the Tsimshian did not favour the bishop's High Church ritual form of worship. The Crown sided with the bishop in a combined attempt to appropriate the land away from the Tsimshian, causing angry residents to expel the Crown's surveyor by force. The threat of violence in 1884 resulted in a commissioners' inquiry held at Metlakatla, which determined that Duncan's leadership had been the problem. Since British authorities intended to avoid direct conflict with the First Nation, a typical colonialist strategy of dominant groups evading the use of force, blaming Duncan was a simpler solution. Besides, the Church Mission Society, an arm of the Anglican Church, had already decided the matter by removing Duncan for insubordination.[13]

During a prolonged land dispute, the Tsimshian of Metlakatla tried several legal avenues to resolve the conflict with Bishop Ridley. Receiving no impartial justice from the magistrate's office, the Tsimshian of Metlakatla dismantled the general store as a form of protest and reappropriated the school house the bishop had appropriated for religious use. Assertions of social and religious rights made by the Tsimshian were the first recorded claims made by First Nations that connected economy and religion. The claim was supported by the *Victoria Daily Colonist* newspaper: "what right have we to make away with their land? But even if we have a title it is only in trust for the benefit of the Indians that we have it. But is it for their benefit to give away their land to religious teachers whom they do not want? There would, I apprehend, be no question here but for the entering into it of the Church of England, a name which is often potent to cover a multitude of sins."[14] Galvanized by the dispute rather than fractured by it, the community of seven hundred Tsimshian and William Duncan left British Columbia to found New Metlakatla on Annette Island, further north along the Alaskan coast. Their wish for a higher level of autonomy and recognised property rights was granted by the US government, ironically, an administration with generally poor Indian relations.

Comparative Case Study: An Elaborate West End for Holy Cross Church, Skookumchuck, BC

In the shadow of the Cascade Mountains of British Columbia, the graceful triple tower of the west end of Holy Cross Roman Catholic Church on the Skatin Nation at Skookumchuck overlooks the rushing waters of the Lillooet River (fig. 6.3). The west end of Holy Cross was most unusual, not only among mission churches in Canada but also among those influenced by European

Fig. 6.3 Holy Cross Roman Catholic Church (Skatin First Nation), Skookumchuck, British Columbia, 1895–1905.

designs; that is, specific antecedents were virtually impossible to find in either the Middle Ages or the nineteenth century. The central spire over the gable is in the position of a bellcote, though its size and verticality also evokes a crossing tower found at the intersection of the nave and transepts on medieval churches. The surprising arrangement originates from postcards of European churches carried by the Oblates engaged in converting the First Nations. With exceptional carpentry knowledge, the Skatin builders ensured the central tower would be structurally supported at the west end, choosing not to blithely copy the positioning of a crossing tower on a rectangular building without transeptal arms.

The planning of Holy Cross in 1895 and its completion in 1905 were the culmination of the proselytizing work of the Oblates of Mary Immaculate begun in 1843. The Oblates received no architectural training, unlike their Anglican counterparts, which explains the western facade's strong medieval vocabulary fused with a long rectangular nave. The combination of a richly designed west end on an otherwise simplified plan is not unusual by Roman Catholic architectural standards of the early twentieth century, especially with respect to mission churches built in Western Canada. British Columbia and Alberta have numerous timber mission churches composed of a single room, with an interior altar space rather than a separate chancel area. Roman Catholic church-builders were not remotely interested in Ecclesiological architectural fashion and its dictates of proportion, truthful use of materials, and doctrine of archaeological antecedents. The round-headed fan window above the main entrance is a reference to Roman arches – an essential reference to the Catholic Church in Rome – but the pointed windows in the nave and rose window in the west gable are Gothic vocabulary. The delicacy of the octagonal towers was a suitable quotation of French medieval design. As if to highlight the hybridity of the interior design, the walls are decorated with boards arranged in a geometric pattern to resemble the bottom of a woven basket. The building exterior is clad with horizontal timbers joined with a three-quarter tongue and groove technique to provide a richer aesthetic than the plain clapboard finish.

The transmission of medieval vocabulary from the French Oblates and their clientele untutored in European architecture occurred through postcard images regularly carried by the Roman Catholic missionaries. The postcards of European churches and cathedrals were revealed to First Nations elders, demonstrating the superiority of the missionary's places of spiritual origin. These images justified Bouillon's choice of elevation and details to the Oblates and First Nation elders at Our Lady of the Rosary in Sechelt. Ely Cathedral's massive octagonal crossing tower was another possible source, though a more direct and aesthetically similar source was published in George Woodward's *Rural Church Architecture* (fig. 6.4). The gabled windows in the tower of Woodward's drawing appears to have influenced the type of gable picked out in wood similarly arranged in churches for First Nations.

The church of St Louis in Bonaparte (1890) (fig. 6.5), a First Nations Reserve in British Columbia, is remarkable not only for its eclecticism but also for its architectural references to other mission churches in the region. The gabled tower and the fan windows were used at the Roman Catholic

Fig. 6.4 Specimen page from *Rural Church Architecture*. George Woodward, 1868.

Church at Fountain, BC (c. 1890–1900). The massive twin towers at the Musquem church of St Michael the Archangel (1902), Vancouver, and St Mary's (1900), Scowlitz, were important antecedents. Yet, the watershed moment for these churches, and especially for Holy Cross, was the construction of Our Lady of the Rosary (1890, destroyed by fire 1906), Sechelt, built by the Belgian-born

Fig. 6.5 Detail of tower from the Roman Catholic Church of St Louis, Bonaparte, British Columbia, c. 1890.

architect Joseph Bouillon. All are related to the architect-designed church in Sechelt, likely visited by numerous First Nations who were given half-price railway tickets to attend the consecration. The event promoted the civilizing effect of missionary work and religion among the Native population and generated goodwill for the CPR, demonstrating the close relation of industry, commerce, and religion.

THE DEVELOPMENT OF NATURAL AND SPIRITUAL RESOURCES IN BRITISH COLUMBIA

Gold discoveries along the Fraser River in 1858 and subsequent finds in the Cariboo region temporarily propelled British Columbia onto the international scene and convinced thousands of profit seekers that their fortunes lay beneath the west coast topsoil and along its streams. Placer gold deposits in the rivers of the Cariboo area brought the town of Barkerville into existence in the 1860s, making a fortune for its founder Billy Barker. His famous antics and subsequent financial ruination from excessive gambling and drinking illustrate that less exciting commercial ventures such as laundry and dry goods sales were stable and lucrative. Exhausted and penniless, many of the gold seekers in northern British Columbia took jobs in the coal mines on Vancouver Island.

Missionaries moved more or less in tandem with groups of workers and settlers, the largest and most rapidly expanding of which were associated with gold mining. For that reason, reports made by missionaries often contained some discussion about the development of mining and other forms of commercial activity near their parishes. Anglican missionaries and Oblates of the Order of Mary Immaculate moved in tandem with the gold seekers in British Columbia, since these folk represented the bulk of population and wealth generation. A significant mineral deposit, they knew, could lead to the establishment of a permanent settlement just as the sudden affluence of its population could build a permanent church in a newly established town.

Case Study: Marketing Failure as Success at St Saviour's Church, Barkerville

In spring 1869, the seasonal runoff from the Cariboo Mountains in central British Columbia flooded the main street of the gold rush town of Barkerville, piling three feet of ice and snow up against the front steps of St Saviour's Anglican church (fig. 6.6). Raising the church up on stilts was a necessity borne of the town's poor location. However, the strategy of raising the building combined with the vertical board-and-batten cladding added a triumphant character, not unlike the vertical articulation of churches published in numerous pattern books including the previous illustration from Woodward's text (see fig. 6.4, page 138). The vertical exterior cladding was a technique used in Maritime churches of New Brunswick, notably those built by the architect Edward Medley, son of Bishop John Medley of the Anglican diocese of that province. An antecedent of that aesthetic form was found in the Ecclesiological Society's pattern book *Instrumenta Ecclesiastica* (see fig. 3.5, page 78). Thus, the use of vertical cladding not only connected the coasts of Canada, unintentionally or no, but also linked Canada with Britain through illustrated publications. The commentary running throughout *Instrumenta Ecclesiastica* proclaimed the superiority of both the Anglican Church and its architectural accomplishments.

The location of St Saviour's church at the head of the only street in town appeared to signal the prominence of the Anglican community among the population of several thousand miners, labourers, and townsfolk in Barkerville. In fact, the opposite was true. The more personable and accessible Methodist minister achieved greater popularity among the townsfolk and miners despite his denunciation of liquor and vice, two major social pastimes in the isolated settlement. As a result, the Anglican Rev. James Reynard encountered significant difficulties.

Fig. 6.6 St Saviour's Anglican Church, Barkerville, British Columbia, 1869.

Arriving several months after a devastating fire that purged the entire town of its wooden buildings and canvas tents, Rev. Reynard was unable to find financial support to construct a church. Compounding Reynard's poor timing was his appearance on the scene after the Methodist preacher, Rev. Thomas Derrick, who had already raised $1,850 to build a church. It exhausted the townsfolk's limited charity. The town's remaining capital had been earmarked for rebuilding homes and businesses. Reynard nevertheless managed to convince a few local supporters, and with the help of contractors Bruce and Mann he completed the most architecturally ambitious project in the town.

Despite the aspirations of the Anglican mission to the goldfields of British Columbia, the speculative attempts to grow either enterprise proved unsustainable in Barkerville. When the mining camp failed in 1870, Reynard aborted his mission and left his newly completed church to the slow decay of the Barkerville ghost town. Reynard's journey south along the Cariboo gold trail was a long one, during which he had many days to contemplate the precariousness of building a religious mission on the flank of speculative mineral exploitation.[15] Undeterred, a new contingent of gold speculators in the Barkerville area resurrected the town in 1898, causing the Anglican Church Mission Society to restore the mission at St Saviour's Church. They dispatched the Rev. Field Yolland, along with his wife and small children, within months of the new gold finds in the area. Again, the Anglican mission to Barkerville proved unsustainable; after two winters Yolland moved his family further west to Quesnel, where he profited from farming part-time. To raise the $250 necessary to construct a modest church in Quesnel, Yolland turned to another British publication: *Work for the Far West*.

MARKETING BRITISH COLUMBIA'S HARDSHIP TO SOLICIT CHURCH-BUILDING FUNDS FROM BRITAIN

While the *Colonists' Handbook No.1* (1882) exaggerated the profitability of Canada's natural resources to British readers, the serialized publication *Work for the Far West* (1898–1914) derived support for church-building by developing sympathy for Anglican missionaries in squalid conditions in British Columbia. *Work for the Far West*, a hybrid diary/newspaper, was not published in Canada. Its place of production and distribution was the textile manufacture town of Tewksbury, Gloucestershire, in the vicinity of England's southwest midlands. Bishop John Dart (1895–1910) of New Westminster, British Columbia, created the journal for several purposes, using it to generate offers of "patterns for churches and other work to be done for the diocese, and will recommend or lend books to be read in working parties."[16] More pointedly, the journal routinely featured articles and letters penned by missionaries and clergymen, describing the hardship of building churches on the formidable west coast of Canada. These stories overstated the negative aspects of life in remote areas of Canada West, since Bishop Dart knew that the Society for the Propagation of the Gospel in Foreign Parts (SPG – a missionary arm of the Anglican Church) intended to cease financial support for west coast missions in 1900. So, *Work for the Far West* was a political appendage of the colonial bishop mobilized to keep money flowing to his colonial diocese. Administrators for the SPG were determined to make the diocese self-sustaining. They claimed that British Columbia's robust economy of abundant natural resources augmented by markets linked through intercontinental rail service could sustain Dart's diocese on its own.[17] However, Dart already knew about the SPG's strategy, having worked as their organizing secretary prior to his installation as colonial bishop. Thus, he plotted to publicize the plight of colonial missions, raise money in the public domain, and embarrass the SPG into an extension of its subsidy.

With the exception of a single large private donation form Baroness Angela Burdett-Coutts, whose gift of £15,000 established the diocese of British Columbia, money for church-building in British Columbia was extracted from many poor people who were least able to afford it, Britain's working classes. The scheme succeeded because Britain's working classes were already predisposed to worry about the disappearance of a village lifestyle in the colonies that they believed was lost to urbanized England; the British working classes imagined the village lifestyle was salvageable in Canada. Demonstrating the tactical strength of the colonial position, church-builders in British Columbia became adept at raising money from overseas in Britain by taking advantage of their belief in the civilizing effect of British culture and currency.

Case Study: Over-expansion in Steveston, British Columbia, St Anne's (1901–2) and St Jerome's (1903)

The underfunded Anglican diocese of New Westminster in British Columbia was closely associated with the St Anne's Society in the working-class manufacture town of Tewkesbury, England. The colonial bishop John Dart was good friends with the Rev. Jerome J. Mercier, trustee for the St Anne's Society and publisher of the serialized journal *Work for the Far West*. Both men were personally acquainted with the impetuous and cantankerous Rev. Joseph McAfee Donaldson (1835–1918), whose immigration to Canada was the result of polygamy charges in Australia. Aware of Donaldson's difficulties Bishop Dart permitted the reverend to establish a parish in 1895 in the small fishing village of Steveston, BC, where he operated as lay minister until an ecclesiastical license could be procured. Donaldson's first order of business was the construction of a small timber church, dedicated to St Anne (fig. 6.7). The church was composed of a simple nave and chancel, seating approximately eighty people. In its simplicity, St Anne's was related to the type of chapel illustrated in the Rev. George Bowler's pattern book *Chapel and Church Architecture with Designs for Parsonages* (1856) (fig. 6.8). It had little architectural pretence comprising a plain silhouette resembling a one-room Prairie schoolhouse, owing to inadequate funding and limited architectural vision.

To obtain money for the church project Donaldson wrote to the journal *Work for the Far West*. His requests found an enthusiastic supporter in Anne Mercier, Rev. Jerome's spouse. Donaldson promised to finish the church at the cost of about £100, noting "half that amount would make it sufficiently

Fig. 6.7 St Anne's Anglican Church, Steveston, British Columbia, c. 1905.

Fig. 6.8 Specimen page from *Chapel and Church Architecture with Designs for Parsonages.*

comfortable to be used during the winter season."[18] The unambitious request appeared to embody the characterization of Anne Mercier's novella *A Home in the Northwest* (1903), where settling farmers succeed in building a church with few financial resources. Similar tales printed in *Work for the Far West* were likely the story's inspiration.

Donaldson's acceptance of funding from Tewksbury in England did not translate into benevolent leadership in Steveston. He held the fishing community and cannery workers in the lowest esteem. His cantankerous character won him few friends, several times accused of keeping stray chickens and livestock that wandered into his yard. The Mounted Police were called to settle a dispute involving his procuring an organ from the defunct Steveston Opera House. A quarrel over an unpaid bill for timber in 1902 resulted in Donaldson chasing his supplier down the main street in full view of the townsfolk and his visiting bishop. The supplier, Mr French, had padlocked the church. What led an intemperate and unpopular lay minister found guilty of infidelity to raise not one but two churches in a small frontier town?

With attendance at Sunday services dropping at St Anne's, Donaldson hatched a plan to build a second church away from the fishermen and closer to landowning farmers, six miles outside of town. Emboldened by the success of his first fundraising effort in Tewksbury, Donaldson sought to increase his request for money from £80 (about $400) to £200. Rather than admit defeat in Steveston, Donaldson was keen to project an image that his parish was expanding as a strategy to raise money for the second church. For the solicitation of one-time gifts to his so-called "expanding" parish Donaldson called upon Anne Mercier at *Work for the Far West*, once again, writing "in order to make the Church more worthy of the honoured name which it is to commemorate, I have made it much better, and therefore more expensive than would otherwise have been necessary or expedient. To do this I have taken upon myself personally the entire responsibility in the matter of finding the necessary funds, which is a venture of faith as well as hope."[19] The connection with the Mercier family must have been fruitful, because St Jerome's Church was built by 1903. It must have been more than coincidence that the dedication name of each of these churches reflects upon the Christian names of Anne and Jerome Mercier. Donaldson was accomplished at raising money from the working classes in Britain. Mobilized by the idea that their donations sustained a simple village lifestyle worthy of their support, the Merciers had little idea that the pastoral life was as imaginary to them as it was in Steveston. Constructing small rural churches helped to sustain the myth intruded upon by the reality of the sixteen-hour work day in both places.

The lack of Sunday attendance at either of his two churches must have confirmed Donaldson's doubts about the onset of technocratic society and concomitant ambivalence to religious enterprise. The sparse silhouette of St Anne's, Steveston, outlines the change in social geography and economy as compared with his previous posting in Mortlake, Australia. There, in 1864, Donaldson hired the London architect Leonard Perry to erect a small but dramatic replica of the thirteenth-century church of St Michael's Long Stanton, Cambridgeshire, showing his commitment to the principles for a town church that George Edmund Street had essayed in the *Ecclesiologist*. St Michael's was illustrated in several pattern books including Raphael and J. Arthur Brandon's *Parish Churches* (1848). With the Ecclesiological conversation more or less extinct by the turn of the century, and the polemics over Humanist and Positivist thought having turned to architectural technology debates, Donaldson retreated to regional vernacular church form. He may have consoled himself that the timber church was a temporary stopgap on the way to a permanent expression in stone or brick, but neither was predestined. At the age of seventy-seven in 1912, Donaldson's cautionary tale of the evaporation of religious institution in Steveston was confirmed by a riot that broke out as striking First

Nations cannery workers were replaced by Asian immigrants willing to accept a fraction of the pay scale. What he failed to understand was that his ministrations to the Anglican community had produced limited effect and that the populace had already learned to manipulate the separation of religion and economy to serve personal ends.

CONNECTING RAILWAY AND RELIGION

Capital was pooled into conglomerates at an unprecedented rate during the last quarter of the nineteenth century to empower a loose contingent of enterprises such as railway, metals manufacture, and print media. The second railway boom of the 1870s, which assembled feeder lines into the CPR project and catapulted it westward on the favourable projections of cargo-shipment profits, was brought into the service of settlement expansion. The estimated £25 million of invested capital in the CPR guaranteed by British loan agreements, given reluctantly, connected numerous small towns across Canada with the apparatus of the British Empire. "The great highway to and from Europe that wielded the commercial scepter of the world"[20] was also reflected in the cultural highway that deepened the communication among the national and transoceanic Anglican hierarchy.

The CPR project was marketed to the Canadian and British publics as an economic and social requirement of the modern world, without revealing its corporate agenda. Aggressive project management of the CPR augmented the growth of some towns while strangling others, depending on the location of railway stations. A northern route across the Prairies was abandoned in favour of a southern one that was more lucrative for the CPR, despite severe spring floods, since the company was paid a $200,000 cash incentive by Winnipeg businessmen. The deal superseded Selkirk as the planned railway hub of the Prairies. Similarly, the western terminus of the CPR in Port Moody in coastal British Columbia was cancelled after businessmen at Hasting's Mill offered the conglomerate free land in exchange for altering the route; their success inaugurated the city of Vancouver in 1885. Other, more scandalous, behaviour transpired as railway management's strong sense of entitlement and power clashed with unscrupulous businessmen. Profiteering railway contractors like Samuel Zimmerman slowed the progress of construction on the Great Western main line in order to extract $470,000 in bonuses for the completion of work already agreed upon. Railway scandal touched the reputation of the Anglican diocese's chief architect at St James Cathedral, Toronto. In his capacity as lead engineer for the Great Western line, Fred Cumberland accepted a $10,000 bribe to sanction substandard work; it brought a swift end to his professional reputation.[21]

Given the habitual financial failure of new railway projects the CPR represented an extreme economic risk to shareholders, the Government of Canada, and loan guarantors in Britain. As a result, and with the blessing of Canadian government officials, the CPR employed a complex method of soliciting and instilling public support. They enlisted artists and writers to create guidebooks that championed the project. Using images of locomotives, railway stations, and the vastness of the Canadian landscape as set pieces in a drama of broad economic and public proportions, the guidebooks solidified the CPR's power base. Locomotives were envisioned as eternal entities crossing the vast land at unprecedented speed. Railway stations became the new gateways to welcoming towns and cities, the largest of which built CPR hotels – the new palaces of luxury travel. The guidebooks blended the technological achievement of engineering with picturesque views of the Rocky Mountains, each a source of danger and mystery. Images of industrial development were omitted in the interest of selling the image of Canada as profound natural environment and augmenting the imagined cultural affinity with England's countryside.

To inspire public support for the CPR's completion, which politicians and industrialists understood as a vast moneymaking business, print media were encouraged to focus on human interest stories rather than dry economic figures. A similar strategy involved the resistance to paying large dividends to shareholders in favour of reinvesting 90 percent of Company revenues, totalling $95 million by 1913.[22] This gave the intended impression that the CPR was a public rather than a private enterprise, sustained by the story that the railway consolidated Confederation. With its hand in many different business opportunities, ranging from canneries to hotel chains, the company appeared as multifaceted as the country itself. CPR management even incorporated several towns once it was discovered that company towns turned profits, though nothing could have been more profitable than the free land that the Company received in 1884 in exchange for moving the planned railway terminus from Port Moody to Granville (now Vancouver). In turn, William Van Horne, general manager of the CPR, made parcels of this land available to religious institutions at reduced cost.

Case Study: St James Anglo-Catholic Church, Vancouver

After the plain timber Anglican church of St James in Vancouver burned on 13 June 1886 – a year after the town was founded in association with land deals favourable to the CPR – the railway company offered at reduced cost two possible parcels of land for the church's relocation. St James' building committee chose the larger site at the corner of Gore and Oppenheimer (Cordova) streets rather than a lot on Richards Street that was too near whisky mills and junk shops. The fire was an opportunity to make a stronger architectural statement aligned with the neo-Gothic fashion of the times. The earlier building's simple rectangular layout and lack of structural expression yielded limited character beyond the obligatory pointed windows with trefoil "cut-outs" imitating medieval window tracery. The San Francisco-based milling firm of Heatly and Company had donated the first site, used until the 1886 fire, showing the close connection between business and religion, not to mention the strong west coast affinities. Despite considerable architectural deficiencies with the first St James, Anglican Bishop Acton Windyer Sillitoe of the New Westminster diocese remembered the modest building for its "taste and orderliness."[23]

The congregation at St James was divided over the site for relocation and a group of dissenters unhappy with the level of ritual in Anglo-Catholic liturgy erupted in 1887 over Holy Eucharist. The remaining High Anglican congregation, led by Father Henry Glynne Fiennes-Clinton's High Church, continued at St James, while the Low Anglican contingent established at new parish at Christ Church (later Cathedral), Vancouver. Clinton was relieved to see them leave, confident that the city's rapidly expanding population would provide the High Church parishioners he sought. He gauged correctly. Vancouver's population nearly doubled in 1888 from 5,000 in 1887. By the time St James Church was consecrated on 1 January 1888, an overcapacity crowd of more than 250 in attendance required many people to sit in the chancel for lack of space. Those in the chancel had a good view of the ceremony in which Bishop Sillitoe displayed the deed for the site from the CPR on the High Altar.

Those remaining with Father Clinton approved of the architect Thomas Sorby's plan to adopt Perpendicular Gothic. It reflected English medieval architecture of the fourteenth and fifteenth centuries, a connection articulated in the half-timbered gables. Architectural quotations from the Early English and Decorated phases of Britain's twelfth and thirteenth centuries were no longer in fashion by the 1880s in Canada as architects generally moved on to newer forms of historicizing trends.

Fig. 6.9 St James' Anglo-Catholic Church, Vancouver, BC.

Sorby, who was also the honorary secretary of the Building Fund would not approve of a stone-clad building on the grounds of expense and capped construction costs at $4,000. The congregation acquiesced since they wanted to remain debt-free in the construction of the new church. Local merchants and service providers assisted by reducing costs, including the timber from Hasting's Mill, the design from Sorby, and labour provided at cost by contractors Whitearce, McDonald, and Manning. After four decades of the congregation's expansion and relatively poor upkeep of the building the roof began to decay.

By the 1920s, the congregation reached its tolerance of the spatial limitations of their church around the same time as the endurance of historicizing Gothic wore out. The religious and community leaders at St James became more amenable to a structural expression of the times. The main protagonists in the redesign of St James Church were a triumvirate of two Anglo-Catholic Priests and one of Britain's leading architectural dynasties: Father Wilberforce Cooper, Father Robert Harker, and the architect Adrian Gilbert Scott. Father Harker accepted a one-year posting at St James in 1921 until replaced by Father Cooper the year following, but it initiated a lifelong affiliation with Vancouver and its Anglo-Catholic church. Sometime after the onset of the Great Depression in 1929 Father Harker offered to help St James replace its old church by donating $25,000 if the congregation could match him dollar for dollar. By 1933, the search for a suitable local architect was not producing the "level of design required," inducing Cooper to hire one from "England or the East."[24] By 1934 they had accepted the London architect Adrian Gilbert Scott,

Fig. 6.10 Postcard of Golder's Green Church, England.

heir to an architectural dynasty begun by Sir George Gilbert Scott. Cooper had initially pursued Giles Gilbert Scott, who was too busy with other projects and referred his brother Adrian, whose All Saint's Anglican Cathedral (1919–1938, demolished), Cairo, blended progressive design with Old World Gothic aesthetics.

The design submitted by Adrian Gilbert Scott was a modern version of fourteenth-century Gothic updated through the use of reinforced concrete and the massing of spaces rising to a broad octagonal central tower (fig. 6.9). Letters between Scott and Father Cooper recounted a significant concern about the difficulty of the site, since the new church was wedged between the parish hall and St Luke's clergy house. Scott's solution brought the main entrance to the street corner, providing a vestibule area that opened into a large octagonal worship area extended to the west and surmounted by a gallery. Though progressive in materials and layout the design was hardly new, since Adrian's more bankable brother had used the very same layout and massing of the centre tower for St Alban's Catholic Church (1918), Golder's Green, London (fig. 6.10). Cooper received two picture postcards of St Alban's, which were referred to in a letter from Father Harker and demonstrated the easy translation of new design concepts to the farthest margins of the British Empire. Though remotely located and seemingly unable to influence his first choice of architect, Father Cooper managed to settle for the brother of the architect he wanted and got the design from his premier choice.

This explains why the correspondence between architect and client dealt almost exclusively with technical matters about experimenting with finishes on concrete surfaces and the decision to replace a costly dome with a cheaper wood-panel ceiling. Scott's elevation is dynamic and free, though neither ahistorical nor unprecedented. The octagonal crossing tower of Britain's fourteenth-century Ely Cathedral is a distant geometric relative, although St Alban's is the parent. The use of concrete in churches in Canada was relatively new, except that the material had been discussed in connection with the fire-proofing of industrial and commercial buildings.[25] Addressing aesthetic concerns of concrete finishes during the opening ceremonies of St James on 25 July 1936, Lieutenant Governor of Canada Lord Tweedsmuir, better known as the author John Buchan, lectured that "we moderns are committed to that material [concrete], and the sooner we get over our false modesty about it, the better for our taste and our pocket-book. To our stubborn minds, concrete still seems naked, and we must cover it up with a costly sham of tile and brick or granite. Its seems hard to learn that mere face-painting is bad architecture. Steel and concrete lend themselves not to petty surface decoration but to severe lines and great masses."[26]

Scott's massing of forms for the St James rebuild ignited the old debates about the way that churches should look, chief among them historicism versus modernism. The variety of visual imagery available to church-builders arrived in the Dominion largely through importing pattern books; prints, magazines, and postcards augmented the disagreement.

Case Study: St John the Divine, Victoria, BC

In 1912, the rebuilding of St John the Divine in Victoria (fig. 6.11) was awarded to the son-in-law architect of that church's Anglican Rev. Percival Jenns. The commission represented the inaugural foray into ecclesiastical architecture for Col. William Ridgway Wilson (1862–1957). Wilson trained in the London offices of architects Searles and Hayes, later specializing in office blocks, residences, and school buildings. At St John the Divine, Wilson's inexperience in ecclesiastical architecture was matched by the congregation's especial lack of architectural knowledge; they had been using a prefabricated cast-iron and sheet-metal building purchased in 1860 from W. Slater & Co. of England and known locally as the "Iron Church." This type of building had been marketed to colonial parishes as cheaper alternatives to the outcome of the architect/client relationship.

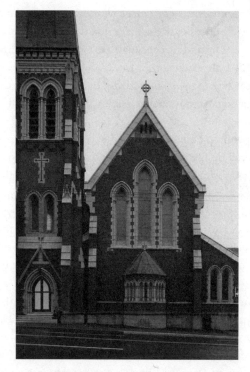

Fig. 6.11 St John the Divine Anglican Church, Victoria, BC.

The founding members of St John the Divine responded positively to prefabricated cast iron, though the same could not be said of their bishop. They did not have to give much thought to what an Anglican church ought to look like, since choosing a design from the manufacturers catalogue limited the aesthetic possibilities. The process of ordering through the catalogue, awaiting shipment, and arranging for someone to assemble the parts highlighted the consumerist aspect of architecture. The Bishop of British Columbia had to be pressed to consecrate the building on account of the temporary nature of iron buildings; bishops preferred not to consecrate temporary structures. Despite the initial novelty of the "Iron Church," its eventual removal proved to have been a good business decision. The streetcars that passed in front of the church must have reverberated at such a decibel inside the building that parishioners were momentarily deafened. Besides, the land had appreciated in value and was sold back to the Hudson's Bay Company for $140,000, a figure representing nearly all of the $170,000 cost of the new land and church construction.

The lack of knowledge about ecclesiastical architecture on the St John's project may have precipitated the building committee's approval, in 1912, of William Ridgway Wilson's historicist quotation of a church design more suited to the 1840s. The economical use of lancet windows, in pairs and triplets, and his judicious use of buttresses with double and triple weatherings were tell-tale signs of George Edmund Streets adaptive Gothic Revival. St John's composition of heavily buttressed corner tower and the gabled west end enclosing a triple lancet window was unexciting by 1920s standards. Wilson struggled to harmonize what amounted to a series of individual gothic motifs, including buttresses, windows, and doorways, as if each element had been cribbed from different church designs. This might certainly seem to be the case, except that the overall design is remarkably close to Arnold Woodroofe's (FRIBA) and Charles Osborn Wickenden's published drawing in the *Canadian Architect and Builder*, in 1903, for a Presbyterian church in Vancouver (fig. 6.12). Except for the gabled west entrance on the sketch of the Presbyterian church, Wilson's design for St John's is a quote of the sketch for the Presbyterian church. The relationship demonstrates the influence of print media and explains how a competent architect augmented his repertoire by looking at pictures of buildings when tackling unfamiliar grammar.

Wilson's adoption of an out-of-date vocabulary was logical given the conservative nature of the leadership at St John the Divine. Jenns was against the idea of empowering a synod of the Anglican Church in Canada to deal with ecclesiastical matters considered beyond the scope of ordinary folk. "As long as I remain in the Church of England I know what her laws are and I value them far too highly to cast them to the winds and be governed by those of so small a church as that of British Columbia."[27]

DIVERSITY AND POLITICS

The Protestant Churches combined social reform and liturgical reform as a focal point of human salvation. The equation had a strong moral imperative, expressed in sermon. A reduction of ritual in worship set them apart from Roman Catholic and Anglican worshipers. For that reason, Methodist religious knowledge was constituted in and guided by printed material and the spoken word. The reciprocal relationship between congregants and their minister, during the church service, was characterized by readings and sermonizing.

In reaction to this structure, the Anglican leadership in Canada was reluctant to recognize the legitimacy of other religious groups and Christian sects, believing that the Common Book of Prayer was the superior expression of Christian ceremony, rites, and sacraments. Cultural intolerance validated their objection to sharing social and economic advantages. Attempts to deny

Fig. 6.12 Design of a Presbyterian Church by Arnold Woodroofe and C.O. Wickenden.

the growth of Methodism in Ontario, Alberta, and British Columbia as well as concentrations of Orthodoxy in Ukranian and Greek Prairie settlements continued to put some Anglican leaders out of touch with the real situation. The immigration of multiple ethnic cultures produced a varied terrain of religious observance. Thrust together geographically in growing towns and cities and in rural places, different religions expressed their identity, and even rivalries, in architectural terms.

However, there was no truly dominant ideology, even though the Anglicans believed that Canada was a "Dominion" under their preserve and specific form of worship. The Anglican Church was ultimately unsuccessful in parlaying its unofficial "compact" with the leading members of Dominion society; it failed to monopolize the consecration of legal marriages and institutionalize Anglican education. Methodist marriages had already become legal in 1830, and the battle to open Anglican colleges was lost in 1850. The Anglican leadership tried to delegitimize the communal nature of Methodism, which focused power at the congregational level, without realizing that Methodists had organized under the umbrella of synods during the 1860s in a manner similar to the Church of England. Still, the similarities did not outweigh the differences and interdenominational rivalries in architecture expressed the serious business of distinction.

Thus, when Methodist church-builders divested themselves of the traditional meeting-house style of church architecture – a two-storey rectangular shell articulated with multi-pane sash windows – to adopt a neo-Gothic vocabulary, they legitimized a new spatial layout. The traditional longitudinal axis was reconfigured into a wider worship hall and, after the 1860s, an amphitheatrical seating arrangement. The removal of nave arcades improved sightlines and acoustics and was thus better suited to sermons from the pulpit. A chancel was not needed because it had a ritual function that was diminished in Evangelical practice. For this reason, the chancel arch became an aesthetic motif used to frame the organ and the pulpit. The change coincided roughly with the reorganization of Methodist faith from its previous focus on the conversion of sinners to its new focus on salvation.[28]

Attendant upon the expanded wealth of Methodist and other Evangelical sects, a new series of architectural pattern books written specifically for tectonic issues raised by nonconformist groups were introduced. Effective layouts and dynamic elevations were included in F.J. Jobson's *Chapel and School Architecture, as Appropriate to the Buildings of Nonconformists, Particularly to those of the Wesleyan Methodists: With Practical Directions for the Erection of Chapels and School-Houses* (1850), George Bidlake's *Sketches of Churches: Designed for the Use of Nonconformists* (1865), James Cubitt's *Church Designs for Congregations* (1870), and Joseph Crouch's *Church, Mission Halls, and Schools for Non-Conformists* (1901).[29] These books appeared at a time when the Evangelical branch of Christianity was searching for a way to define how churches should look. Some books, like Jobson's, were written exclusively for Methodist congregations and emphasized the importance of flexible interior spaces that could be converted into classrooms to teach the Gospel. Others were almost entirely picture books with little textual explanation, depicting modified neo-Gothic versions of churches acceptable to Anglicans. All three books were printed in Britain and filtered into booksellers in Canadian towns, where the expansion of the merchant classes augmented the Methodist ranks. Many shop assistants, mechanics, and day-labourers who earned a meagre living felt marginalized by their inability to contribute to the financial needs of the Anglican Church and found acceptance in the Methodist body.[30] Its proclivity for religious reform lead naturally to calls for social reform, fiery sermons, and public demonstrations for temperance.

The emergence of pattern books written specifically for Evangelical church-builders expressed the growing legitimacy of nonconformist spiritual choice. Architecture was a visible manifestation of difference, demonstrated in a series of books produced in the US by the architect Gurdon P. Randall of Chicago, Illinois. Between the 1860s and 1880s he marketed an eclectic assortment of neo-Renaissance and Free Classicist designs whose titles reflected the book's contents: *Descriptive and Illustrated Catalogue, Containing Plans in Perspective, of Colleges, School Houses, Churches, and Other Buildings, and Suggestions Relative to Their Construction, Heating and Ventilation* (1866). The book's rhetoric promoted the supremacy of an architect's knowledge and taste over that of a builder while simultaneously advertising the manufacture of goods and services pertaining to church construction. The incongruence of these two practices eroded the architect's traditional heroic public persona. Randall's self-promotion was explicit when he reissued his earlier book under a slightly different title two years later without changing a word. This was the hallmark of an architect attempting to vault himself into celebratory status using print media.

Comparative Case Study: Metropolitan Methodist Church,
Victoria, BC (1890)

The growth of the Methodist population in Victoria, British Columbia, in the 1880s coincided with a lull in the production of architectural pattern books addressing the architectural requirements of Evangelical churches. George Bidlake's *Sketches of Churches: Designs for the Use of Nonconformists* (1865) was outdated by the standards of the 1880s, and its reliance on the longitudinal plan and neo-Gothic format typical of Anglican churches was unacceptable to the Methodist individuality. In response, the building committee at Victoria's Metropolitan Methodist Church hired a local architect, Thomas Hooper (1857–1935), and sent him on an ambitious study of architecture in Eastern Canada and the US.[31]

The Methodist building committee wanted a progressive design and an open-minded architect. They selected Hooper because of his impressive design for Homer Street Methodist Church (1888) in Victoria (fig. 6.13), which

Fig. 6.13 Homer Street Methodist Church, Victoria, BC.

offered a viable alternative to the Gothic Revival style. The architect's close acquaintance with the Methodist missionary, Ebenezer Robson, brother of British Columbia Premier John Robson, was particularly useful for the commission.[32] In meetings with the architect, the building committee outlined their desire to have a large facility capable of housing offices, Sunday school, and worship hall under one roof. They were also concerned that the exterior of the new premises not resort to neo-Gothic, which had strong ceremonial and ritual associations with the Anglican and Roman Catholic Churches.

Hooper returned to Victoria from the eastern United States with a new appreciation for the Romanesque Revival, particularly the musculature of Henry Hobson Richardson's Holy Trinity Anglican Church in Boston (1872–77). The brawny round arches and sculptural richness combined with a mature compositional massing of load bearing walls influenced Hooper's choices for Metropolitan Methodist in Victoria. The strong play of light and shadow on Richardson's rusticated envelope, deepened in the recessed windows, was qualified for Canadian consumption by the *Canadian Architect and Builder*'s 1888 depiction of Palmerston Baptist Church by the firm Langley and Burke (fig. 6.14). Embarking on his journey only a few months after the publication of the Palmerston church, Hooper set out to see, firsthand, what Romanesque Revival looked like and determine its usefulness.

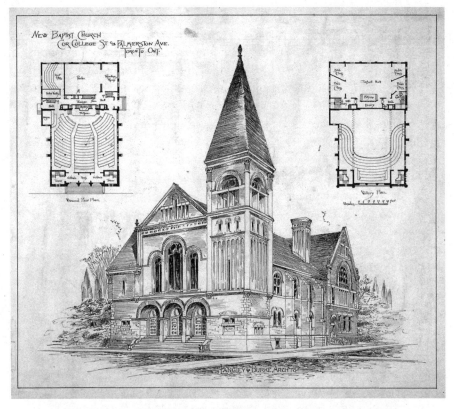

Fig. 6.14 Prospective design for Palmerston Baptist Church by Henry Langley and Edmund Burke.

Upon his return to Victoria and conscious to avoid associations with what the Anglican cohort were doing in architecture, Hooper combined the robust massing of Romanesque Revival with the privileged class associations of Scottish Baronial motifs. He grafted circular hanging turrets onto the Richardsonian tectonics, resulting in the amalgamation of round corner tower and gabled ends joined at right angles into a new Romanesque Revival recipe. This recipe did not initially include the expensive rusticated masonry popularized by Richardson, although the building committee ordered their contractor, Mr W.H. Burkholder, to use it. The change in materials put grave financial pressure on Burkholder, whose $50,224 accounted for timber only. The rich exterior and eclectic flair went largely unnoticed in the local press. The *Victoria Daily Colonist* remarked on the ornamental and handsome rose window and pleasing neutral tint of the interior wall finishes as though describing a newly built home.[33]

RELIGIOUS DIVERGENCE

Unwavering conviction described the positions of the Abrahamic faiths with regard to each groups' claims to religious purity and social respectability. Few religious institutions recognized the legitimacy of other groups. Each was sustained by its own doctrine's narrow interpretations of religious thought. This divergence extended to congregational intrarelationships, tearing into social cohesion. The emergence of religious synods, conferences, and assemblies on a national scale mirrored Canada's efforts to self-govern but also veiled these internal disputes. Religion was part of the agenda in the 1837 Papineau Rebellion in Lower Canada, which raised the issue of race, French identity, and nationality. The 1837 Mackenzie Rebellion manifested as a response to the social and economic privileges of the Family Compact, which spread an Anglican bias.

The Anglican contingent excelled in claims to social superiority, confirmed by economic advantage, that they metaphorically engraved onto the Anglican Book of Common Prayer. This position legitimized the award of land and choice political appointments to family and friends of the Compact's patriarch, D'Arcy Robinson. Disregarding the will of a weak elected legislative assembly, the Compact's actions raised the ire of Methodist, Presbyterian, and other settlers. It resulted in a fear of the spread and escalation of localized violence that ultimately prompted the British Colonial Office to suspend the Constitution in the Dominion and appoint Lord Durham (John Lambton) to the post of Governor General. It effectively made his post into a constitutional monarch in the Dominion. Durham's famous 1839 Report accepted the minority view of the English-speaking business community in Montreal: that French-Canadian society – resolutely Roman Catholic – was "priest-ridden and unprogressive."[34] Lord Durham urged the British Crown to "settle the matter" of Anglican minority in Lower Canada by adopting a policy favouring the union of Upper and Lower Canada in order to make the French a minority and undermine the quest for French nationalism. Flying Britain's regimental flags and the Union Jack, Britain's national emblem, from the pillars of Anglican churches was an intentional demonstration of social continuity. "Those who claimed to be descendants of natives of Scotland, Ireland, England, or France were the same class of people with the same customs, institutions, and laws."[35] For this reason, the flag – like church pattern books – were a visible means of expressing settlement expansion under the influence of the established Church, thereby recalling Old World privilege and social prestige.

Comparative Case Study: The Episcopal Church of Our Lady, Victoria BC

In 1855, a permanent rift developed among the Anglican contingent in Victoria, BC, because of fundamental disagreements in theology that grew between the chaplain of the Hudson's Bay Company, Edward Cridge, and the bishop of the diocese George Hills. The two men came into direct conflict over the bishop's authority, which culminated in Hills censure of Cridge's Low Church position, writ publicly as disloyalty to the bishop. Cridge became incensed by the bishop's invitation to Archdeacon W.S. Reese of Vancouver to preach a High Church sermon at the newly consecrated cathedral in 1874. The tempo of the situation escalated in the print media as each party reported inflammatory things about the other, and a crescendo was reached during a protracted court battle that was part media circus. In the end, the Evangelical Cridge was ousted from the cathedral and consequently assembled a large contingent of dissatisfied members, forming a branch of the US Episcopal Church in Victoria. He was elected missionary bishop of the Episcopal Church in 1875, giving some credence to the supposition that his arguments with Bishop Hills was as much a matter of personal politics as it was of churchmanship.

In 1874, Cridge's delegation found itself immediately in need of a new church building. They benefited from the power, prestige, and money given by one of their more prominent members, Sir James Douglas, the second governor of Vancouver Island and a former factor of the Hudson's Bay Company. He donated two town lots for the new church and also supplied 10 percent of the total $9,700 building cost. Wasting little time, they hired the local architect John Teague, who had designed several churches and public buildings in Victoria. He was given the mandate to produce a set of drawings for a church that reflected their Evangelical character. Teague was instructed to forego architectural associations with the Anglican Church – muscular arcading, historical references to specific medieval periods and precedents – yet the building committee readily accepted the Gothic vocabulary that the Church of England had dominated for so many years. Teague settled on the US variety of Carpenter's Gothic, popularized in pattern books by well-known US architects A.J. Davis and A.J. Downing. Yet, the exterior cladding and simple rose window in the west gable resembled a model published in the Ecclesiological Society's pattern book *Instrumenta Ecclesiastica* (1856) (see fig. 3.5, page 78). The drawings he gave to Cridge, eventually dedicated as the Reformed Church of Our Lady (fig. 6.15), shared architectural features with a Presbyterian church published in *A Hand Book of Designs, Containing Plans*

Fig. 6.15 The Reformed Episcopal Church of Our Lord, Victoria, BC.

in Perspective (1868) by the Chicago architect Gurdon P. Randall. The architectural features included a western gable enclosing a round window, surmounted by a bellcote and symmetrical finials. Teague also benefited from the extra width of the church designed by Randall, visually moderated by the vertical articulation of the board-and-batten cladding. The choice to clad the church with California Redwood was at least peripherally related to the promotion of Red Pine in US pattern books such as Samuel Sloan's *The Model Architect* (1852). The influence of US architecture and the Episcopal Church in Victoria is ironic but not isolated regardless of the city's reputation for "Englishness."

SOURCES OF PRESBYTERIAN CHURCHES FOR BRITISH COLUMBIA

The Scottish ancestry of the majority of those allied with the Presbyterian Church accounted for a large, but not exclusive, part of that ministry. Because the aesthetics of church buildings reflected the cultural heritage of its congregants, the Scottish Baronial style became a viable architectural fashion for many Presbyterian groups. The relatively quick increase in the Presbyterian population strained the finances of individual congregations. Internal divisions developed such as the one between the Rev. Thomas Somerville and a group of congregants, which resulted in the establishment of St Andrew's Presbyterian Church in Victoria. Wanting to erect a new church quickly, the building committee advertised a premium payment of $100 to the architect who supplied the most appropriate design. In 1868, the architect Hermann Otto Tiedemann was selected. By the late 1880s, and roughly coincident with the fire of 1889 that destroyed large parts of urban Victoria, the congregation decided to erect a larger church that was more consistent with the Scottish heritage of the core part of the congregation.

COMPARATIVE CASE STUDY: ST ANDREW'S PRESBYTERIAN CHURCH, VICTORIA, BC (1890)

Before construction began on the Presbyterian church of St Andrew's on Douglas and Broughton, the building was already pronounced "comfortable and complete in all its appointments" as well as "the most beautiful and imposing [church] in Victoria."[36] Rev. Macleod described it as "commodious" prior to being able to set foot inside the church structure. The sale of new subscriptions to raise 2/3 of the building costs, estimated to be a total of $40,000 prompted the optimism.

The round-headed windows of Trimen's Romanesque Revival design were as far from Gothic as a medieval revival church could come without attaching itself to neo-Renaissance and Roman Catholicism. However, the "real" innovation was the building's auditorium plan and amphitheatrical seating, in which "everyone commands views of the pulpit platform and a back seat is as good as one in the front."[37] The architect's attention to acoustics and improved lighting were evident in the arched ceiling and the use of the new technology of electric light. The eclectic use of polychromatic brickwork and a diaper-patterned roof demonstrated the design was fairly up to date.

Other Romanesque Revival churches of the day were illustrated in the *Canadian Architect and Builder;* these included the Palmerston Baptist Church by the partnership of Langley and Burke, and St Andrew's Presbyterian by the architectural partnership of Power and Son. These illustrations demonstrate the centrally planned auditorium-style arrangement of space as opposed to the longitudinal axis. From the exterior, the centrally planned church appears to have two main facades, though one is usually primary as is the case with the Douglas St Entrance of St Andrew's. The adoption of two facades on the centrally planned church emphasized the structural massing of spatial components, resulting in a heavier aesthetic.

The Presbyterian Church's interest in using the Romanesque Revival as a way to determine what a church of their order should look like was demonstrated in their pattern book *Designs for Village, Town and City Churches*. The book illustrates a design for a church in Assiniboia by W.A. Langton of Toronto, who noted the stepped gables, which was amplified in Trimen's earlier design for St Andrew's. Within three years of the completion of St Andrew's Church the congregation was undergoing another serious internal dispute that threatened to cause a split. In a public display of temper the Rev. Macleod notified the congregation about his displeasure over having his stipend reduced. The congregation had been facing financial difficulties for several years and had accumulated $12,340 in interest charges on a mortgage of $50,283. The annual revenues were only $2,262, which was barely enough to pay their reverend's $2,000 stipend.

The financial troubles contributed to some internal tensions that had been brewing for some time. Rev. Macleod and some prominent members of the congregation blamed each other for the church's financial problems. The situation became so heated that a church tribunal was called with testimony heard from the clergyman and Mrs Ballantyne, who challenged the Rev. Macleod on moral grounds, highlighting the connection between morality, economy, and religion.

Eclectic uses of architectural typologies grew as the general public became accustomed to seeing a wide variety of churches illustrated and constructed. The pattern books justified whatever version of historicism an architect chose to champion, whether it was one founded on archaeological precedent or one that supported the development of style. Architects used pattern books to promote individual self-interest, to shut down the values held by others, and to convert claims to taste into professional prestige. However, the same architects, in loose cooperation with the viewing public, merely succeeded in widening a market that was uncontrolled by any one theory, style, or practitioner.

Viewers and users of buildings became increasingly interested in newness, though it continued to be veiled in some aspect of history. The Scottish Baronial style that was loosely considered to be under the banner of "modern gothic" was valued by some Protestant church-builders for cultural associations no less than as a device to highlight cultural difference. Responding to a more complex set of social cues, builders of Jewish synagogues in urban settings often adopted Renaissance vocabulary in order to blend in with their religious and secular surroundings. Persecution during the pogroms of Eastern Europe drew some Jewish groups to the Prairies to pursue farming and related businesses. A small Winnipeg community of 1,164 Jews in 1871 grew substantially by the 1890s, requiring the construction of a purpose-built synagogue. The congregation, naming itself Rosh Pina, chose to use a neo-Gothic language for their elevation that was not unlike those examples found in various pattern books used by nonconformist church-builders. Cognizant of anti-Semitism in Canada, the builders of Rosh Pina wished to veil the exterior of the worship hall with socially acceptable architecture. Synagogue architecture had no strict historical antecedents, so cultural references like the onion-shaped turrets illustrated the Russian ancestry of the community.

Nowhere did this widening medieval vocabulary and development of modern gothic stand out more clearly than in the confidence applied by US architects. This trait was apparent in every one of the church pattern books produced in the United States, showing that US architects were adept self-promoters eventually organizing large architectural practices into virtual factories of production employing dozens of draughtsmen.

7

THE INFLUENCE OF US ARTISTIC, CULTURAL, AND ECONOMIC CAPITAL

PRESSURE FROM US ARCHITECTS

The US publishing business eventually influenced the importation of pattern books to Canada. Overland rail and waterway transport made it possible for New York and Philadelphia publishers to ship directly to markets in Toronto, Winnipeg, and even Vancouver. The mergers and buyouts among Canadian booksellers in the 1880s resulted from the perceived threats of US book distribution.[1] John Sebastian Helmcken (1824–1920), speaker of the British Columbia Legislature and an Anglican (later a reformed Episcopalian after a schism with Bishop Hills in Victoria) expressed the threat, remarking on the probability that "not only this colony, but the whole Dominion of Canada, will be absorbed by the United States."[2] With the majority of Canadian book sales being comprised of US titles, Canada's importers worsened the situation by advertising that they could get books from Boston and New York within a week of their publication at a quarter the price of British first editions.

What made the church pattern books produced by US architects popular was that their authors embraced the eclecticism of High Victorian Gothic with vigour and panache. Their infatuation with structural polychromy (black and red bands and zigzag patterns in brickwork), dramatically asymmetrical floorplans, curved motifs used in towers, and a great sense of aesthetic liberty appeared infectious among many church-builders in Canada. The influence of John Ruskin's *Stones of Venice*, showing the richness of Italian brickwork, not only influenced William Butterfield at All Saints, Margaret Street, London, but had a wider effect on the authors of US pattern books. The showmanship of High Victorian Gothic was something that US architects could sink their teeth into. Henry Hudson Holly's use of structural polychromy is a fine example that runs throughout many of his designs in *Church Architecture* (1871).

Case Study: St Mary's Roman Catholic Church (1899–1902), Indian River, PEI

On 4 August 1896, St Mary's Roman Catholic Church in Indian River was struck by lightning as the Reverend Monsignor D.J. Gillis stood on a nearby veranda saying his rosary. On or about the same time he was struck with the idea of creating a new church in the image of one he particularly admired in Kinkora, PEI, which featured an impressive groined ceiling of lightly stained birch wood. The architect William Critchlow Harris (1854–1913) produced a satisfactory set of drawings, and skilled carpenters were hired to complete the new church (fig. 7.1). Like at St Malachy's at Kinkora, Harris adopted a mix of French neo-Gothic based on the fashions occurring at the time in Quebec, Britain, and the polychromatic vocabulary popular in the United States. Though Harris visited Montreal on several occasions to inspect churches similar to his final design for St Mary's he was generally not a well-travelled architect. Besides some time working in Winnipeg, Manitoba, Harris spent

Fig. 7.1 St Mary's Roman Catholic Church, Indian River, Prince Edward Island.

most of his life on Prince Edward Island, a bachelor living in a modest apartment. His apprenticeship to the architect David Sterling, who was a fine practitioner but not a major exponent of High Victorian Gothic, could not have ignited Harris's imagination. It is difficult to deny that Harris's flair for injecting an additional level of drama into High Victorian Gothic design is also found in the US pattern books in the 1870s and 80s.

The polychrome picked out in the painted detail at St Mary's Church was a trademark of Harris's vocabulary. He appreciated the deep contrast in tones, a robust addition to his sense of asymmetrical planning. The rounded corner tower distinctly accentuated an otherwise standard cruciform church design. The tower's round form stands out like the major note of a scale, when played in a chord, increasing its resonance. The rounded forms of the interior timber-vaulted ceiling designed to improve acoustics had clear references to French medieval models illustrated in pattern books. Raphael and J. Arthur Brandon's *Open Timber Roofs of the Middle Ages* asserted itself as the essential text on its niche subject. The subject of acoustics was taken up by the US architect and pattern book author Charles P. Dwyer, who prescribed that, "in taking up the subject of church construction, there are some points worthy of particular attention; namely, the absolute necessity for hearing distinctly in every part of the building ... and perfect accommodation of the auditory."[3] The merits of designing a church to act as an acoustic instrument closely resembled Harris's design ideas. He was an avid amateur musician.

A MOSTLY DIRECT PATH

The technical advances and stylistic experimentation evident in US publications appeared to provide a competitive advantage to US architects entering competitions in Canada from their offices in the United States. Canadians complained about the loss of local jobs and their concerns about cross-border competition prompted the formation of professional organizations on a regional scale. Intentional restriction of competition from the US and the promotion of Canadian architecture occupied the discussions of these nascent organizations. The merits of establishing architecture schools in Canada as a means of improving the standards and quality of architectural output was a significant consequence of US competition.

Awarding large projects to US architects drew criticism from the Ontario Association of Architects as well as the *Canadian Architect and Builder*. The journal published the OAA's letter of complaint to the Manufacturer's Life Association, which had hired, in 1907, the Detroit firm of Donaldson & Meyer to design their new headquarters on Bay Street in Toronto. "There seems to be every reason why a company chiefly supported by the citizens of Canada should carry out the principle of not procuring outside of Canada what can be got at home and there is no reason to question the ability of Toronto architects to properly design and erect a building of twelve stories," they charged, adding: "it lies with the capitalists of the city to give [Canadian architects] that opportunity."[4] Using British Columbia as a counterexample it is evident that a clutch of architects, engineers, and surveyors, whose careers had matured in the US, did not lack for opportunities to erect churches; among them: the architect Charles Clow of Detroit (1860–1929), who emigrated in 1883 and designed the Reformed Episcopal Church, New Westminster, in 1899; Thomas McKay (1842–1887), who moved north from California and made the leap from contractor to architect with the design of St Peter's Catholic Church, New Westminster, in 1886; the architect, J. Eugene Freeman (1856–1926), who exemplified the cross-border architectural relationship between BC and California with regards to church-building and economy. Freeman trained two years in San Francisco under the prominent architect William F. Smith, advanced himself to partner, and then attached himself to the Dunsmuir family of California, wealthy mine owners and industrialists. He was commissioned by them to build Grace Methodist Church (1894) in Cumberland, BC, where the prestigious family maintained a second residence.

US political economy attached itself to the development of architecture in Canada through the men who influenced Canadian infrastructure. The two Americans appointed to oversee the CPR, Cornelius William Van Horne (1843–1915, born Frankfort, Illinois) and his successor, Thomas Shaughnessy (1853–1923, born Milwaukee, Wisconsin), exposed Canadians to US marketing methods. They gambled successfully that increasing the number of luxurious Pullman sleeping cars, produced at the Pullman facility near Chicago, Illinois, would translate into proportionately higher passenger service.[5] The Pullman cars were too heavy for the steep inclines through the Rockies, so the company ventured into the hotel business, initially to ensure passengers were able to dine in style around the mountain passes. The combined business and tourist rail travellers accommodated on new routes at recently completed CPR hotels translated into record profits for the company. This exuberant promotion combined with scientific marketing, which increased the traffic of an affluent clientele on the CPR rail lines, also increased the trafficking of taste in the pattern books.

The matter-of-fact layout of illustrations in early pattern books by architects such as Andrew Jackson Downing influenced the easy-to-read format adopted by the next generation of US authors such as Frederick Withers and

Henry Hudson Holly. The staple of Withers's book *Church Architecture: Plans Views and Perspectives of Twenty-One Churches* (1873) was two-dimensional elevation drawings and sections of churches peppered with the odd picturesque views to add panache. Henry Hudson Holly employed something of the picturesque in his drawings, although he included simple full-page plans that provided just enough information to promote a particular design. It was a typical ploy among US architects to offer the complete set of plans by mail, inviting building committees to make contact. All of this was intended to keep builders out of the architecture profession, especially prior to the period before accredited schools developed. The architect Amos Bicknell included technical data and sample contracts in *Bicknell's Victorian Village* (1873) to arm customers against unscrupulous contractors. Similar attitudes existed in Canada.

The US sensibility that John Teague adapted to the Carpenter's Gothic of the Reformed Episcopal Church of Our Lord in Victoria established the architect's heroic character. Teague's practice was encouraged by the apparent civic and cultural expansion of the City of Victoria, believing itself to be the recipient of the CPR terminus until its disappointment in 1885, when Vancouver (formerly Hasting's Mill) was chosen as the railway's terminus. Teague was a fierce competitor, ousting the leading practitioner in Victoria, H.O. Tiedemann, into retirement. He received more than 350 commissions during his long career, completing many buildings on Vancouver's Island and in the capital city of Victoria. It was clear that Teague had adopted the bravado of the US architects A.J. Davis and A.J. Downing by reading their pattern books. He harvested the best samples of bargeboard cut-out patterns from house designs in their books and installed them in the gables of his churches. At the same time he borrowed the majestic hammer-beam roof for the open timber ceiling from Raphael and J. Arthur Brandon's pattern book *Open Timber Roofs*. Archaeological precedent was modified by Teague, who seemed content to procure motifs from history as one would flip through the pages of designs laid out like mail-order catalogues. It was expert self-promotion and a personal "manifest destiny" that appeared to launch Teague to the top of his profession in the region.

Architects who used self-promotion to their advantage approached it with care while others were more deliberate. US pattern book authors like George Woodward advertised the sale of previous volumes inside the pages of new books: *Woodward's Architecture and Rural Art* contained ads for *Woodward's National Architect*. The idea seems to have been to create a dynasty of book volumes that never became stale. The purpose of this type of marketing was the attempt to set Woodward up as the source for an inexperienced clientele searching for a design and an architect. However, the price point demonstrated that new material was more highly valued by the reading public even if the designs contained in the new books were not appreciably different from the old. Older editions of Woodward's books sold for less than $2.00, as compared to new volumes of *National Architect* priced at $12.00, meaning that customers might upsell themselves after exhausting the cheaper edition. On the basis of pricing alone, it was difficult for Woodward to establish the dynasty of knowledge he appeared to have desired.

While the inclusion of advertisements positioned the church pattern books as nascent magazines, marketing architectural fashion as taste, some US authors added full-page illustrations of interior church scenes whose purpose blatantly marketed historical ideals. Henry Hudson Holly's *Church Architecture* contained contrasting interiors – "The Reformation" and "The Deformation" – that depicted the merits of the Episcopal Church versus pre-nineteenth century forms of worship (fig. 7.2). In "The Deformation," two lonely parishioners – a man and his wife – sit on a cold and uncomfortable bench listening to the sermon from one of three different preachers, each removed to a pulpit. The sleeping husband and his distracted wife have their backs to the officiating clergy. The dilapidated building is in disarray. The Gothic arch, which appears to frame a gallery and not the chancel, has been pushed dangerously out of vertical by the slanted roof of the aisle. A depressed archway related to neo-Classical domestic interiors frames the triple pulpit. In the foreground, the octagonal font, though constructed in a form reminiscent of medieval fonts, is used to hold the gentlemen's hats instead of Holy Water. The shabbiness of the church in "The Deformation" stands in direct opposition to that in "The Reformation," whose consistent vertical lines and pristine condition evokes piety, humility, and social stability. An attentive congregation faces the high altar, encompassed by the verticality of the stone rib-vault above the chancel. The vaulted interior allows the chancel to be pierced by a full suite of triple lancet windows encompassed by a framing arch with plate tracery at its apex. The congregation is depicted listening dutifully to the sermon delivered from the pulpit located not at the extreme east but in the crossing arch beneath the tower, an arrangement indicative of a cathedral. The clear model for Holly's polemical set of drawings, published in the 1870s, was Augustus Welby Pugin's first book, *Contrasts* (1836), in which is shown the social benefits of an archaeologically "correct" medieval gothic architecture. A famous pair of contrasting images in Pugin's book shows the medieval versus the modern town, in which the former retains its connection with religion through a proliferation of church spires while the latter depicts tax houses and insane asylums in the foreground. The connections between truth,

Fig. 7.2 Specimen page of "The Deformation and the Reformation" in the House of God from *Church Architecture*.

taste, beauty, and religion no less than architectural function were described by Holly as the antithesis of "bad architecture and shams of all kinds [that] exemplify the fraud and neglect of ecclesiology which so militate against true art."[6]

The image of a church spoiled by misuse and careless religious observance resonated with audiences in the late nineteenth and early twentieth centuries. It indicates that Anglican churchmen continued to be concerned about the future of their stations, something that showed in complaints about poor and casual attendance at Sunday sermon. What worked to the advantage of the clergy were social pressures to conform with a way of life that was approved of by religious authorities. The same concerns and social pressures were at the heart of the illustration in Holly's pattern book, which operated as a serious condemnation and as a humorous distraction. The drawing's dramatic presence among a series of architectural patterns shows that the supporters of religious institution still believed that they had plenty of work to do in guiding the conscience of society.

CONCLUSION

The commercial orientation of the social fabric was a significant factor in settlement expansion. Its characterization in the spread of religious enterprise was exemplified in the distribution and use of church pattern books. Architects and church-building committees used the pattern books differently, though each participated in a "commerce of taste" that marketed the transience of fashion as the enduring qualities of taste. The social and economic claims associated with taste invigorated free choice, competition, and variety while also maintaining the exclusivity and privilege held by dominant groups. Through the variety of designs promoted in the pattern books, architects inadvertently empowered the clients they sought to control. The spread of the pattern books proved that taste-cum-fashion was available to all, ultimately disrupting the heroic character of the architect.

The argument seemed always to return to the idea of taste as the trump card played to decide a close contest. Taste was often mentioned in association with an aesthetic appeal anchored by the pragmatics of economy as though the latter was the one undeniable factor. A review of the pattern book by the US author Reverend George Bowler, *Chapel and Church Architecture* (1856), pursued exactly this mix of special qualities: "That the plans and sketches of church architecture, designed and drawn by our brother, Rev. George Bowler, evince, in a high degree, *correctness of taste* and skill in execution, combining in themselves, to an extent seldom equalled, *beauty, economy, and convenience*; and we feel confident that the publication of the work would be of essential service to the churches in this country."[1]

Validating the pattern book and highlighting the connective tissue holding together economy, taste, and religious architecture the review applauded Bowler for presenting attractive designs that ranged in cost between $1,500 and $20,000. It further noted that the purpose of Bowler's book was to "enable committees to decide on some style previous to making application to an architect, so that they may convey their ideas and wishes clearly." According to this, taste was available at virtually any price, though exclusive to those who played along. Playing along meant that one asserted claims about the way churches should look, disregarding the claims of all others.

Church-building committees – composed of influential businessmen, lawyers, and senior-level members of the clergy, wielding the power of aesthetic choice – had to be guided through varied architectural vocabulary. The pattern book was the expedient tool of choice. The rapidly expanding book trade and the spread of religious institution across multiple Christian denominations resulted in numerous iterations of the Gothic Revival church. The slipperiness of taste in a social context, underlined by the effects of capitalism on religion, required a framework that visualized human interactions as relationships in oscillation.

Selling mechanically reproduced visual imagery liquidated the apparent authenticity and mystifying elements of the original work of art but also commodified the value of representation. Like the heroic character of the architect in society, the mystical authority employed by religious institution, was disrupted by modern science and technology. The mechanical spread of print-based visual and verbal imagery brought about a varied and opportunistic use of church illustrations. That the debates coalesced around the way churches should look meant that the agency of the pattern books was both embraced and contested in the context of imperial and colonial authority.

The spread of church architecture masked fashion as science and knowledge as did civil and consumer society. Wealthy and powerful people who benefited from the uneven situation of capitalism veiled Canada's social inequities behind egalitarian terms that included *prosperity*, *progress*, and *science*. On the one hand, the exchanges of cultural, economic, and artistic capital appeared to offer social mobility to any participant. The distribution of church pattern books certainly appeared to make taste (or more properly fashion) available to all. On the other hand, the social elite and the architects they employed continued to claim that the "truly" enduring qualities of taste related to one's pedigree, education, and wealth. As a result, a large part of the social apparatus, contemporaneously advertised as egalitarian, was used to deny social mobility to a large portion of the working class and poorer populace. The pattern books illustrated churches as societal commodities, virtually in a department-store fashion. This indicated the depth to which the corporate strategy had permeated other areas of cultural and religious production. The focus of architecture in the public domain, aided by the pattern books' presentation of plastics, largely drove issues of aesthetics rather than liveability.

The potency of church-building and of the pattern books' imagery emanated from configurations of public taste. Similar patterns of public taste in the late-nineteenth and early twentieth centuries were constituted in the new commercial practices existing in department stores. The cycle of production and consumption was awakened by objectives to create and market new knowledge systems, including new construction techniques in church-building. The spread of these new knowledge systems connected settlement expansion with the enactment of civil society. The book trade in Canada spread the imagery of civil society, particularly in relation to the importance of religion, whether or not piety was actually at the heart of the new commercial society. Thus, the church pattern books demonstrated how new marketing schemes were adopted to sell the old ideas of religion in societies still making transition from agrarian to commercial structures, an activity representative of mapmaking, planning, and communication systems.

In the view of European settlers, the spread of knowledge in books contrasted sharply with the oral traditions of indigenous peoples. The juxtaposition served to enhance Western ideology and Anglican doctrine. Thus, national imaginings more ephemeral than actual were equated with the westerly spread of booksellers and thus of European knowledge. Despite the social freedoms marketed alongside the development of Canada, the constrained rules of imperialism and monopoly resonated with the public. The transfer of knowledge from Europe and the US to Canada indicated the power of British culture and the hegemony of the US commercial market. The pattern books followed the grand historical narratives of dominant cultures constituted as such by advanced capital. The pattern books also represented the categorization of architectural styles, nuanced by the variety of imagery on display. They were part of the national imaginings inherent in the unfinished business of Confederation, marketed as the final stage of building the country while denying legitimacy to First Nations and Métis.

Many religious institutions forged new territory, creating a regulatory infrastructure ahead of the political apparatus. This explains why Alberta and Saskatchewan established Anglican "provinces: within the larger Church structure before the two regions entered into political union with the Dominion of Canada. As an important component in identity formation, settlement expansion in the Prairies was felt in regional rather than national terms. The railway project to connect the coasts across an unimaginable distance was emblematic of the ambitions of church-builders to unify specific but distant communities through religion. In reality, religion was offered to everyone, even though churches benefited from the wealthy and thus provided residual benefits accordingly. Thus, churches were not places of social equality that the pattern books advertised.

The variety and sheer number of neo-Gothic churches built across the Dominion vied for – and complicated – national identity. A satisfactory compromise was never achieved because the heterogeneous viewing public did not officially champion a single style for Canada. The sense of disorder was equally reflected in the inability of architects to organize even regional self-regulatory bodies based on a standard set of principles. Many attempts to organize self-regulatory bodies resulted in their disbanding due to internal squabbling.

The ideology and identity in printed legislation and in journals of architectural criticism that influenced church-building were sustained by the larger economic, religious, and cultural apparatus. Economy and print reproduction combined in pattern books of churches to create a textural surface of concentrated settlement, consecrated under the auspices of religious and secular governments. Taken together the pattern books presented a deliberate attempt to order patterns of public taste through economy, and this affected not only architecture but also the deployment of religion.

APPENDIX: BIOGRAPHIES OF PATTERN BOOK AUTHORS

RAPHAEL BRANDON (1817–1877)

Raphael Brandon completed numerous restorations of medieval buildings, primarily churches and chapels. In 1846–48 he worked on the restoration of St Martin, Leicester with his brother J.A. Brandon, again in 1851–52 with Robert Richie, in 1857 while in partnership with Freshwater, and finally in 1861–62 with Broadbent.

He built several railway stations and engine houses on the London-Croydon line in the 1840s, in which chimneys were disguised as the bell towers of early Gothic churches. He designed the Apostolic Church in Gordon Square (1851–55), the actors' church (near Picadilly Circus, demolished April 1854), and St Peter's, Great Windmill St (1860–61). He was predeceased by his wife and child, went into depression, and committed suicide in 1877 by self-inflicted gunshot wound to the head. Brandon was best known for architectural books of the Gothic Revival, including *An Analysis of Gothic Architecture* (1849), *Open Timber Roofs of the Middle Ages* (1849), and *Parish Churches* (1848).

Source
Transactions of the Jewish Historical Society of England, vol. 18 (1954): 127–41.

JAMES KELLAWAY COLLING (1816–1905)

James Kellaway Colling described himself as a draughtsman more than as an architect. He completed the lithographic plates for other architects' pattern books. He knew Raphael Brandon, having completed the lithographic plates for Brandon's pattern book *Parish Churches* (1848).

Between 1849 and 1855 Colling drew architectural subjects on wood for the *Illustrated London News,* including the 1851 Exhibition building, Houses of Parliament, and Northumberland House. His pattern books included *Gothic Ornaments, Being a Series of Samples of Enriched Details* (1846), *Details of Gothic Architecture: Measured and Drawn from Existing Examples* (1852), *Art Foliage, for Sculpture and Decoration, with an Analysis of Geometric Form, and Studies from Nature of Buds, Leaves, Flowers, and Fruit* (1865), and *English Medieval Ornament* (1874).

His buildings included Hooton Hall, Cheshire; the Albany, Liverpool (a large block of offices); St Paul, Cheshire, Hooton; Ashewicke Hall, Gloscestershire; Coxwold Hall, Lincolnshire; Popham Church, Hants, 1875 (demolished). In 1891–93 he designed the National Portrait Gallery with Ewan Christian, who was a fellow pupil of Habershon nearly fifty years earlier. His restoration commissions included Eye Church, Suffolk; Hingham Church, Norfolk; Arthingworth Church and Kelmarsh Church, Northamptonshire; Scole Church, Norfolk; Melbury Church, Dorset; Oakley Church, Suffolk; and the Chapel of the Mercers Company, London; new Grammar school at Eye.

Colling was an important drawing teacher to William Eden Nesfield. Colling died at the age of ninety on 1 September 1905. He had been an associate of RIBA 1856 and Fellow 1860, resigned 1885. He helped found the Architectural Association, and he founded the Architectural Draughtsmen in 1842. In 1851, he established an architectural museum, an outgrowth of Cottingham's Museum.

His books were not without their controversy. *The American Architect,* in 1905, wrote that his books had a most unhappy influence on American architecture because students of medieval design thought that his books were treasuries of Gothic ornamentation. According to that journal's editors, students believed that the integration of some of Colling's designs into their would accomplish a perfected Gothic design.

Sources

RIBA *Journal* vol. 9 (1902): 44.

Obituary, *The Builder* vol. 89 (1905): 281.

Margaret Henderson Floyd," A Terra Cotte Cornerstone for Copley Square: Museum of Fine Arts, Boston 1870–76 by Sturgis and Brigham," *JSAH* vol. 32, no.83 (1973): 103.

Jill Franklin, *The Gentleman's Country House and Its Plan: 1835–1914* (London: Routledge, 1981).

Quentin Hughes, *Seaport: Architecture and Townscape in Liverpool* (London: Lund Humphries, 1964).
Owen Jones, *The Grammar of Ornament*, 100-103.
Andrew Saint, *Richard Norman Shaw* (London: Yale University Press, 1976): 3, 440.
John Summerson, *The Architectural Association 1847–1947* (1947).
Theodore Turak, "French and English Sources of Sullivan's Ornament and Doctrine," *Prairie School Review* vol. 11, no. 4: 5, 28.

HENRY HUDSON HOLLY (1834–1892)

Henry Hudson Holly, born in New York, NY, was an architect and pattern book author. His first book, *Country Seats*, was published in 1863, and it was followed in 1871 by *Church Architecture*. He practiced in partnership with Horatio F. Jelliff after 1887. His architectural credits include the Virginia Military Institute at Lexington, St Luke's Memorial Hall at the University of the South, and a palatial residence in Colorado reported to have cost $400,000.

Source
Obituary, *American Architect and Building News* 9 July 1892; see also 3 November 1878.

FRANK E. KIDDER (1859–1905)

Franklin E. Kidder, born in Bangor, Maine, was in practice as an architect and engineer for only a short period and thereafter devoted his time to writing books. He was well known as the author of *Kidder's Architects' and Builders' Handbook*, first published in 1884 and later undergoing eighteen editions up to 1944. His architectural training occurred at Cornell University's School of Architecture, and in 1880 he graduated in Engineering from the Massachusetts Institute of Technology. Poor health forced him to abandon an attempt to start an office in Boston. He moved to Denver about 1888 and continued to work in that city until 1891, associated for a time with John J. Humphreys.

Source
Obituary, AIA *Bulletin*, December 1905.

WILLIAM EDEN NESFIELD (1835–1888)

William Eden Nesfield was born in Bath, England, and graduated Eton College in 1851. He was a man of independent means who disliked architectural competitions and openly chided architects for their use of professional advertising.

In the London offices of the architect William Burn, Nesfield met Richard Norman Shaw, who had worked for the prominent British architect George Edmund Street in 1858, and together they shared offices from 1862 to 1876 and an official partnership 1866–69. Afterward Nesfield worked for James Kellaway Colling and Colling's uncle, the esteemed architect Anthony Salvin.

He claimed to have won a travelling Studentship from the Royal Academy in the Architectural School that took him to Italy, France, Athens, Constantinople, and Salonica with James Donaldson, the son of an English professor of architecture. The story was refuted in a letter to the editor of *The Builder*, dated 14 April 1888, from R. Phene Spiers, who remarked that Nesfield could never have travelled on a Royal Academy Studentship because he never attended the Academy.

Upon his return (regardless of how he travelled) in the early 1860s he prepared drawings for a pattern book, *Specimens of Medieval Architecture*, which used selected examples of the twelfth- and thirteenth-century buildings he documented on his travels. The book was dedicated to Lord Craven, for whom Nesfield enlarged the country house Coombe Abbey, Warwickshire. Nesfield claimed that the book lifted him to the front ranks of the profession, though the rise in standing was more likely a result of his patron. Because Nesfield's architectural practice had become busy almost immediately he was prompted to hire Day and Son, Lithographers to the Queen, to finish the plates. Nesfield was acutely aware of his reputation and social station. Among Nesfield's his early commissions were the lodges at Kew Gardens and Regent's Park awarded by the Hon. Mr Cowper-Temple. In 1887, Nesfield married Mary Annetta Gwilt, eldest daughter of John Sebastian Gwilt the draughtsman and brother of Joseph Gwilt, a prominent author of books on architecture, especially *Gwilt's Encyclopaedia of Architecture*.

Sources
Journal of the Royal Institute of British Architects, 23 May 1903, 396.
The Builder vol. 54, 7 April 1888, 244.
Architectural Review vol. 1 (1897): 241, 289–92.

Country Life vol. 146 (1969): 542–5, 614–17; vol. 164, 20 July 1978, 158–61; vol. 163, 16 March 1977: 678–81; vol. 163, 23 March 1977: 766–9.
The Victorian Country House (1979): 318–28.
Architectural Review vol. 2 (1897): 29.
Obituary, *The Builder*, vol. 54, 31 March 1888.

George Truefitt (1824–1902)

George Truefitt was articled at age fifteen to the British architect Lewis Nockalls Cottingham (the elder). Truefitt later worked for Sancton Wood (1815–86), and afterward with Eginton of Worcester. With Calvert Vaux (1824–95) he travelled throughout the English countryside to document medieval architecture with sketchbooks. Vaux went on to practice professionally with Andrew Jackson Downing and Frederick Law Olmsted in New York.

Truefitt had an extensive architectural practice but built few buildings considered historically important. He erected buildings in twenty-five different counties of England and worked internationally in fifteen countries. He produced sixteen churches and chapels, including St George's Tufnell Park, St George's Worthing, St John's Bromley, Kent, and Davyhulme Church, Cheshire. He is credited with the restoration of 10 medieval churches. He erected 8 rectory houses, 7 schools, 13 banks in major cities, 7 large halls and church rooms, 170 houses and mansions, and 44 cottages. He was the architect of Tufnell estate for over twenty-five years. He was involved in extensive renovations at Aboyne Castle, Aberdeenshire, the residence of the Marquis of Huntly. Truefitt retired from architecture in 1899 and died at Worthing in 1902 at the age of eighty-nine.

He was elected a Fellow of RIBA in 1860. He was the author of two pattern books and contributed several articles to the journal *The Builder*; to its editor, Mr Godwin, he claimed early success on account of publishing designs in the journal that solicited several important commissions.

Sources

Obituaries in *The Builder*, 16 August 1902, 153, and *The Building News* vol. 83 (1902): 252.
Building News vol. 59, 1 August 1890.
RIBA *Journal* vol. 30, no.8 1902.

GEORGE WIGHTWICK (1802–1872)

George Wightwick was born in Wales and trained in London. He was an architect and architectural journalist. In the late 1820s he practiced with John Foulston in Plymouth. With Foulston he completed several civic projects, including the Bodmin County Lunatic Asylum, the Plymouth Mechanics' Institute, Athenaeum Terrace, the Esplanade, the Devon and Cornwall Female Orphan Asylum, and the Devonport Post Office.

His views on church architecture differed from the leading churchmen and ecclesiological architects of the day, and he published these ideas in *Weale's Quarterly Papers on Architecture* in 1844–45. His pattern books include *Hints to Young Architects: Comprising Advice to Those Who Are Destined to Follow the Profession* (1846 with new editions in 1847, 1860, 1875 and 1880) and *The Palace of Architecture: A Romance of Art and History* (1840).

FREDERICK WITHERS (1828–1901)

Frederick Withers trained in England and immigrated to New York with his friend Calvert Vaux. He moved to Newark, NJ, to work for the landscape architect Andrew Jackson Downing. After Downing's unexpected death, Withers returned to New York and entered into a six-year partnership with Vaux beginning in 1866. Important commissions included the old Jefferson Market, and the Court House and Prison group of buildings, designed in Victorian Gothic. Withers and Vaux were the architects of the Hudson River State Hospital for the Insane, one of the most costly and pretentious early public buildings in New York State.

Withers was best known as a church architect completing commissions in New York State and New England. Important ecclesiastical commissions included the First Presbyterian (1867) in Newburgh, NY, and in 1874 St Luke's Episcopal, Beacon, NY, Zabriski Memorial Church, Newport, RI, and St Thomas, Hanover, NH. Withers was an early member and fellow of the American Institute of Architects and served a term as secretary of the national organization.

Source

Obituary, AIA *Quarterly Bulletin*, April 1901.

NOTES

CHAPTER ONE

1 Canadian Pacific Railway Company, *The Canadian Pacific: The New Highway to the Orient*, 114.
2 The social classifications of taste remain relevant in Bourdieu, *Distinction*, 7.
3 Bourdieu, *The Field of Cultural Production*, 147.
4 Truefitt, *Designs for Country Churches*, iv.
5 The location of taste was present in specific works of antiquity according to the view of Haskell, *Taste and the Antique*, 6.
6 Slater, *Consumer Culture and Modernity*, 157.
7 Upton, "Pattern Books and Professionalism," 105–50.
8 Bourdieu, *The Field of Cultural Production*, 64–72.
9 Bowler, *Chapel and Church Architecture with Designs for Parsonages*.
10 Ibid.
11 Hart, *Designs for Parish Churches*, 4.
12 *The Church* (22 December 1853): 2.
13 Slater, *Consumer Culture and Modernity*, 144 and 51.
14 Eastlake, *Hints on Household Taste*, 8–9.
15 Wills, *Ancient English Ecclesiastical Architecture*, 10.
16 *Ecclesiologist*, "Montreal Cathedral," vol. 18 (1857): 359.
17 *Illustrated London News*, "New Cathedral at Montreal," (3 March 1860): 205.
18 A robust source for the book collector continued to be John Britton's *A Catalogue Raisonne of a Unique Collection of Books on Cathedral and Architectural Antiquities; with Proofs and Etchings* (London: Longman and Co., 1837). Another of Britton's numerous publications, *The Architectural Antiquities of Great Britain* (London: Longman, Hurst, Rees, and Orme, 1809, several reprints), was used by the Canadian architects Cumberland and Storm to connect the medieval design of gatehouse at Bury St Edmunds abbey with their design for the main entrance to University College.

19 The Ontario Architectural Association considered building a curriculum that involved a series of well-respected British architectural books, including John Henry Parker's *An Introduction to the Study of Gothic Architecture* (1829, numerous reprints into the early twentieth century), Matthew Bloxam's *Gothic Architecture* (accurately titled *The Principles of Gothic Ecclesiastical Architecture*, 1841, numerous reprints), Thomas Rickman's *Gothic Architecture* (accurately titled *An Attempt to Discriminate the Styles of Architecture in England*, 1825, numerous reprints), and James Fergusson's *History of Architecture* (1855). The same magazine article listed books recommended by the Quebec Architectural Association, including Gwilt's *Encyclopaedia of Architecture* (1888 ed.), Fergusson's *Handbook of Architecture* (1855), and Raphael Brandon's *Analysis of Gothick Architecture* (1847 numerous reprints). See: critique of Ontario Association of Architects recommended curriculum published in *Canadian Architect and Builder*, 4 September 1891, 91–2.

20 The idea that medieval gothic architecture originated in Britain was not universally accepted in the Empire. Ruskin's *The Stones of Venice* and Street's *Some Account of Gothic Architecture in Spain* each point to the importance of Continental sources.

21 Fergusson, *History of the Modern Styles of Architecture*, vol. 2, 3.

22 Ibid, 427.

23 Ibid.

24 *Canadian Architect and Builder*, "The Influence of the Modern Christian Church upon the Ecclesiastic Architecture of the Dominion," vol. 12. No. 4 (April 1899): 79–80.

25 Benjamin, "The Work of Art in the Age of Mechanical Reproduction," 217–51.

26 *Canadian Architect and Builder*, "A Dominion Architectural Association," vol. 2, no. 2 (February 1889): 15.

27 *Canadian Architect and Builder*, "The Advisability of the Registration of Architects," vol. 8, no. 9 (September 1895): 106–7.

28 Fleming and Lamonde, eds, *History of the Book in Canada*, 198.

29 Anderson, *Imagined Communities*, 67.

30 See Thomas Flanagan, "Aboriginal Title" in Gilbert et al., eds, *Reappraisals in Canadian History: Post-Confederation*.

31 *Manitoba Morning Free Press* (15 December 1899): 5.

32 Morris, *Heaven's Command*, 337.

33 An analysis of the architecture associated with monopoly appeared in Carr, "New Building Technology in Canada's Late Nineteenth-Century Department Stores," 124–42.

34 *Victoria Daily Standard* (17 October 1872): 3, and (29 June 1872): 3. For more about Hibben's, see Fleming and Lamonde eds, *History of the Book in Canada*, 223–4.

35 *Bookseller and Stationer*, "What Men in the Trade are Doing," (January 1908): 22.
36 Report from the *Proceedings of the First Annual General Meeting of the Canadian Booksellers' Association*, 1876, 19.
37 Fleming and Lamonde, eds, *History of the Book in Canada*, 201.
38 Canadian Pacific Railway Company, *The Canadian Pacific: The New Highway to the Orient*, 6.
39 Language describing neo-Gothic, such as *correct*, *proper*, and *solemn*, was used to challenge the Classical idiom's three-hundred year-dominance of British ecclesiastical architecture. More telling of the neo-Gothic proponents' position was an adjacent use of the terms *debased*, *decayed*, and, most damning of all, *pagan* to describe post-Reformation Classicizing, and Georgian style, churches. As a derogatory term, *pagan* was associated architecturally with the "impious" polytheism of the pre-Christian world. Initially, ecclesiological "correctness" was transmitted by Augustus Welby Northmore Pugin (1812–52), who advocated precise archaeological study, and thus truthful, modelling of original medieval designs. Pugin promoted his principles through the distribution of two books, *Contrasts* (1839) and *True Principles* (1841). The publications were polemical vehicles fusing together moral rhetoric with a series of architectural principles. His principles were directed both to architects and to a general audience of architectural consumers. Though Pugin's architectural practice was curtailed by his conversion to Catholicism, which somewhat limited his clientele to less financially affluent, mainly Irish-Catholic congregations, book production made him into a contemporary heroic figure. Then, architecture and painting critic John Ruskin promoted the ethics of "truth," "beauty," "sacrifice," and "obedience," interfaced with the belief in nature as a source of revelation, see Ruskin, *The Seven Lamps of Architecture* (1849) and the three-volume series of *The Stones of Venice* (1851–53). Ruskin built upon the "dry and practical" nature of Pugin's polemics with an impassioned prose that captured the emotional complexity of architecture, showing the warmth, richness, and colour of Continental examples, see Brooks, *John Ruskin and Victorian Architecture*, 9.
40 See also, Pugin, *True Principles*.
41 Hay, "Architecture for the Meridian of Canada," 253–5.
42 See Diocesan Archives of Eastern Newfoundland (Anglican), letter 18, 20 May 1845, Feild to Scott. For a complete analysis of the construction of St John's Anglican cathedral, see Coffman, "Sectarian Rivalry, Sectarian Identity, and Gothic Revival Architecture in Newfoundland." My gratitude to Peter Coffman for making available data from the Anglican diocesan archives in Newfoundland.
43 Lord Elgin (son-in-law to Lord Durham and appointed governor general in 1848) attempted to have Britain direct the colonies' trade and foreign policy. Lord Durham resigned as a result of sharp attack by political enemies in Britain, led by

Lord Brougham, over Durham's withdrawal of charges against the 1837 rebellion participants, except Mackenzie and Papineau. See McNaught, *The Penguin History of Canada*, 104.

44 House of Assembly, 8 June 1866. See Ajzenstat, *Canada's Founding Debates*, 133.
45 Webster, "*Temples... Worthy of His Presence*," 18.
46 Wills, *Ancient English Ecclesiastical Architecture*, 5–6.

CHAPTER TWO

1 Legislative Assembly, 8 February 1865; see Ajzenstat, *Canada's Founding Debates*, 133.
2 *Ecclesiologist*, "On the Future of Art in England," vol. 19 (August 1858): 232, from a paper read at the Anniversary Meeting of the Ecclesiological Society, 1 June 1858.
3 Correspondence in the archives of the Oxford Architectural Society references letters from colonial churchmen and bishops asking for sets of drawings for new churches, including: "The president undertake to make a communication to Mr Herchman to the effect that the Society would undertake to furnish tracings of any church, if he could hold out any hope of a sufficient sum being raised for the erection of a church-like building," 10 May 1845; "The president read a letter from the Rev. E Hawkins, mentioning that the Bishop of Toronto was in want of designs for churches. It was agreed to forward to the Bishop a set of the Society's Publications, with the exception of the working drawings of Littlemore," 15 November 1845; and, "Agreed to send set of publications to Bishop of New Brunswick," 8 February 1845. My gratitude to William Westfall for providing notes on the Oxford Society's holdings.
4 Rather than public rebellion, the Maritime colonies tended toward institutional change like that provided by Lord Durham, which sometimes had the effect of hiding conflicts and contestations.
5 Ketchum, *The Life and Work of the Most Reverend John Medley*, 52.
6 The pattern book by Coleman, *Designs for Parish Churches*, also contains a similar reference to Shottesbrooke as a model.
7 Medley, letter 209, 14 December 1844, Ashmolean Museum. The dating of Medley's letter is likely correct since the OAS Reports of Committee Meetings 6 December 1844 to 22 April 1847 contain notes dated 25 January 1845 that mention a letter was read from the bishop elect of New Brunswick, requesting copies of the Society's publications.
8 *Ecclesiologist*, "Colonial Church Architecture Chapter IX," vol. 9 (April 1848): 362.
9 Bailey, "The Basis and Persistence of Opposition to Confederation in New Brunswick." Bailey convincingly argues that the reasons for New Brunswick's resistance to Confederation was not out of Loyalist duty to England but because of local economics and politics.

10 *Ecclesiologist*, "Colonial Church Architecture – Chapter XII, Fredericton," vol. 9 (August 1848): 192. See also *Ecclesiologist*, "Colonial Church Architecture Chapter IX," vol. 9 (April 1848): 361–3.
11 From about 1841 to 1851 the journal included a section dealing with churches in the colonies, though Ceylon, Guyana, and India figured prominently, which paralleled the Empire's greater economic and social investments in the East.
12 John Medley, letter 209, 14 December 1844, Ashmolean Museum, Oxford, Publications of the Oxford Architectural Society. There was a recent history of importing architectural books into the diocese in New Brunswick from Britain since Frederick Coster had written to J.L. Richards, rector of Exeter College, on 29 April 1843 thanking the Society for sending *View and Details of Four Churches* (publication date and place unknown). He noted that he would be glad to receive the whole series, implying that the publication was a pamphlet. See letter 155, Ashmolean Museum, Publications of the Oxford Architectural Society.
13 OAS meeting minutes, 8 February 1844, Ashmolean Museum.
14 John Medley, letter 208, 15 July 1844, Ashmolean Museum.
15 Ketchum, *The Life and Work of the Most Reverend John Medley*, 133.
16 *The New York Ecclesiologist*, "Cheap Churches," vol. 1 (October 1848).
17 *The New York Ecclesiologist*, "Reality in Church Architecture," vol. 2 (April 1848).
18 Heeney, *Leaders of the Canadian Church*, 121.
19 Kalman, *A History of Canadian Architecture*, 282. Bishop Medley was in Cambridge to deliver an address to the Ecclesiological Society on Tuesday, 9 May 1848; see *Ecclesiologist*, "Colonial Church Architecture – Chapter XII, Fredericton," vol. 9 (August 1848): 192–3.
20 *Ecclesiologist*, "Colonial Church Architecture Chapter IX," vol. 9 (April 1848): 362.
21 Ibid.
22 Ibid., 361.
23 Medley, *Elementary Remarks on Church Architecture*, 8. I thank Malcolm Thurlby for pointing out this reference in Medley's prodigious writings.
24 Heeney, *Leaders of the Canadian Church*, 121.
25 *Ecclesiologist*, "Colonial Church Architecture Chapter IX," vol. 9 (April 1848): 361.
26 Medley, *The Advantage of Open Seats*, 10.
27 Ibid., 2.
28 For a discussion on Keely and his influences, see Thurlby, "Joseph Connolly in the Roman Catholic Archdiocese of Kingston, Ontario," 25–38, especially 30.
29 *Charlottetown Herald* (12 August 1885): 4.
30 McKendry, *With Our Past before Us*, 19–21.

CHAPTER THREE

1 *The Report of the Incorporated Society for the Propagation of the Gospel in Foreign*

Parts for the Year 1838 (SPG, 1838) noted that the colony of Newfoundland had "forgotten that she was a Christian nation."

2 I owe a good deal of gratitude to Peter Coffman for providing access to his considerable body of scholarship on Maritime architecture, published in his book *Newfoundland Gothic*. Beginning as clerk-of-works for the Newfoundland cathedral, Hay later became an important figure in the development of neo-Gothic architecture in the Dominion. For a broader discussion of William Hay in connection with colonial church-building in Bermuda, see Magrill, "'Development' and Ecclesiology in the Outposts of the British Empire," 15–26.

3 Coffman, "St John's Anglican Cathedral and the Beginnings of Ecclesiological Gothic in Newfoundland," 16.

4 Diocesan Archives of Eastern Newfoundland (Anglican), Feild to William Scott, 23 June 1846.

5 The drawings do not survive, but Archdeacon Thomas Bridge commented on them as being too rural for the metropolis of St John's. See Provincial Archives of Newfoundland and Labrador, Bridge to Ernest Hawkins, 24 August 1846.

6 *Ecclesiologist*, "The Ecclesiology of Newfoundland," vol. 14 (March 1853): 156.

7 Diocesan Archives of Eastern Newfoundland (Anglican), Feild to William Scott, August 1844.

8 Diocesan Archives of Eastern Newfoundland (Anglican), Feild to Ernest Hawkins, 19 June 1845.

9 House of Commons Papers, Reports &c, vol. 36, no. 30: 43. The queen's letter produced approximately £16,000, not including other funds from the SPG and SPCK, with which only the nave of the cathedral was completed.

10 Provincial Archives of Newfoundland and Labrador, Bridge to Ernest Hawkins, 24 August 1846.

11 Wix, *Six Months of a Newfoundland Missionary's Journal*, 6.

12 Public Records Office, Colonial Office Correspondence, no. 548, 3 January 1850 "Erection of New Cathedral."

13 Truefitt, *Designs for Country Churches*, vi.

14 Truefitt's earlier and little known text *Architectural Sketches on the Continent* (1847) was produced after a period of travel on the Continent, evoking the status of a Grand Tour. *Architectural Sketches* included sixty pages of different subjects that ranged from aisle windows to church spires, gleaned from travel to St Omer, Chalons-sur-Marne, Strasbourg, and Cologne. The book's illustrations were based on "original sketches, in all completed on the spot, being produced in etchings by the author."

15 Truefitt, *Designs for Country Churches*, iv.

16 Ibid.
17 *Ecclesiologist*. Street, "The True Principles of Architecture and the Possibilities of Development."
18 Ibid.

CHAPTER FOUR

1 Robertson, *Landmarks of Toronto*, 37 and 260.
2 Westfall, *Two Worlds*, 111–12.
3 The Anglican Church in Canada had believed itself the sole beneficiary of the Clergy Reserves by claiming it was the only true "Protestant" Church.
4 *The Church*, vol. 17, no. 24 (24 March 1853): 300.
5 Robertson, *Landmarks of Toronto*, 14.
6 The lands were offered through a forty-two-year lease extendable at a price of $3 per foot, see *The Church*, 1850: 119, advertisement signed by the churchwardens Thomas Harris and Lewis Moffat.
7 The bishop did not stomach selling pews to the congregants at full price, because it would mean that they had had to finance two churches in as many decades. As a result, the building committee initially approved of the idea of selling the churchyards but left the matter in the hands of the Vestry, see "Report of the Committee Appointed by the Vestry of St James' Church to Report on the Rebuilding of the Church," Toronto, 1849, Archives of St James' Anglican Cathedral. Later, the committee withdrew their approval of the sale and openly opposed it.
8 Bramhill's pamphlet is found in the Archives of St James' Cathedral.
9 "St James' Church," a letter from F.R.S. to the *Globe* editor, 3 December 1849. Archives of St James' Cathedral.
10 Ibid.
11 Strachan, *Letter to the Right Hon. Lord John Russell*, 1. The sale of the Clergy Reserves – 2 million acres of land once set aside by governments for the benefit of religious institutions in Canada – appeared both imminent and likely to accrue little to the established Church.
12 Strachan, "Letter to the Hon. A.N. Morin," 4.
13 *Ecclesiologist*, "Montreal Cathedral," 359.
14 Clark, *The Developing Canadian Community*, 4.
15 Robertson, *Landmarks of Toronto*, 40. The property purchased from Mr Alcorn was valued at $18,000 in 1888.
16 Robertson, *Landmarks of Toronto*, 36.
17 Ibid., 11.
18 Ibid.

19 Ibid.
20 *Anglo-American Magazine*, "Colonial Chit-Chat-Toronto," vol. 3, no. 4 (August 1854): 362.
21 *Globe* (10 August 1874): 4.
22 Census of Upper Canada, 1860–61, table 2.
23 Canadian Pacific Railway, *The Canadian Pacific: The New Highway to the Orient*, 14.
24 Robertson, *Landmarks of Toronto*, 17.
25 Woodward, *Woodward's National Architect*.
26 Presbyterian Committee on Church Architecture, *Designs for Village, Town, and City Churches*, 4.
27 See *Canadian Architect and Builder*, "Presbyterian Church Competition," vol. 3, no. 2 (1890): 24; vol. 5, no. 1 (1892): 3, and vol. 5, no. 7 (1892): 71.
28 Robertson, *Landmarks of Toronto*, 229.
29 Ibid., 124.
30 Butler, "St Andrew's Presbyterian Church, Toronto," 181.
31 Robertson, *Landmarks of Toronto*, 126.

CHAPTER FIVE

1 "The Land Corporation of Canada." which offered "80 acres of land absolutely free to each settler and his family ... besides many rare privileges not afforded by any other company." See *Regina-Leader Post*, 27 March 1888.
2 Mercier, *A Home in the North-West*, 61.
3 Ibid., 68.
4 *Colonists' Handbook No.1: Canada*.
5 The Métis were of mixed Euro-Canadian and First Nations "ancestry who had developed their own shared culture, customs, traditions, way of life, and collective identity separate from those of their Indian foremothers (many of them Cree, Ojibway, Chipewayan, and Saulteaux) and their European forefathers, primarily French and Scottish." See Goulet, *The Metis*, 15.
6 *Saskatchewan Herald*, "Church of England Missions" (5 October 1885).
7 *The Diary of Rev. Hunt*. Unpublished, 29 December 1853 and 10 April 1854.
8 Ibid., 29 March 1856 and 24 July 1858.
9 Ibid., 23 August 1858. Rev. Hunt wrote: "this felt passed its first winter in this country at York factory; the next at Norway House; the next at red River, having been sent thither by mistake; the next at Norway House again on its way hither and the next in the storeroom here being the fifth year since it left England: it is still in a state to be unrolled and useful to the Church instead of to my house."
10 George Edmund Street's comments on the truthful articulation of the Gothic

Revival style appeared in a paper read before the Oxford Architectural Society, later published under the title "The True Principles of Architecture and the Possibility for Development." It outlined his position on massiveness, contour, colour, tracery, and the undisturbed space of the wall, which were related to opinions of Ruskin in *The Stones of Venice* regarding structural truth and beauty in nature and architecture.

11 By the 1870s, the Métis of Scottish ancestry tended toward farming and other capitalist pursuits while the Métis of French descent tended toward a nomadic and hunter lifestyle, following the buffalo. See Giraud, *The Métis in the Canadian West*, 113. See also Taylor and Baskerville, eds, *A Concise History of Business in Canada*, 96–8.

12 Hildebrandt, *The Battle of Batoche*, 89.

13 *Saskatchewan Herald*, 2 May 1884. Riel and the Métis in 1885 found the news press and public opinion set against them. Few people outside of the Métis or the Prairies cared about the decimation of the buffalo and of the Métis' economic base of trade in the Assiniboia with the Hudson's Bay Company. Editorials declared the central government was doing its best to settle "half-breed" land claims along the Saskatchewan despite the "unreasonableness" of the Métis. The press not only described Riel as a megalomaniac lunatic but also helped to make him a martyr in the weeks after his execution in November 1885. See *Regina-Leader Post*, 21 April 1885, 4; 9 November 1885, 4; and 14 December 1885, 4.

14 *Saskatchewan Herald*, "Church of England Missions" (5 October 1885): 3.

15 The Métis have been improperly characterized as a backward culture but recent evidence suggests that they were both resourceful and economically sophisticated. For instance, after 1850, following years of dealing exclusively with the HBC the Métis began to compete against the Company, on account of the American Fur Company, whose steamboats on the Red River and railway links between St Paul, Minnesota, and New York beat out the HBC's slower transport. The Métis position is not difficult to understand, since their strong sense of identity began to challenge "not simply the Company's economic prerogatives, but also its political and judicial powers in the fur-trade interior." See Taylor and Baskerville, eds, *A Concise History of Business in Canada*, 103.

16 Giraud, *The Métis in the Canadian West*, 442.

17 *Regina-Leader Post*, 24 May 1883, 4.

18 Wheeler, "The Evolution of Architecture in Western Canada." See also Kidder, *Building Construction and Superintendence*.

19 *Canadian Architect and Builder*, "Manitoba Association of Architects," vol. 19, no. 12 (1906): 190–3.

20 Wheeler, "The Evolution of Architecture in Western Canada," 8.

21 Ibid.
22 *Canadian Architect and Builder*, "Convention of the Ontario Association of Architects," vol. 2, no. 12 (1889): 137.
23 Crossman, *Architecture in Transition*.
24 Storm, "An Appeal for Organization."
25 *Canadian Architect and Builder*, "Convention of the Ontario Association of Architects," vol. 2, no. 12 (1889): 183.
26 Ibid., 185.
27 *Canadian Architect and Builder*, vol. 3, no. 9 (1890): 99–100.
28 Hart, *The Selling of Canada*, 88.

CHAPTER SIX

1 British Columbia, *The Province of British Columbia*, 5.
2 The census of 1881 recorded approximately 50,000 people, half of them First Nations, living primarily along the Fraser River, the Straight of Georgia, and on the west coast of Vancouver Island. Harris, *The Resettlement of British Columbia*, 138.
3 *Colonists' Handbook* no. 1, 11 and 23.
4 British Columbia, *The Province of British Columbia*, 11–15.
5 Father Clinton's letter, dated Vancouver, 3 April 1886, is found in Reeve, *Every Good Gift*, 15.
6 Harris, *The Resettlement of British Columbia*, 10.
7 McKee, *Treaty Talks in British Columbia*, 19–20.
8 Madill, *British Columbia Indian Treaties in Historical Perspective*, 7–13. The welfare of First Nations became a federal responsibility after British Columbia entered Confederation in 1871.
9 See Usher, *William Duncan of Metlakatla*. A focused perspective on education and industry can be had in MacIvor, "Science and Technology Education in a Civilizing Mission."
10 Kidder, *Building Construction and Superintendence*, 27.
11 Usher, *William Duncan of Metlakatla*, 138.
12 McDonald, *From Ceremonial Object to Curio*, 203.
13 Metlakatla Inquiry British Columbia, *Report of the Commissioners*, 136–7.
14 *Victoria Daily Colonist*, 4 October 1884, 3.
15 Weir, *Canada's Gold Rush Church*.
16 *Work for the Far West*, January 1898, 23.
17 Ibid, 5.
18 *Work for the Far West*, April 1902, 18.
19 Ibid.

20 *The Illustrated London News*, 16 February 1861, 1. The investment in the Canadian railway represented only 2.5 percent of Britain's National Debt and 6 percent of the outlay used to construct England's rail system.
21 Webb, *Economics of Railroad Construction*, 20–1.
22 Hart, *The Selling of Canada: The CPR*, 88.
23 See Gowan, *Church Work in British Columbia*, 10, 93, 110.
24 St James' Cathedral archives, architect letter file, Father Harker folio.
25 *The British Colonist*, 28 June 1908, 12.
26 Reeve, *Every Good Gift*, 106.
27 Underhill, *The Iron Church*, 35.
28 Westfall, *Two Worlds*, 51.
29 See Thurlby, "Nonconformist Churches in Canada 1850–1875," 58–9.
30 Marks, *Revivals and Roller Rinks*, 63.
31 *Canadian Architect and Builder*, "Personals," 116.
32 Hooper's practice was, for a time, one of the largest on the West Coast. A series of financial reversals in the 1890s caused the architect to retire penniless but not after having tried to restore his practice in New York City between 1915 and 1927.
33 *Victoria Daily Colonist*, 21 February 1890, 4.
34 McNaught, *The Penguin History of Canada*, 91–96. In effect, the 1840 Act of Union did create a single province in the St Lawrence and Great Lakes areas, which included equal legislative assembly representation from what was then called Canada East and Canada West, although immigration unbalanced such short-lived legislative equalities.
35 Joseph Arsenault of PEI addressing the House of Assembly, 10 March 1868. See Ajzenstat, *Canada's Founding Debates*, 258.
36 *Victoria Daily Colonist*, 12 January 1890, 4.
37 Ibid., 5 January 1890, 4.

CHAPTER SEVEN

1 A survey of international sources of book supply, including the Canadian Book Imports and Exports Database, housed in the History of the Book in Canada project, confirmed that the US was the Dominion's principal source for books. See Fleming, ed., *History of the Book in Canada*, 207.
2 J.S. Helmcken addressing the Legislative Council, 9 March 1970. See Ajzenstat, *Canada's Founding Debates*, 194.
3 Dwyer, *The Economy of Church, School, and Parsonage Architecture*, 9.
4 *Canadian Architect and Builder*, "Rights of Canadian Architects," vol. 20, no. 4 (1907): 60.

5 By increasing the number of its Pullman luxury sleeping cars by a factor of four between 1901 and 1912, the CPR increased its passengers from 4,337,799 in 1901 to 15,480,934 in 1913. See Hart, *The Selling of Canada: The CPR*, 88.
6 Holly, *Church Architecture*, 60.

CONCLUSION

1 Bowler, *Chapel and Church Architecture*, 223–8.

BIBLIOGRAPHY

Ajzenstat, Janet. *Canada's Founding Debates*. Toronto: University of Toronto Press, 2003.

Anderson, Benedict. *Imagined Communities*. Revised ed. New York: Verso, 2000.

Arnold, Dana. *Re-presenting the Metropolis: Architecture, Urban Experience and Social Life in London 1800–1840*. Aldershot, UK: Ashgate Publishing, 2000.

Arnold, Dana, and Stephen Bending, eds. *Tracing Architecture: The Aesthetics of Antiquarianism*. Oxford: Blackwell Publishing, 2003.

Arthur, Eric and Stephen Otto. *Toronto: No Mean City*. 3rd ed. Toronto: University of Toronto Press, 1986.

Bagshaw, Roberta L. *No Better Land: The 1860 Diaries of the Anglican Colonial Bishop George Hills*. Victoria, British Columbia: Sono Nis Press, 1996.

Bailey, Alfred. "The Basis and Persistence of Opposition to Confederation in New Brunswick." *Confederation*, Carl Berger, ed. Toronto: University of Toronto Press, 1967, 71–93.

Barman, Jean. *The West beyond the West*. Toronto: University of Toronto Press, 1991.

Baudrillard, Jean. *The Consumer Society*. London: Sage Publications, 1998.

Beaud, Michel. *A History of Capitalism, 1500–2000*. New York: Monthly Review Press, 1983 (2001).

Belcher, Margaret, ed. *The Collected Letters of A.W.N. Pugin*. Oxford: Oxford University Press, 2001.

Bellanance, Claude and Pierre Lanthier, ed. *Les territoires de l'entreprise*. Sainte-Foy, PQ: Les presses de l'université Laval, 2004.

Benjamin, Walter. "The Work of Art in the Age of Mechanical Reproduction." Harry Zohn, trans. *Illuminations*. London: Fontana, 1973, 217–51.

Bennett, Vicki. *Sacred Space and Structural Style: The Embodiment of Socio-Religious Ideology*. Ottawa: University of Ottawa Press, 1997.

Berger, Carl. *The Writing of Canadian History*. 2nd ed. Toronto: University of Toronto Press, 1986.

Boorman, Sylvia. *John Toronto: A Biography of Bishop John Strachan*. Toronto: Clark, Irwin, 1969.

Bourdieu, Pierre. *Distinction: A Social Critique of the Judgement of Taste*. Cambridge, MA: Cambridge University Press, 1984.

– *The Field of Cultural Production*. New York: Columbia University Press, 1993.

– *The Social Structures of the Economy*. Chris Turner, trans. Cambridge: Polity Press, 2005.

British Columbia, Metlakatla Inquiry. *Report of the Commissioners, Together with the Evidence*. Victoria: Richard Wolfenden, 1885.

British Columbia. *The Province of British Columbia, Canada: Its Resources, Commercial Position, and Climate*. Canadian Pacific Railway, 1890.

Brooks, Chris. "Building the Rural Church." *The Victorian Church: Architecture and Society*, Andrew Saint and Chris Brooks, eds. Manchester: Manchester University Press, 1995.

– *The Gothic Revival*. London: Phaidon Press Limited, 1999.

– "'The Stuff of Heresiarch': William Butterfield, Beresford Hope, and the Ecclesiological Vanguard." *A Church as It Should Be*, Christopher Webster, ed. Stamford: Shaun Tyas, 2000, 121–40.

Brooks, Chris, and Andrew Saint, eds. *The Victorian Church: Architecture and Society*. Manchester: Manchester University Press, 1995.

Brooks, Michael. *John Ruskin and Victorian Architecture*. New Brunswick, NJ: Rutgers University Press, 1987.

Brosseau, Mathilde. *Gothic Revival in Canadian Architecture*. Ottawa: Parks Canada, 1980.

Buckley, Kenneth. *Capital Formation in Canada 1896–1930*. Ottawa: McClelland and Stewart, 1974.

Buggeln, Gretchen. *Temples of Grace*. Hanover and London: University Press of New England, 2003.

Bumsted, J.M. *The History of the Canadian Peoples*. Toronto: Oxford University Press, 2003.

Butler, Janine. "St Andrew's Presbyterian Church, Toronto's 'Cathedral of Presbyterianism,'" *Ontario History* vol. 83, no.3 (1991).

Cain, P.J., and Anthony Hopkins. *British Imperialism 1688–2000*. New York: Longman, 2002.

Cambridge Camden Society. *A Few Hints on the Practical Study of Ecclesiastical Architecture and Antiquities*. 4th ed. Cambridge: University Press, 1843.

– *A Few Words to Churchwardens on Churches and Church Ornaments, No. 1 Suited to Country Parishes*. 8th ed. Cambridge: University Press, 1841.

– *A Few Words to Church Builders*. 1st ed. Cambridge: University Press, 1841.

– *Few Words to Churchwardens on Churches and Church Ornaments, No. 1 Suited to Town and Manufacturing Parishes*. 2nd ed. Cambridge: University Press, 1841.

Canadian Pacific Railway Company. *The Canadian Pacific: The New Highway to the Orient, across Mountains, Prairies and Rivers of Canada*. Montreal, 1890.

Carr, Angela. "From William Hay to Burke, Horwood and White: A Case History in Canadian Architectural Draughting Style." *Society for the Study of Architecture in Canada* vol. 15, no. 2 (1990): 41–51.

– "New Building Technology in Canada's Late Nineteenth-Century Department Stores: Handmaiden of Monopoly Capitalism." *Journal for the Society of Architectural Historians* vol 23, no. 4 (1998): 124–42.

– *Toronto Architect Edmund Burke: Redefining Canadian Architecture*. Montreal: McGill-Queen's University Press, 1995

Carrington, Philip. *The Anglican Church in Canada*. Toronto: Collins, 1963.

Chodos, Robert. *The Canadian Pacific Railway: A Century of Corporate Welfare*. Toronto: James Lewis and Samuel, 1973.

Clark, Kenneth. *The Gothic Revival: An Essay in the History of Taste*. London: Constable & Co. Ltd., 1928.

Clark, S.D. *The Developing Canadian Community*. 2nd ed. Toronto: University of Toronto Press, 1971.

Clarke, Basil. *Church Builders of the Nineteenth Century*. London: Society for Promoting Christian Knowledge, 1938.

Coates, Colin M., ed. *Imperial Canada, 1867–1917*. Edinburgh: University of Edinburgh, 1997.

Coffman, Peter. *Newfoundland Gothic*. Quebec: Multimondes, 2008.

– "Sectarian Rivalry, Denominational Identity, and Gothic Revival Architecture in Newfoundland." PhD thesis. Queen's University, 2006.

– "St John's Anglican Cathedral and the Beginnings of Ecclesiological Gothic in Newfoundland," *Journal of the Society for the Study of Architecture in Canada* vol. 31, no.1 (2006): 16.

Colonists' Handbook No.1: Canada, Containing Statistical and Other Information from Government Sources and Useful Councels to Emigrants. London: The Society for Promoting Christian Knowledge, 1882.

Cram, Ralph Adams. *Church Building: A Study of the Principles of Architecture in Their Relation to the Church*. Boston: Small, Maynard and Company, 1901.

– *Convictions and Controversies*. reprint ed. Freeport, NY: Books for Libraries Press, 1935 (1970).

– *The Gothic Quest*. 2nd ed. Garden City, NY: Doubleday, Page and Company, 1918.

– *Six Lectures on Architecture*. Freeport, NY: Books for Libraries Press, 1917.

Crang, Mike and Nigel Thrift, ed. *Thinking Space*. London: Routledge, 2000.

Creighton, D.G. "Economic Nationalism and Confederation." *Confederation.* Carl Berger, ed. Toronto: University of Toronto Press, 1967, 1–8.

Crossman, Kelly. *Architecture in Transition: From Art to Practice 1885–1906.* Kingston and Montreal: McGill-Queen's University Press, 1987.

Cruikshank, Ken. "Policy Entrepreneurs and Regulatory Innovation: Simon James Mclean, William Lyon Mackenzie King and Business-Government Relations in the Age of Laurier." *Canadian Papers in Business History*, Peter A. Baskerville, ed. Victoria, BC: The Public History Group, 1993.

Dane, Joseph. *The Myth of Print Culture: Essays on Evidence, Textuality, and Bibliographical Method.* Toronto: University of Toronto Press, 2003.

Davis, Clarence and Kenneth Wilburn, Jr, ed. *Railway Imperialism.* New York: Greenwood Press, 1991.

Davis, Terence. *The Gothick Taste.* London: David and Charles, 1874.

de Certeau, Michel. *The Practice of Everyday Life.* Steven Randall, trans. Berkeley and Los Angeles: University of California Press, 1984.

Dempsey, Hugh. *The Canadian Pacific Railway West: The Iron Road and the Making of a Nation.* Vancouver: Douglas & McIntyre, 1984.

Dixon, Roger, and Stephan Muthesius. *Victorian Architecture.* New York: Oxford University Press, 1978.

Downs, Barry. *Sacred Places: British Columbia's Early Churches.* Vancouver: Douglas & McIntyre, 1980.

Eagle, John A. *The Canadian Pacific Railway and the Development of Western Canada, 1896–1914.* Montreal: McGill-Queen's University Press, 1989.

Elliott, John and Christopher Webster, eds. *"A Church as It Should Be."* Stamford: Shaun Tyas, 2000.

Epstein, Clarence. "Church Architecture in Montreal during the British Colonial Period 1760–1860." University of Edinburgh, 1999.

Evans, Richard J. *In Defense of History.* New York: W.W. Norton, 1999.

Fleming, Patricia and Yann Lamonde, , eds. *History of the Book in Canada* vol. 1, *Beginnings to 1840.* Toronto: University of Toronto Press, 2004.

Flyvbjerg, Bent. *Making Social Science Matter.* Cambridge: Cambridge University Press, 2001.

Fortier, Robert, ed. *Villes industrielles planifiées.* Montreal: Boréal, 1996.

Foucault, Michel. *The Archaeology of Knowledge.* A.M. Sheridan Smith, trans. London and New York: Routledge, 1969.

Gibson, John, ed. *Sticks and Stones: Some Aspects of Canadian Printing History.* Toronto: Toronto Typographic Association, 1980.

Gilbert, A.D., C.M. Wallace, and R.M. Bray, eds. *Reappraisals in Canadian History: Post-Confederation.* Scarborough: Prentice Hall Canada Inc., 1992.

Giraud, Marcel. *The Métis in the Canadian West*. Edmonton: The University of Alberta Press, 1986.

Goulet, George, and Terry Goulet. *The Métis: Memorable Events and Memorable Personalities*. Calgary: Fabjob Inc., 2006.

Gowan, Rev. Herbert H. *Church Work in British Columbia; Being a Memoir of the Episcopate of Acton Windeyer Sillitoe, DD, DCL, First Bishop of New Westminster*. London: Longmans, Owen, 1899.

Gowans, Alan. *Building Canada: An Architectural History of Canadian Life*. Toronto: Oxford University Press, 1966.

– *Looking at Architecture in Canada*. Toronto: Oxford University Press, 1958.

Grant, John Webster. *A Profusion of Spires*. Toronto: University of Toronto Press, 1988.

Halasz, Alexandra. *The Marketplace of Print: Pamphlets and the Public Sphere in Early Modern England*. Cambridge: Cambridge University Press, 1997.

Harris, Cole. *Making Native Space: Colonialism, Resistance, and Reserves in British Columbia*. Vancouver: University of British Columbia, 2002.

– *The Resettlement of British Columbia: Essays on Colonialism and Geographical Change*. Vancouver: University of British Columbia Press, 1997.

Hart, E.J. *The Selling of Canada: The Canadian Pacific Railway and the Beginnings of Canadian Tourism*. Banff: Altitude Publishing, 1983.

Harvey, R.G. *Carving the Western Path by River, Rail, and Road through BC's Southern Mountains*. Surrey, British Columbia: Heritage House, 1998.

Haskell, Francis. *Taste and the Antique: The Lure of Classical Sculpture 1500–1900*. London: Yale University Press, 1981.

Hawkes, Terence, ed. *The Return of the Reader*. London: Methuen, 1987.

Hay, William. "Architecture for the Meridian of Canada." *Anglo-American Magazine* vol. 2, January (1853): 253–5.

– "The Late Mr Pugin and the Revival of Christian Architecture." *Anglo-American Magazine* vol. 2, June (1853): 70–3.

Hedges, James B. *Building the Canadian West: The Land and Colonization Policies of the Canadian Pacific Railway*. New York: Russell and Russell, 1939.

Heeney, William Bertal. *Leaders of the Canadian Church*. Toronto: The Musson Book Company, 1918.

Hildebrandt, Walter. *The Battle of Batoche: British Small Warfare and the Entrenched Métis*. Ottawa: National Historic Parks and Sites, 1989.

Hitchcock, Henry-Russell. *Early Victorian Architecture in Britain*. New Haven: Yale University Press, 1954.

Hobsbaum, Eric. *The Age of Capital, 1848–1875*. New York: Charles Scribner's Sons, 1975.

– *The Invention of Tradition*. Cambridge: Cambridge University Press, 1992.

Hodgins, Bruce, ed. *Canadian History since Confederation*. Georgetown, ON: Irwin-Dorsey, 1979.

Hodnett, Edward. *Image and Text*. London: Scolar Press, 1982.

Hunt, the Rev. Robert. *The Diary of Rev. Hunt* (unpublished). Saskatchewan Archives, transliterated by Margaret Wynne.

Innis, Harold. *The Fur Trade in Canada*. Toronto: University of Toronto Press, 1999.

– *A History of the Canadian Pacific Railway*. Toronto: University of Toronto Press, 1971.

Jameson, Frederic. *Postmodernism or, the Cultural Logic of Late Capitalism*. Durham: Duke University Press, 1991.

Jandl, Katherine Cole Stevenson and H. Ward. *Houses by Mail: A Gide to Houses from Sears, Roebuck and Company*. Washington: The Preservation Press, 1986.

Jauss, Hans Robert. *Towards an Aesthetic of Reception*. trans. Timothy Bahti. Minneapolis: University of Minnesota Press, 1982.

Kalman, Harold. *A History of Canadian Architecture*. 2 vols. Toronto: Oxford University Press, 1995.

Kenneally, Rhona Richman. "Depictions of Progress: Images of Montreal in Contemporary Guidebooks 1837–1907." *Journal of the Society for the Study of Architecture in Canada* vol. 23, no.1 (1998): 7–13.

– "The Tempered Gaze: Medieval Church Architecture, Scripted Tourism, and Ecclesiology in Early Victorian Britain." Dissertation, McGill University, 2002.

Keshen, Jeffrey, and Suzanne Morton. *Material Memory: Documents in Post-Confederation History*. Don Mills: Addison-Wesley, 1998.

Ketchum, William Quintard. *The Life and Work of the Most Reverend John Medley*. Saint John, New Brunswick: J & A McMillan, 1893.

King, Anthony, ed. *Buildings and Society: Essays on the Social Development of the Built Environment*. London: Routledge & Kegan Press, 1980.

Kowsky, Francis. *The Architecture of Frederick Clarke Withers and the Progress of the Gothic Revival in America after 1850*. Middletown, CT: Wesleyan University Press, 1980.

– *Country, Park, and City: The Architecture and Life of Calvert Vaux*. New York: Oxford University Press, 1998.

Lamb, W. Kaye. *History of the Canadian Pacific Railway*. London: Collier Macmillan, 1977.

Lambton, John (Lord Durham). *Lord Durham's Report on the Affairs of British North America*. Oxford Oxford Press, 1839 (reprinted 1912).

Landow, George P. *Victorian Types Victorian Shadows: Biblical Typology in Victorian Literature, Art, and Thought*. Boston, London, and Henley: Routledge and Kegan Paul, 1980.

Leach, Neil, ed. *Rethinking Architecture*. London: Routledge, 1997.

Lefebvre, Henri. *The Production of Space*. 2004 ed. Donald Nicholson-Smith, trans. Oxford: Blackwell Publishing, 1974.

Liscombe, Rhodri Windsor. "A 'New Era in My Life': Ithiel Town Abroad." *Journal for the Society of Architectural Historians* vol. 5, no. 17 (1991): 5–17.

– "The Commodification of Civic Culture in Early Nineteenth-Century London." *London Journal* vol. 29, no. 2 (2004): 17–32.

Little, J.I. *Borderland Religion: The Emergence of an English-Canadian Identity, 1792–1852*. Toronto: University of Toronto Press, 2004.

Lizars, Robina Macfarlane. *In the Days of the Canada Company: The Story of the Settlement of the Huron Tract and a View of the Social Life of the Period 1825–1850*. Toronto: William Briggs, 1896.

Lowe, Lisa. "Discourse and Heterogeneity: Situating Orientalism." *Critical Terrains: French and British Orientalisms*. Ithaca: Cornel University Press, 1991.

Luxton, Donald. *Building the West*. Vancouver: Talon, 2003.

– "Taming the West: The Thirty-Year Struggle to Regulate the Architectural Profession in British Columbia." *Journal of the Society for the Study of Architecture in Canada* vol. 23, no. 4 (1998): 108–23.

MacIvor, Madeleine. "Science and Technology Education in a Civilizing Mission." University of British Columbia, 1993.

MacRae, Marion. *Hallowed Walls: Church Architecture of Upper Canada*. Toronto: Clarke, Irwin & Company, 1975.

Madill, Dennis. *British Columbia Indian Treaties in Historical Perspective*. Ottawa: Research Branch, Corporate Policy Indian and Northern Affairs Canada, 1981.

Magrill, Barry. "'Development' and Ecclesiology in the Outposts of the British Empire: William Hay's Gothic Solutions for Church Building in Tropical Climates (1840–1890)." *Journal of the Society for the Study of Architecture in Canada* vol. 29, nos 1–2 (2004): 15–26.

Marks, Lynne. *Revivals and Roller Rinks: Religion, Leisure and Identity in Late Nineteenth Century Small Town Ontario*. Toronto: University of Toronto Press, 1996.

Maxwell, Richard, ed. *The Victorian Illustrated Book*. Charlottesville and London: University of Virginia, 2002.

McDonald, Joanne. *From Ceremonial Object to Curio: Object Transformation at Port Simpson and Metlakatla, British Columbia in the Nineteenth Century*.

McKee, Christohper. *Treaty Talks in British Columbia*. 2nd ed. Vancouver: UBC Press, 2000.

McKendry, Jennifer. *With Our Past before Us: Nineteenth-Century Architecture in the Kingston Area*. Toronto: University of Toronto Press, 1995.

McNaught, Kenneth. *The Penguin History of Canada*. London: Penguin, 1988.
McNeil, John Thomas. *The Presbyterian Church in Canada*. Toronto: General Board, Presbyterian Church in Canada, 1925.
Medley, John. *The Advantage of Open Seats*. Oxford: I. Shrimpton, 1843.
– *Elementary Remarks on Church Architecture*. London: P.A. Hannaford, 1841.
Mercier, Anne, and Violet Watt. *A Home in the North-West, Being a Record of Experience*. London: Society for Promoting Christian Knowledge, 1903.
Merriam, Sharan. *Case Study Research in Education: A Qualitative Approach*. Oxford: Jossey-Bass Publishers, 1990.
Morris, James. *Heaven's Command: An Imperial Progress*. London: Faber and Faber, 1973.
Musto, Sylvia. "Social Crisis and the Imaging of England's History: Representing Medieval Norfolk in the Early Nineteenth Century." University of British Columbia, 2001.
Myers, Robin and Michael Harris, eds. *The London Book Trade: Topographies of Print in the Metropolis from the Sixteenth Century*. London: Oak Knoll Press and The British Library, 2003.
Nasson, Bill. *Britannia's Empire*. Stroud, Gloucestershire: Tempus Publishing, 2004.
Nicholas, Thomas. *Colonialism's Culture: Anthropology, Travel, and Government*. Cambridge: Polity Press, 1994.
– *Entangled Objects: Exchange, Material Culture, and Colonialism in the Pacific*. Cambridge, MA: Harvard University Press, 1991.
Norrie, Kenneth, Douglas Owram, and J.C. Herbert Emery. *A History of Canadian Economy*. Scarborough, ON: Nelson, Thomson, 2002.
O'Gorman, James. *American Architects and Their Books to 1848*. Amherst: University of Massachusetts Press, 2001.
Ondaatje, Kim. *Small Churches of Canada*. Toronto: Lester & Orpen Dennys, 1982.
Otto, A.J.H. Richardson and Stephen. "John Try: A Master Carpenter, Builder, and Architect in Old Montreal." *Journal of the Society for the Study of Architecture in Canada* vol. 22, no. 2 (1997): 32–9.
Pacey, Elizabeth. *More Stately Mansions: Churches of Nova Scotia 1830–1910*. Hantsport, Nova Scotia: Lancelot Press, 1984.
Parker, George L. *The Beginnings of the Book Trade in Canada*. Toronto: University of Toronto Press, 1985.
Pascoe, C.F. *Two Hundred Years of the Society for the Propagation of the Gospel: An Account of the Society for the Propagation of the Gospel in Foreign Parts 1701–1900*. London: Society for the Propagation of the Gospel, 1901.
Pastor, Monica Leigh. "Imaging the Metlakatlas: Shifting Representations of a North West Coast Mission Community." University of British Columbia, 1999.
Peake, Frank A. *The Anglican Church in British Columbia*. Vancouver: Pitchell Press, 1959.

Peck, Linda Levy. *Consuming Splendor: Society and Culture in Seventeenth-Century England*. Cambridge: Cambridge University Press, 2005.

Preston, Richard and Russworm, Lorne, ed. *Essays on Canadian Urban Process and Form II*. Waterloo, Ontario: Department of Geography, University of Waterloo, 1980.

Pugin, Augustus Welby. *Contrasts: Or, A Parallel between the Noble of Edifices of the Middle Ages, and Corresponding Buildings of the Present Day; Shewing the Present Decay of Taste* (1836, reprinted 1841).

– *The True Principles of Pointed or Christian Architecture* (1841).

Ralko, Joe. *Building Our Future: A People's Architectural History of Saskatchewan*. Calgary: Red Deer Press, 2005.

Reeve, Phyllis. *Every Good Gift*. Vancouver, BC: St James' Church, 1981.

Reiff, Daniel D. *Houses from Books: Treatises, Pattern Books, and Catalogs in American Architecture, 1738–1950: A History and Guide*. Pennsylvania: The Pennsylvania State University Press, 2001.

Resnick, Philip. *The European Roots of Canadian Identity*. Toronto: Broadview Press, 2005.

– *Thinking English Canada*. Toronto: Stoddart Publishing Co., 1994.

Richardson, Douglas Scott. "Hyperborean Gothic; or, Wilderness Ecclesiology and the Wood Churches of Edward Medley." *Architectura* vol. 2 (1972): 48–74.

Roman, Donald W. "Railway Imperialism in Canada, 1847–1865." *Railway Imperialism*. Clarence B. Davis, ed. New York: Greenwood Press, 1991, 7–24.

Romney, Paul. *Getting It Wrong: How Canadians Forgot Their Past and Imperilled Confederation*. Toronto: University of Toronto Press, 1999.

Ruskin, John. *The Seven Lamps of Architecture*. New York: Noonday Press, 1849 (reprinted 1961).

– *The Stones of Venice*. London: Penguin, 1851 (reprinted 2001).

Russell-Corbett, Jane. "'The Ecclesiologist' and Anglican Church Architecture in the Canadian Colonies." *Journal of the Society for the Study of Architecture in Canada* vol. 21, no. 4 (1996): 89–94.

Sandilands, R., ed. *Architecture of the Fraser Valley*. Vancouver: Opportunities for Youth, 1972.

Schivelbusch, Wolfgang. *The Railway Journey: The Industrialization of the 19th Century*. Berkeley: University of California Press, 1977.

Scott, Sir George Gilbert. *A Plea for the Faithful Restoration of Our Ancient Churches: A Paper Read before the Architectural and Archaeological Society for the County of Bucks, at Their First Annual Meeting in 1848 … to Which Are Added Some Miscellaneous Remarks on Other Subjects Connected with the Restoration of Churches, and the Revival of Pointed Architecture*. London: Parker, 1850.

– *Lectures on the Rise and Development of Medieval Architecture*. London: J. Murray, 1879.

– *Remarks on Secular & Domestic Architecture, Present & Future.* London: J. Murray, 1858.

Segger, Martin. *Victoria: A Primer for Regional History in Architecture.* Victoria: Heritage Architectural Guides, 1979.

Shinn, Rev. George Wolfe. *King's Handbook of Notable Episcopal Churches in the United States.* Boston: Moses King Corporation, 1889.

Simmins, Geoffrey. *Fred Cumberland: Building the Victorian Dream.* Toronto: University of Toronto Press, 1997.

Sinnema, Peter W. *Dynamics of the Pictured Page: Representing the Nation in the Illustrated London News.* Aldershot: Ashgate, 1998.

Slater, Don. *Consumer Culture and Modernity.* Cambridge: Polity Press, 1997.

Smeins, Linda E. "Pattern Books and the Queen Anne Style in America." PhD dissertation. The University of British Columbia, 1989.

– *Building an American Identity: Pattern Book Homes and Communities.* Walnut Creek and London: Altamira Press, 1999.

Smith, Donald B., R. Douglas Francis, and Richard Jones. *Destinies: Canadian History since Confederation.* 4th ed. Toronto: Harcourt Canada, 2000.

Smith, H.M. Scott. *The Historic Churches of Prince Edward Island.* Ottawa: SSP Publications, 2004.

Stacey, C.P. "Britain's Withdrawal from North America 1864–1871." *Confederation.* Carl Berger, ed. Toronto: University of Toronto Press, 1967, 9–22.

Stafford, Barbara Maria. "Presuming Images and Consuming Words: The Visualization of Knowledge from the Enlightenment to Post-Modernism." *Consumption and the World of Goods.* John and Roy Porter Brewer, eds. London and New York: Routledge, 1993.

Stamp, Gavin, ed. *Personal and Professional Recollections by Sir George Gilbert Scott.* Stamford: Paul Watkins, 1995.

Stanton, Phoebe B. *The Gothic Revival & American Church Architecture: An Episode in Taste, 1840–1856.* Baltimore: Johns Hopkins Press, 1968.

Storm, William George. "An Appeal for Organization." *Canadian Architect and Builder* vol. 1, no. 2 (1888): 3.

Strachan, Bishop John. *The Clergy Reseserves: A letter from the Bishop of Toronto, to the Hon. A.N. Morin, Commissioner of Crown Lands.* Toronto: Thompson & Co., 1854.

– *Letter to the Right Hon. Lord John Russell on the Present State of the Church in Canada.* London: George Bell, 1851.

– *Thoughts on the Rebuilding of the Cathedral Church of St James.* Toronto: The Diocesan Press, 1850.

Street, George Edmund. *Brick and Marble in the Middle Ages: Notes of Tours in the North of Italy.* 2nd, 1874 ed. London: John Murray, 1855.

- *Some Account of Gothic Architecture in Spain* (1865, reprinted 1869, 1914)
- *Unpublished Notes and Reprinted Papers*. 2nd ed. New York: The Hispanic Society of America, 1916
- "The True Principles of Architecture and the Possibility for Development." *Ecclesiologist* vol. 13 (1852): 247–62," *Ecclesiologist* vol. 19 (August 1858): 232.

Summerson, John. *Architecture in Britain 1530–1830*. Middlesex: Penguin, 1953. 1979.

Tansil, Charles C. *The Canadian Reciprocity Treaty of 1854*. Baltimore: The Johns Hopkins Press, 1922.

Taylor, Graham D., and Peter A. Baskerville, eds. *A Concise History of Business in Canada*. Toronto: University of Toronto Press, 1994.

Thomas, Christopher. "High Sense of Calling: Joseph Connolly, A.W. Holmes, and Their Buildings for the Roman Catholic Archdiocese of Toronto, 1885–1935." *Canadian Art Review* vol. 13, no.2 (1986): 97–120.

Thompson, Paul. *William Butterfield*. London: Routledge and Kegan Paul, 1971.

Thurlby, Malcolm. "Joseph Connolly in the Roman Catholic Archdiocese of Kingston, Ontario" in the *Journal of the Society for the Study of Architecture in Canada*, vol. 30 no. 2 (2005): 25–38.

- "Nonconformist Churches in Canada 1850–1875." *Ecclesiology Today* vol. 34, January (2005): 53–73.

Tuck, Robert. *Gothic Dreams*. Toronto: Dundurn Press, 1978.

- *Gothic Dreams: The Architecture of William Critchlow Harris 1854–1913*. Charlottetown, PEI: Confederation Centre Art Gallery and Museum, 1995.
- *Churches of Nova Scotia*. Toronto: The Dundurn Group, 2004.

Ullmann, Walter. "The Quebec Bishops and Confederation." *Confederation*, D.G. Creighton, ed. Toronto: University of Toronto Press, 1967.

Underhill, Stuart. *The Iron Church 1860–1985*. Victoria: Braemar Books Ltd, 1984.

Upjohn, Everard. *Richard Upjohn: Architect and Churchman*. New York: Da Capo Press, 1968.

Upton, Dell. "Pattern Books and Professionalism: Aspects of the Transformation of Domestic Architecture in America, 1800–1860." *Winterthur Portfolio* vol. 19, no. 2/3 (1984): 105–50.

Urquhart, M.C. *Gross National Product, Canada, 1870–1926: The Derivation of the Estimates*. Kingston and Montreal: McGill-Queen's University Press, 1993.

Usher, Jean. *William Duncan of Metlakatla*. Ottawa: National Museum of Man, 1974.

Vaudry, Richard W. *Anglicans and the Atlantic World: High Churchmen, Evangelicals, and the Quebec Connection*. Montreal and Kingston: McGill-Queen's University Press, 2003.

Veillette, John, and Gary White. *Early Indian Village Churches*. Vancouver University of British Columbia Press, 1977.

Viloria, James. "The Politics of the 'We' in the Construction of Collective Identities in Histories of Architecture in Canada." *Journal of the Society for the Study of Architecture in Canada* vol. 24, no. 4 (1999): 10–16.

Walsh, H.H. *The Christian Church in Canada*. Toronto: The Ryerson Press, 1956.

Webb, Walter Loring. *Economics of Railroad Construction*. 2nd ed. New York: John Wiley and Sons, 1906 (1912).

Webster, Christopher, ed. *'Temples ... Worthy of His Presence': The Early Publications of the Cambridge Camden Society*. Oxford: Spire Books, 2003.

Weedon, Alexis. *Victorian Publishing: The Economics of Book Production for a Mass Market, 1836–1916*. Aldershot, UK: Ashgate, 2003.

Weir, Joan. *Canada's Gold Rush Church*. Quesnel: Anglican Diocese of the Cariboo, 1986.

Wellcome, Henry Solomon. *The Story of Metlakatla*. London: Saxon, 1887.

Westfall, William. "The Sacred and the Secular: Studies in the Cultural History of Protestant Ontario in the Victorian Period." University of Toronto, 1976.

– *Two Worlds: The Protestant Culture of Nineteenth-Century Ontario*. Kingston and Montreal: McGill-Queen's University Press, 1989.

Westfall, William and Malcolm Thurlby. "Church Architecture and Urban Space: The Development of Ecclesiastical Forms in Nineteenth-Century Ontario." *Old Ontario: Essays in Honour of J.M.S. Careless*, David Keene, ed. Toronto: Dundurn Press, 1990.

Wheeler, Charles H. "The Evolution of Architecture in Western Canada." *Canadian Architect and Builder* vol. 10, no 1 (1897).

White, J.F. *The Cambridge Movement: The Ecclesiologists and the Gothic Revival*. Cambridge: Cambridge University Press, 1962.

Wix, Edward. *Six Months of a Newfoundland Missionary's Journal from February to August, 1835*. London: Smith Elder, 1836.

Work for the Far West (1898–1905).

Yukon, Archivists of the Ecclesiastical Province of British Columbia and. *Guide to the Holdings of the Archives of the Ecclesiastical Province of British Columbia and Yukon*. Toronto: Anglican Church of Canada, 1993.

Zeller, Suzanne. *Inventing Canada: Early Victorian Science and the Idea of a Transcontinental Nation*. Toronto: University of Toronto Press, 1987.

– *Land of Promise, Promised Land: The Culture of Victorian Science in Canada*. Ottawa: Canadian Historical Association, 1996.

CHURCH PATTERN BOOKS

Arnot, David Henry. *Gothic Architecture Applied to Modern Residences: Containing Designs of All the Important Parts of a Private Dwelling, Exhibited in Elaborate Perspective Drawings.* New York and Philadelphia: D. Appleton and Company; G.S. Appleton, 1851.

Bidlake, George. *Sketches of Churches: Designed for the Use of Nonconformists.* Birmingham: S. Birbeck, 1865.

Bowler, George. *Chapel and Church Architecture with Designs for Parsonages.* New York and Boston: Sheldon Blakeman and Co., 1856.

Brandon, Raphael, and J. Arthur Brandon. *An Analysis of Gothick Architecture.* London: P. Richardson (also sold by authors), 1847.

– *The Open Timber Roofs of the Middle Ages: Illustrations by Perspective and Working Drawings of Some of the Best Varieties of Church Roofs: With Descriptive Letter-Press.* D. Bogue, 1849.

– *Parish Churches: Being Perspective Views of English Ecclesiastical Structures, Accompanied by Plans Drawn to a Uniform Scale, and Letter-Press Descriptions.* London: George Bell 1848 (numerous reprints).

Brooks, Davey James. *Examples of Modern Architecture Ecclesiastical and Domestic.* Birmingham: S. Birbeck, 1873.

Butterfield, William. *Elevations, Sections etc., of St John the Baptist at Shottesbrooke.* Oxford: Oxford Society for Promoting the Study of Gothic Architecture, 1844.

Colling, James Kellaway. *Art Foliage, for Sculpture and Decoration; with an Analysis of Geometric Form, and Studies from Nature, or Buds, Leaves, Flowers, and Fruit.* London: the author, 1865

– *Examples of English Medieval Foliage and Coloured Decoration, Taken from Buildings of the Twelfth to the Fifteenth Century: With Descriptive Letterpress.* London: B.T. Batsford, 1874.

– *Gothic Ornaments, Being a Series of Examples of Enriched Details and Accessories of the Architecture of Great Britain.* London: G. Bell, 1850.

Crouch, Joseph, and Edmund Butler. *Church, Mission Halls, and Schools for Nonconformists.* Birmingham: Buckler and Webb, 1901.

Davidson, Ellis. *Gothic Stonework: Containing the History and Principles of Church Architecture, and Illustrations of the Characteristic Features of Each Period, the Arrangement of Ecclesiastical Edifices, and a Glossary of Terms.* London: Cassell, Peter, and Galpin, 1874.

Dwyer, Charles P. *The Economy of Church, School, and Parsonage Architecture Adapted to Small Societies and Rural Districts.* Buffalo: Phinney and Co., 1856.

Eastlake, Charles. *Hints on Household Taste in Furniture, Upholstery, and Other Details.* London: Longmans, Green, 1878.

Eastlake, Charles L. *A History of the Gothic Revival.* New York: Humanities Press, Leicester University Press, 1872. 1970.

Fergusson, James. *History of the Modern Styles of Architecture.* 2 vols. London: John Murray, 1891.

Hart, J. Coleman. *Designs for Parish Churches, in the Three Styles of English Church Architecture with an Analysis of Each Style: A Review of the Nomenclature of the Periods of English Gothic Architecture, and Some Remarks Introductory to Church Building, Exemplified in a Series of over One Hundred Illustrations.* New York: Dana and Co., 1857.

Holly, Henry Hudson. *Church Architecture Illustrated with Thirty-Five Lithographic Plates from Original Designs.* Hartford, CT: M.H. Mallory and Company, 1871.

Jobson, F.J. *Chapel and School Architecture, as Appropriate to the Buildings of Nonconformists, Particularly to Those of the Wesleyan Methodists: With Practical Directions for the Erection of Chapels and School-Houses.* London: Hamilton, Adams, & Co., 1900.

Kidder, Frank, and Harry Parker. *Kidder-Parker Architects' and Builders' Handbook.* 18th ed. New York: John Wiley and Sons, Inc, 1944.

Kidder, Frank E. *Building Construction and Superintendence, Part Three: Trussed Roofs and Roof Trusses.* New York: The William T. Comstock Company, 1910.

King, Thomas H. *The Study-Book of Medieval Architecture and Art: Being a Series of Working Drawings of the Principal Monuments of the Middles Ages, Whereof the Plans, Sections, and Details Are Drawn to Uniform Scale.* London: Bell and Daldy, 1868 repinted 1893.

Medley, John. *Elementary Remarks on Church Architecture.* Exeter: P.A. Hannaford, 1841.

Mickelthwaite, John Thomas. *Modern Parish Churches; Their Plan, Design, and Furniture.* London: Henry S. King and Co., 1874.

Nesfield, Eden. *Specimens of Medieval Architecture.* London: Day and Son, 1862.

Paley, Frederick Apthorp. *A Manual of Gothic Architecture With Directions for Copying Them and for Determining Their Dates.* London: J. Van Voorst, 1846.

– *A Manual of Gothic Mouldings: A Practical Treatise on Their Formations, Gradual Development, Combinations, and Varities.* London: J. Van Voorst, 1845.

– *The Church Restorers: A Tale, Treating of Ancient and Modern Architecture and Church Decorations.* London: J. van Voorst, 1844.

Parker, John Henry. *A B C of Gothic Architecture.* London: Parker and Co., 1881.

– *An Introduction to the Study of Gothic Architecture.* 3 ed. Oxford: J. Parker, 1867.

– *A Manual of Gothic Stonecarving.* Oxford: J. Parker, 1855.

Patterson, W. *A Manual of Architecture: For Churches, Parsonages, and Schoolhouses ...* Nashville, TN: Publishing House of the Methodist Episcopal Church South, 1875.

Presbyterian Committee on Church Architecture. *Designs for Village, Town, and City Churches*. Toronto: General Assembly of the Presbyterian Church in Canada, 1893.

Pugin, Augustus Welby Northmore. *Contrasts: Or, a Parallel between the Noble Edifices of the Middle Ages, and Similar Buildings of the Present Day, Shewing the Present Decay of Taste Accompanied by Appropriate Text*. 2nd ed. London: Charles Dolman, 1836, 1841.

– *The True Principles of Pointed or Christian Architecture Set Forth in Two Lectures Delivered at St Marie's, Oscott*. London: John Weale, 1841.

Robertson, J. Ross. *Robertson's Landmarks of Toronto, a Collection of Historical Sketches of the Old Town of York from 1792 until 1837 and of Toronto from 1834 to 1904, also Nearly Three Hundred Engravings of the Churches of Toronto Embracing the Picture of Every Church Obtainable from 1800–1904*. Toronto: J. Ross Robertson, 1904.

Scott, Sir George Gilbert. *Examples of Modern Architecture, Ecclesiastical and Domestic ... Churches and Chapels, Schools, Colleges, Mansions, Town Halls, Railway Stations*. Boston: James R. Osgood, 1873.

Scratton, George. *A Manual for Country Building: In Advocacy of Certain Principles of Plan and Construction to Meet the Times*. London: the author, 1865.

Sharpe, Edmund. *Architectural Parallels; or, the Progress of Ecclesiastical Architecture in England through the Twelfth and Thirteenth Centuries, Exhibited in a Series of Parallel Examples Selected from the Abbey Churches [of] Fountains, Kirkstall, Furness, Roche, Byland, Hexham, Jervaulx, Whitby, Rievaulx, Netley, Bridlington, Tintern, St Mary's, York, Guisborough, Selby and Howden*. London: Van Voorst, 1848.

– *A Treatise on the Rise and Progress of Decorated Window Tracery in England: Illustrated with Ninety-Seven Woodcuts and Six Engravings on Steel*. London: J. van Voorst, 1849.

– *Decorated Windows: A Series of Illustrations of the Window Tracery of the Decorated Style of Ecclesiastical Architecture*. London: J. Van Voorst, 1849.

– *Illustrations of the Conventual Church of the Benedictine Abbey of St Germain at Selby: An Example of the Geometrical and Curvilinear Periods of English Architecture Consisting of Interior and Exterior Perspective Views, Plans, Elevations, and Sections*. London: J van Voorst, 1870.

– *Illustrations of the Conventual Church of the Cistercian Abbey of St Mary, at Netley, an Example of the Lancet and Geometrical Periods of English Architecture; Consisting of Interior and Exterior Perspective Views and Plans, Elevations and Sections*. London: J. van Voorst, 1870.

– *Illustrations of the Priory Church of St Mary at Bridlington : An Example of the Lancet and Geometrical Periods of English Architecture Consisting of Interior and Exterior Perspective Views, Plans, Elevations, and Sections*. London: J. van Voorst, 1870.

– *Illustrations of the Sculpture, Foliage, and Other Ornamental Details of the Following*

Abbey Churches – Whitby, Rievaulx, Netley, Bridlington, Guisborough, Howden, Selby – Containing Examples of the Carved Work of the Lancet, Geometrical, Curvilinear, & Rectilinear Periods of English Architecture. London: J. Van Voorst, 18?.

– *Supplement to "Architectural Parallels"; Containing the Full-Sized Mouldings of … Abbey Churches.* London: J. van Voorst, 1848.

Sholl, Charles. *Working Designs for Ten Catholic Churches.* New York: D. and J. Sadoir and Co., 1869.

Sloan, Samuel. *The Model Architect.* Philadelphia: E.S. Jones and Co., 1852.

Smith, George T. *Art in House Building. Twenty Designs of Modern Dwellings … Costing from $600 Upwards, Including Designs of a Church & Schoolhouse.* Pittsburgh: J. Eichbaum and Co., 1890.

Society, Cambridge Camden. *Instrumenta Ecclesiastica.* London: John Van Voorst, 1856.

Tress, Richard. *Modern Churches: Designs, Estimates, and Essays; also Plans, Elevations, Working Drawings, and Specifications of Modern Churches Already Erected.* London John Williams, Library of the Fine Arts, 1841.

Truefitt, George. *Architectural Sketches on the Continent.* London: Joseph Masters, 1847.

– *Designs for Country Churches.* London: Joseph Masters, 1850.

Upjohn, Richard. *Upjohn's Rural Architecture: Designs, Working Drawings and Specifications for a Wooden Church and Other Rural Structures.* New York: George P. Putnam, 1852.

Valk, Lawrence B. *Church Architecture: General Descriptions of Some of the Most Prominent Buildings Recently Erected in Iron, Brick and Stock Together with Full Explanation of the New Form of Plan for Churches Invented By.* New York: Holt Brothers, 1873.

Various. *Specimen Book of One Hundred Architectural Designs, Showing Plans, Elevations and Views of Suburban Houses, Villas, Sea-Side and Camp-Ground Cottages, Homesteads, Churches, and Public Buildings also Several Original Designs for Modern Styles of Mantles and Furniture, Prepared Especially for This Work.* New York: Bicknell and Comstock, 1880.

Walcot, Mackenzie. *Church and Conventual Arrangement: With Copious References, a Complete Glossary, and an Index. And Illustrated by a Series of Ground-Plans and Plates of the Arrangements of Churches in Different Countries and at Successive Periods, and of the Conventual Plans Adopted by the Various Orders.* London: Atchley and Co, 1861.

Wightwick, George. *The Palace of Architecture.* London: James Fraser, 1840.

Wills, Frank. *Ancient English Ecclesiastical Architecture and Its Principles, Applied to the Wants of the Church at the Present Day.* New York: Stanford and Swords, 1850.

Withers, Frederick. *Church Architecture; Plans, Elevations, and Views of Twenty-One Churches and Two School-Houses, Photo-Lithographed from Original Drawings with*

Numerous Illustrations Showing Details of Construction, Church Fittings, Etc. New York: A.J. Bicknell, 1873.

Woodward, George Everston. *Rural Church Architecture ... by Upjohn, Renwick, Wheeler, Wells, Auston, Stone, Backus, Reeve, and Eveleth.* New York: George E. Woodward, 1868. 1875.

— *Woodward's National Architect: A Victorian Guide Book of 1869.* New York: George E. Woodward, 1869.

INDEX

Page numbers in italics denote illustrations.

Ancient English Ecclesiastical Architecture. See Frank Wills
Architectural journals. *See The Builder; Canadian Architect and Builder*
Architectural Sketches on the Continent. See George Truefitt
Art Foliage. See James Kellaway Colling

Banff, Alberta, St George's-in-the-Pine's, *125*, 126–7
Barkerville, British Columbia, St Saviour's Church, 140–2, *141*
Batoche, Saskatchewan, St Antoine de Padoue, 115–16
Bicknell, A.J., 36, 41, 78, 170
Bidlake, George, 42, 104, 156–7
booksellers, 22, 37–40, 116–17, 123, 166; Bookseller's and Stationer's Association of Ontario, 38; Canadian Booksellers Association, 40; Ontario Booksellers Association, 37, 40; spread of, 175
Bourdieu, Pierre, 11, 34; habitus, 13
Bowler, George (Rev.), 20, 143, 173
Brandon, Raphael and J. Arthur, 7, 168, 177; *An Analysis of Gothick Architecture*, 39; *Open Timber Roofs*, 43, 110, 120; *Parish Churches*, 17, 28, 58, 76, 127
British Colonist, The, 90
Builder, The, 21
Building committees, 4–9, 16, 37, 83; composition, 11, 91, 174; use of pattern books, 173
Butterfield, William, 65

Canadian Architect and Builder, 21, 123–4, 154
Canadian Illustrated News, 21, 50
Canadian Pacific Railway. *See* railway
Catholicism, 44, 163
Chapel and Church Architecture. See George Bowler (Rev.)
Church Architecture. See Henry Hudson Holly
Clergy Reserves, 48–9, 82–5, 90–1
Colling, James Kellaway, 34–5, 39, 177–8, 180
colonialism, 4, 7, 124, 143; colonial society, 9, 19, 45
commerciality, of pattern books, 41
commodification, 19, 105; of taste and history, 15–16, 19
Comstock, William, 30, 40–1

Corn Laws, British Repeal of, 65
cultural capital, 4
Cumberland, Fred, 37, 89; bribery accusation, 148; pattern book collection, 65–6; Storm partnership, 79–80

Designs for Churches. See George Truefitt
Designs for Village Town and City Churches, 7, 101–3, *102*, *104*, 110. *See also* Presbyterian Church
distinction, social, 19, 21, 94
Donaldson, Joseph McAfee, 143–6
Douglas, James, 130, 161
Downing A.J., 161, 181–2
Dwyer, Charles: *Economy of Church, Parsonage and School Architecture*, 35, 168

Eastlake, Charles, 22
Ecclesiology: Ecclesiologist and Cambridge Camden Society, 25, 41–7, 51–8, 70, 74–5, 91, 172; *Instrumenta Ecclesiastica*, 65, 78, 140, 161
elitism, 20, 68, 85, 174
Episcopal Church, 32, 161–2

Feild, Edward (bishop of Newfoundland and Bermuda), 43–5, 50; Newfoundland Cathedral, 67–71
Fiennes-Clinton, Henry, 129, 149
finance, 3, 105; problems with, 84–6, 162
First Nations: acculturation, 115, 124, 136, 175; disruption to cultural continuity, 39, 109–11, 130–2
Fort George, British Columbia, St George's (The English Church), 11, *12*
Fredericton, New Brunswick, Christ Church Cathedral, 26, 52–8, *53*, 60, 68, 118

Fredericton, New Brunswick, St Anne's Chapel, 51, 55–9, *60*
Fripp, Robert M., 34
Fulford, Francis (bishop of Montreal), 24, 43, 46, 50
fundraising, 69–70, 146

Gilbert Scott, Sir George, 28; Adrian Gilbert Scott, 150–1; Anglican Cathedral of St John's Newfoundland, 68, 72; Giles Gilbert Scott, 151
gold rush, 8, 110, 128, 139–42
Grand Trunk Railway. *See* railway

Harris, William Critchlow, 167–8
Hibben, T.N., 22, 40, 116
Holly, Henry Hudson, 31, 36, 118, 166, 170–2, 179
Hunt, Robert (Rev.), 111–13, 116

Illustrated London News, 21, 26, 49–50, 178
Indian River, PEI, St Mary's Roman Catholic Church, *167*, 168

Keith, J.C.M., 39
Kidder, Frank, 43, 133–4, 179

land: Canada Company, 49; church property, 82–4, 91, 105, 107, 109, 153; controversial sale, 86–90; discount purchases, 110; donations, 8, 50, 149; government negotiations, 46, 148–9; mortgages, 110, North West Land Co., 107; speculation, 84–5, 91
Lane, Henry Bower, 85
Langley, Henry, 81, 91–4; Langley and Burke, 158, 163; Langley, Langley and Burke, 103
London, England, All Saints Margaret Street, 94, 112, *113*, 166

Longstanton, Cambridgeshire, England, St Michael's, 58, *60*, 76, 101, 108, 146

Maugerville, New Brunswick, Christ Church, *18*
Medley, John (bishop of New Brunswick), 43, 50–2; *Elementary Remarks on Architecture,* 56, 59; Fredericton Cathedral, 51–8; pattern books, 52; St Anne's Chapel, 59
Methodism, 154–6; Methodist Church, 8, 42, 75, 104, 140–1; Methodist Meeting House, 43; Metropolitan Methodist Church (Toronto), 93, 96; Metropolitan Methodist Church (Victoria), 157–8
Metlakatla, 131; St Paul's Church, 131–4; Tsimshian and controversy, 131–5; William Duncan, 132, 135
missionaries, 50–1, 110–11, 130–1, 140–2
modernity, 15–16, 124
Montreal, Christ Church Cathedral, 23

Nesfield, William Eden, 27–8, 178–80
New York Ecclesiologist, 31, 56

Ontario Association of Architects, 101, 123, 168
Open Timber Roofs. See Brandon
Oxford Architectural Society (Oxford Movement), 43, 51, 54, 56
Oxford Mills, Ontario, St John the Evangelist, *77*

Parish Churches. See Brandon
Presbyterian Church, 48, 84, 154–5, 162–4. See also *Designs for Village Town and City Churches*
professionalism of architects, 120
profiteering, 147

publishers: British pattern books, 4–10, 21–2, 25, 72; Canadian, 38; distribution, 40, 116–18, 130, 166; marketing, 13–16, 35, 49, 99–103, 164; production, 32, 34–5; US pattern books, 9, 30, 65–6, 166
Pugin, Augustus Charles, 42
Pugin, Augustus Welby, 42, 63, 69, 74–5, 79, 94, 171

Railway, 22, 72, 107, 118, 147–9; Canadian Pacific Railway, 8, 41, 101–11, 115, 122–4, 128–30, 139; CPR guidebooks, 106; Grand Trunk Railway, 96; William Van Horne, 126, 169
recession, global (1873), 94, 131
reciprocity, agreement with US, 65
Ridley, William (bishop), 134–5
Riel, Louis, 109–10. *See also* Batoche
rivalries, architectural, 9, 13, 68, 95, 131, 155–6
Roberston, John Ross, 92
Ruskin, John, 80, 166

seating, preferential, 98; free (or open) in churches, 50, 59–60
Sharpe, Edmund, 28; *Architectural Parallels,* 42
Shottesbrooke, St Mary's Church, 52, *54,* 65. See also William Butterfield
Sillery, Quebec, Roman Catholic Church of Saint Michel, 59, *61*
Sillery, Quebec, St Michael's Anglican Church, 58–9, *61*
Sketches of Churches Designed for the Use of Nonconformists. See George Bidlake
Skookumchuck, British Columbia, Holy Cross, 135–9, *136*
Smith and Gemmell, 91

Snettisham, Norfolk, England, St Mary's, 23, 24, 52, 53, 56
social privilege, 8, 23, 45, 131, 160, 173; Anglican Church, 83–5, 89, 91
Society for the Promotion of Christian Knowledge, 85
Society for the Propagation of the Gospel in Foreign Parts, 51, 70–1, 83, 85, 142
Specimens of Medieval Architecture Chiefly Selected from Examples of the 12th and 13th Centuries in France and Italy. *See* William Eden Nesfield
Stanley Mission, Saskatchewan, Holy Trinity, 111–14, *112*
Steveston, British Columbia, St Anne's Church, 143–7, *144*
Steveston, British Columbia, St Jerome's Church, 143–6
St John's, Newfoundland, Cathedral of St John the Baptist, 68–71, *69*
Storm, William George, 37, 65–6, 80, 94, 103, 122. *See also* Fred Cumberland
Strachan, John (Bishop), 49, 85–91; printed pamphlets, 88–9
subscriptions to pattern books, 39

Teague, John, 161–2, 170
Tignish, PEI, St Simon and St Jude, 62, 63, 65
Toronto, Ontario, St David's Presbyterian Church, 104–6, *105*
Toronto, Ontario, St James Cathedral, 86–97, *87*, *93*, *97*
Toronto, Ontario, St James the Less, 79–82, *80*
Toronto, Ontario, St Michael's Roman Catholic Church, 93–6, *95*
towers and spires, 18, 27, 58–9, 97–8; architectural rivalries, 93–6

treaties with First Nations, 130. *See also* James Douglas
Truefitt, George, 15, 36, 74–5, 181; *Architectural Sketches on the Continent*, 7; *Designs for Churches*, 72, 73, 81, 119, 127
Twenty-One Churches. *See* Frederick Withers

Vancouver, British Columbia, St James' Anglo-Catholic Church, 149–52, *150*
Van Horne, William, 148, 169
Victoria, British Columbia, Metropolitan Methodist Church, 157–9, *158*
Victoria, British Columbia, Reformed Episcopal Church, 161, *162*
Victoria, British Columbia, St Andrew's Presbyterian Church, 163–5
Victoria, British Columbia, St John the Divine, 152–4, *153*

Wheeler, Charles, 119–22
Wickenden, Charles Osborne, 110, 154
Wills, Frank, 7, 20, 30, 89; *Ancient English Ecclesiastical Architecture*, 37, 99; Christ Church Cathedral Montreal, 23–5, 90; Fredericton Cathedral, 51–6, New York, 57; St Anne's Chapel, 65, 76–7
Winnipeg, Manitoba, Holy Trinity Anglican Church, 119–22, *120*
Withers, Frederick, 31, 169–70, 182; *Church Architecture*, 7, 28, 36, 42; pattern books and advertisements, 99; *Twenty-One Churches*, 119–20
Woodward, George: commercialism, 100, 170–1; *Rural Church Architecture*, 42, 63, 133, 137; *Woodward's Architecture and Rural Art*, 99